OLD LOYALTIES, NEW TIES

Therapeutic Strategies with Stepfamilies

by
EMILY B. VISHER, Ph.D.
and
JOHN S. VISHER, M.D.

 BRUNNER/MAZEL *Publishers* • New York

Library of Congress Cataloging-in-Publication Data

Visher, Emily B.
  Old loyalties, new ties.

  Bibliography: p. 243
  Includes index.
  1. Family psychotherapy.   2. Stepparents—Psychology.
3. Stepchildren—Psychology.   4. Family—Mental health.
I. Visher, John S.   II. Title.
[DNLM: 1. Family.   2. Family therapy—methods.
3. Parent-Child Relations.   WM 430.F2 V8290]
RC488.5.V56   1988   616.89′156   87-23899
ISBN 0-87630-489-7

Copyright © 1988 by Emily B. Visher and John S. Visher

Published by
BRUNNER/MAZEL, INC.
19 Union Square
New York, New York 10003

MANUFACTURED IN THE UNITED STATES OF AMERICA

10   9   8   7   6   5   4   3   2   1

For stepfamilies—
and those who help them
achieve their rich potential

Contents

Acknowledgments

As we look back over the past ten years, we realize the considerable debt we owe to many clinicians and researchers interested in family dynamics. We wish to thank in particular: Constance Ahrons, Elizabeth Keller Beach, Eulalee Brand, Glenn Clingempeel, Ann Getzoff, Robert Jay Green, Sharon Hanna, Judith Landau-Stanton, Helen Coale Lewis, Monica McGoldrick, Patricia Papernow, and Kay Pasley for their valuable input during the preparation of this book.

Unfortunately, it is not possible to acknowledge the specific contributions of many of our colleagues because their wisdom has been woven together in our minds and has blended into all of our thinking about therapeutic work with stepfamilies. If they recognize, in somewhat altered form perhaps, their thoughts and skills, we hope they will accept our gratitude for their contributions to our thinking.

Introduction

Over 200 years ago Samuel Johnson said, "To marry again represents the triumph of hope over experience." During the past decade we have met and talked with hundreds of "hopeful" people, and we have come to believe that knowledge about and validation of stepfamilies as a rewarding and valuable type of family can help many individuals to develop competent and effective stepfamilies that bring their members personal growth and many satisfactions.

During these years, we have specialized in working therapeutically with remarriage families, leading workshops, and giving presentations for mental health practitioners and other professionals who work with stepfamily members. We have listened to their questions and concerns, and we have learned much from each of them. In addition, we have come to know many stepfamilies through Stepfamily Association of America. This book is the direct result of these interchanges and sharing of professional experience.

The first chapter will help readers, we hope, to keep the problem-oriented remainder of the book in perspective, while Chapter 2 contains some basic theoretical concepts, many of which we have found helpful to stepfamily adults as well as to therapists and counselors. Chapter 3 outlines therapeutic strategies we believe to be of particular importance when working with stepfamilies, and Chapter 4 describes a number of factors we think need to be considered when assessing whom to see in therapy.

The remaining chapters illustrate what we believe to be major areas of difficulty that can impede the search for a satisfying stepfamily identity and describe ways in which therapists can help family members to deal with these challenges. In closing, we have written a summary of ways in which we view stepfamily therapy as differing from therapeutic work with nuclear families.

In 1981 we were made acutely aware of the continuing dearth of general knowledge about the special structure and dynamics of stepfamilies when a newspaper report on the data from the census lumped together "traditional two-parent households" with remarried families:

The new figures show that, for all the talk of new life styles, the traditional family is still the norm in this country. If divorce is common, so is remarriage, and about three-fourths of all children under age 18 live in traditional two-parent households. (*San Francisco Chronicle,* Nov. 19, 1982, p. 5)

A further example of this kind of confusion about stepfamily structure and dynamics appeared in a recent research report in a scientific journal:

Although her parents separated when she was five, her mother remarried when she was eight. She was raised thereafter in an intact home that included her only sibling, a brother five years older than she. (Warren & Tomlinson-Keasey, 1987)

Our hope is that therapeutic knowledge and skills will contribute to public validation of stepfamiles as positive and viable units with unique structures that are not imperfect copies of nuclear families, but rather, complex family systems created from the integration of old loyalties and new ties.

Palo Alto, California, 1987   Emily and John Visher

Prologue

The changes in American families have been dramatic. The divorce rate has risen 111% since 1970, and at the present time 79% of divorced men and 75% of divorced women remarry; 60% of these have children. It is estimated that one child in five under the age of 18 is a stepchild and that by the year 2000 this type of family will actually outnumber all other kinds of American families (Glick, 1984; Glick & Lin, 1986). No longer is a stepfamily an "alternative" family; it is a normative family with its own challenges and rewards.

OLD LOYALTIES, NEW TIES

Therapeutic Strategies with Stepfamilies

CHAPTER 1

American Stepfamilies
of the 1980s

*Everybody goes through trauma and everybody survives. At the beginning
I thought I wouldn't get through. Now I think I'm stronger for it.*
                    —Teenager living in a stepfamily

"Confusion," "complexity," "resentment," "jealousy," "guilt," "chaos"—these
are a few of the associations that therapists give in response to the word
"stepfamily." The pattern of their associations is consistent. There are also
phrases like "hidden agendas," "alienation," "walking on eggs," "never enough
time," "not as good." Once in a while a timid voice mentions "love," "challenge,"
"humor," "exciting," and a phrase such as "parental happiness," but usually
the word "stepfamily" conjures up a negative image. While the word "family"
may denote hearth and home, pictures of Cinderella shivering by the ashes of
the fire tend to accompany "stepfamily."

Therapists are not alone in their negative associations. In fact, they may be
reflecting not only their own experience working with stepfamilies, but also
the influence of cultural stereotypes. We do not know whether or not we
would receive the same responses to descriptive synonyms such as "blended,"
"remarriage," "synergistic," or "reconstituted" families. There are, however,
no substitute designations for "stepparent," and several studies have tested
the image of "stepmother and stepfather" as compared to "mother and
father" with the conclusion that "step" appears to be pejorative, signifying a
more negative image (Ganong & Coleman, 1983).

In contrast to their more experienced colleagues, counselors who were
inexperienced viewed stepfamilies less positively than nuclear families, seeing
stepparents as less potent and less well-adjusted than adults they believed to
be from nuclear families. Adolescents who were evaluated by the inexperienced counselors were also seen as less potent, less active, and less well-

3

adjusted if they were said to have been from a stepfamily (Bryan, Ganong, Coleman, & Bryan, 1985).

Over 700 college students were found to have utilized family structure as a cue to form stereotypes of a negative character (Bryan et al., 1986). In this study stepparents were seen more negatively than married or widowed parents, and stepchildren were ranked even more negatively than stepparents, falling below children of all other family types tested, including those living with a never-married parent or with a divorced parent who had not remarried. The authors comment, "Though the term *wicked* is readily associated with stepmother and *abusive* has recently been linked with stepfather, it may be that the frequent use of *stepchild* to mean poor, neglected, and ignored has had an insidious impact on attitudes over time" (p. 173). Indeed, this picture of stepchildren may affect stepfamilies in ways not generally recognized, the children at times gaining unproductive power in the suprafamily system as the adults attempt to "make up to them" for the disadvantaged position they are thought to be in.

Another instance comes to mind in which a group of stepfamilies met together shortly before Christmas, the children and the adults meeting in separate discussion groups at the beginning of the evening. They joined together for a holiday party later. The adults were surprised to learn that during the discussion time the children had expressed feelings of happiness and contentment, and had very few negative responses to their family status. It seems that the adults may have been reacting to an inner perception of the children that was stereotypically based.

Stepfamily stereotypes are formed early. A three-year-old expects her friend's stepmother to make her sweep the house, and a seven-year-old says to her stepmother, "You can't be my stepmother, you're not mean enough." No wonder many stepfamilies, wishing to receive the approval of society, conceal their "stepfamilyhood" and pretend that they are nuclear or biological families. Reversing or at least neutralizing this negative stereotype will not be easy since the stories of Cinderella, Snow White, and Hansel and Gretel have yet to be replaced by popular tales featuring benign stepparents.

It has been our impression that most reports from clinicians tend to emphasize the problems in stepfamilies, probably because they have contact with a population which has sought help because of its difficulties, while the empirical researchers who are looking at nonclinical populations tend to have a more positive view of stepfamily life. This impression has been verified by Ganong & Coleman (1986).

Thinking of this matter reminded us of a pediatrician we knew who said, "I'm never going to have any children of my own because they're always sick." Just as he had a biased view because of the restricted population he served, clinicians and researchers may be reacting to different subsamples of the total population—clinicians dealing with families who are talking about their difficulties and reseachers working with families who are willing to be interviewed and answer questionnaires (often because they feel proud of the progress they have made in integrating their stepfamily and want to share their experiences with others).

We believe it is extremely important for therapists to remain aware of the strengths and rewards in stepfamilies while helping them deal with their difficulties. Since the focus of this book is on the "roadblocks" to stepfamily integration, we will be discussing problem areas. In light of this, we consider that it is crucial to remain sensitive to the larger, more objective, stepfamily context. Only a few of the total number of stepfamilies will ever seek therapeutic help, while many will utilize generally available information to guide them along their way. Of those who seek a therapeutic contact, many will do so not because of personal weakness but because they have psychological awareness and strength. They turn to therapy as a valuable tool to help them create a rewarding family life for themselves and their children. This outlook is supported by a considerable body of research and clinical observation showing the stepfamily to be a viable and positive family type.

Among the older studies, Duberman (1975) found that 64% of her stepfamilies rated themselves as having excellent relationships, while only 18% said they were experiencing poor relationships. Bernard (1956) cautiously concluded that stepfamily relations may in many cases be mutually supportive and healthier than the problem-filled family involved in a disruptive first marriage. Burchinal (1964) studied 1500 Iowa high school students and concluded that there were no findings that divorce or remarriage had any long-term significant detrimental effects. Wilson et al. (1975) performed a statistical analysis of two national surveys and concluded that there were no measurable outcome differences between individuals who had experienced stepfather families as compared to other types of family arrangements. In summary, these older studies seem to indicate that children arrive at the same place, but get there by different routes.

More recent studies report similar findings. For example, Santrock, Warshak & Elliott (1982) found that there were few differences in social behavior between stepchildren and children (aged 6-11 years) in nuclear or single-parent households. They also found, as a result of direct observation in a controlled experimental situation, that the social development of boys from stepfamilies was more competent and mature, although girls tended to be more anxious. Furstenburg (1981) has studied remarriage and intergenerational relations. He says, ". . . remarriage has the consequence of distributing a diminishing pool of children among a larger circle of adults. For children it means being connected, albeit sometimes only weakly, to a great number of adults who are prepared to treat them as kin" (p. 136). Family networks are reinforced, and parenting can be shared by a larger kinship group. Bohannan & Yahraes (1979) reported the results of a random survey in San Diego, California. They found that stepchildren view themselves as being just as happy as biological children, as well as just as successful and achieving. These children reported getting along with their stepfathers as well as the biological children reported getting along with their fathers. However, the stepfathers tended to view themselves as less successful, and their stepchildren as less happy, a perception with which their wives did not agree. In fact, living in this type of family has been found to ameliorate many of the negative effects of divorce for children (Chapman, 1977; Peterson & Zill, 1986).

Another study examined remarried families' perceptions of their strengths (Knaub, Hanna, & Stinnett, 1984), and while most of the families reported that there were changes they would like to have been able to make, their scores were high on family strength, marital satisfaction, and perception of family adjustment. Some clinical writers have also looked at stepfamily strengths, and Crohn et al. (1982), writing about the positive aspects of remarriage, say:

> A successful (remarriage) family has a great deal to offer adults and children. It provides exposure to a variety of life styles, opinions, feelings, and enriching relationships. In (remarriage), an adult forms a new love relationship with a partner, which is often strengthened by maturity, life experience, and stability in identity and grows through the gaining of independence and free choice as opposed to desperation and fear. The previously divorced adult, wiser from hindsight, forms a new type of marital relationship, with the opportunity to parent and to benefit from a supportive suprasystem. In (remarriage), children can learn to appreciate and respect differences in people and ways of living, can receive affection and support from a new stepparent and the new suprasystem, and can observe the remarried parent in a good and loving marital relationship, using this as a model for their own future love relationships. If an only child, he or she may gain the experience of cooperation that a subsystem with other children offers (p. 162).

Sager et al. (1983) also write about the positive potential of remarriage from the viewpoint of the child, crediting Dicks (1967) with these points:

> There are many positive aspects of the multiplicity of (remarriage) for the child. After seeing a destructive marital relationship between his

bio-parents, he may gain positive models and a feeling of stability from the loving interaction of the (remarriage) couple. He may get care and attention from his stepparents, sibs, and grandparents that add to the bounty from bio-parents. The multiplicity of personalities, styles of living and values may give the child the rich mosaic of life in an extended family without its structural certitude and monolithicity. A stepparent offers the child opportunities for selective identification and may compensate for limitations in the bio-parents. A child whose mother is a stern, distant person may look to the warmth and gentleness of his stepmother as a way of getting some other needs gratified. His father may love him but have a limited education; the child may find intellectual stimulation in a brighter or more educated stepfather. His breadth of choice of a future mate is broadened insofar as he is influenced by parental introjects and projections. (pp. 237-238)

The chances of having a successful stepfamily experience are enhanced when the milieu surrounding the family is accepting and supportive (Knaub, Hanna, & Stinnett, 1984). With 30% of all marriages being the remarriage of at least one of the adults (Glick & Lin, 1986), a revision of the family life cycle seems in order. As Goldner (1982) states it, "If the first marriage is no longer the happy ending to childhood, but rather the first in a series of stages that characterize a more demanding adult life, family therapists need to recast their understanding of family structure and development with this in mind" (p. 190).

Morawetz (1984) goes a step further when she says that perhaps family therapists are contributing to, rather than ameliorating, problems of step-families by not being "open to the view that couples and families may cope better if their expectations of marriage and family life include the idea of separation and divorce" (p. 572); we would add "remarriage." Even the popular press is commenting on the issue: "The prevalence of a remarriage hardly suggests a demise of the institution of marriage. Rather, countless couples like those interviewed here indicate that the concept of marriage is being expanded to included divorce, cohabitation, and remarrying as parts of a whole life cycle of coupling. It is a concept that places high value on personal growth and fulfillment and permits individuals to strive for better relationships. It is a concept that reaffirms the ideas on which a successful marriage is built" (Dahl, 1984, p. 274).

The message seems clear. At the present time the tightly knit nuclear family is no longer meeting the needs of a great many people. There are a number of reasons for this: because of the increased life span, there is a potential for couples to be married longer, and this gives more opportunity for partners to change and drift apart; the women's movement has altered women's expectations of marriage; religious values have shifted; and the focus of many individuals has changed from concerns about survival to concerns about the quality of their lives. Perhaps the move from an agricultural to an urban society has also put a strain on families; no longer are there extended kin to help with the raising of the children. With the present mobility of American society, many families no longer have roots in one familiar community. The proliferation of stepfamilies may be an adaptation to these changes. While other adaptations may appear, this type of family is likely to be a prominent family form for the forseeable future and a more positive view seems desirable:

> Stepfamilies and professionals who work with them need to know that their family complexity can bring richness and diversity to their members. Building new relationships makes stepfamily members sensitive to the importance of communication and emotional touching. (They) can experience the deep satisfaction and bonding that result from working together to meet difficult challenges. Learning to cope effectively with the pain of loss can produce an ability to deal creatively with the inevitable changes and losses that are a part of life itself. (Visher & Visher, 1982, p. 119)

Stress does not necessarily signal dysfunction, and pain does not necessarily lead to psychological damage. Both can facilitate growth and an appreciation of the importance of caring relationships.

CHAPTER 2

Theoretical Considerations

Recognition of transitional conflict is the key to helping families in cultural transition.

—Judith Landau-Stanton (1985, p. 369)

The basic goal of all families is to provide an atmosphere in which important needs of the adults and children are met, so that the adults find happiness in their lives and the children grow and develop into productive and mature adults. To provide this, stepfamily individuals first must move from diverse previous family cultures to an integrated stepfamily culture. Knowledge of what to expect and ways to make the transition go more smoothly can do much to reduce the transitional stresses and the time involved to accomplish the necessary changes. Even after integration has occurred, the complexity of the suprafamily system may lead to therapeutic contact at times of family transition. Individual problems can occur at any time.

This chapter is devoted to exploring the norms of stepfamilies, their tasks, and their basic therapeutic needs. The remainder of the book describes certain areas of distress and ways in which therapists can help with the delicate process of stepfamily integration and validation.

We define a stepfamily as a household in which there is an adult couple at least one of whom has a child from a previous relationship. We include in our definition households in which the children may reside for periods of time varying from none to full time. Because of basic similarities, we include couples who may not be legally married, but who do have a significant commitment to one another.

TRANSITIONAL FOCUS WITH STEPFAMILIES

Judith Landau-Stanton has written extensively about therapy with families in transition (Landau, 1982; Landau-Stanton, Griffiths, & Mason, 1982; Landau-Stanton, 1985). We find these concepts valuable since we see functioning stepfamilies as families which have made a successful transition from previous family cultures to a new stepfamily culture. We have found that the majority of stepfamilies which seek therapeutic help are asking for assistance with this transition, and "the conflicts arising from transitional factors must provide the initial focus for therapy" (Landau-Stanton, Griffiths & Mason, 1982, p. 368). According to these authors, transitional conflicts arise when individuals or family subsystems do not adapt to the new culture in a synchronous manner. Resulting conflicts may produce considerable stress and symptomatology which cannot be considered pathological per se, but can be viewed as behavior that is the result of the transitional difficulties.

As a rule, stepfamily individuals progress at different rates along the continuum of adaptation to the new family pattern. Bounded by the environmental characteristics outlined in Table 1, adults and children move towards

TABLE 1

Stepfamily Characteristics	Stepfamily Tasks
1. Begins after many losses and changes	1. Dealing with losses and changes
2. Incongruent individual, marital, family life cycles	2. Negotiating different developmental needs
3. Children and adults all come with expectations from previous families	3. Establishing new traditions
4. Parent-child relationships predate the new couple	4. Developing a solid couple bond and forming new relationships
5. Biological parent elsewhere in actuality or in memory	5. Creating a "Parenting Coalition"
6. Children often members of two households	6. Accepting continual shifts in household composition
7. Legal relationship between stepparent and children is ambiguous or non-existent	7. Risking involvement despite little societal support

integration and solidity, with typically different rates of speed. Mapping the suprafamily system (see section on genograms in Chapter 3) and assessing the adjustment difficulties of family members can help clarify the source of stepfamily tensions and suggest the initial therapeutic focus. In stepfamilies in which only one adult has children, we find a typical pattern to be the following:

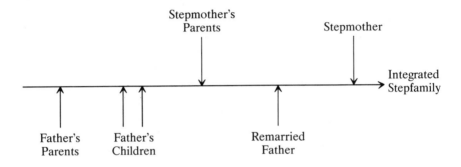

In this pattern, common difficulties are: difficulties between the couple; severe stress and anxiety on the part of the stepparent; disturbed relationships for the remarried parent; manipulative behavior by the children.

When both adults have children, both have strong pulls towards the new pattern and at the same time have pulls from their children, and perhaps from their families of origin, towards the past. In these stepfamilies, while both adults may be closer together in their adaptation to the stepfamily culture, the contradictory nature of the forces both are experiencing may result in their remaining "stuck" in their attempts to change.

Kim and Thomas are a couple who, as in the typical diagram above, illustrate a progression in therapy from transitional issues to marital and personal therapy. They were seen initially because of the chaos in their stepfamily. Kim, the stepmother, was anxious and distraught and Thomas found himself caught between his desire to move forward and his children's wishes to return to the past. The couple had little "glue" in their relationship and were seen as a couple, with the focus on these transitional stepfamily issues. These issues settled down relatively quickly and in this family the two children were never included in therapy since the couple working together reduced the effectiveness of the children's divisive behavior and moved them in the direction of contributing to the new unit.

Once the turmoil had subsided, intimacy issues between the couple led to marital therapy. Upon termination of therapy as a couple, Thomas decided to continue in individual therapy. He wished to deal with several important areas that had surfaced during the therapy sessions — his reactions to his own parents' divorce and to his mother's remarriage when he was eight years old. Thus, the therapy progressed from the "transitional" level to the "individual" intrapsychic level.

Much has been written about working therapeutically with marital and individual issues. Because of the importance of the initial therapeutic focus being on transitional interpersonal stepfamily dynamics, we have put the emphasis in this book in this direction.

RELATIONSHIP CHANGES

The relationship patterns in stepfamilies progress through predictable stages and are different from those in other types of families. Figures 1, 2, and 3 are examples of relationship patterns in functional nuclear families and functional new and mature stepfamilies. These diagrams are simplified, showing only the relationships and bonds between the parenting adults and children, although other relationships can be extremely important, such as grandparents and steprelationships in the other households. The thickness or character of the connecting lines signifies the strength of the relationships.

THE BASIC INTEGRATIVE TASKS

The basic task for stepfamilies is a dual one:

1. To redefine and maintain existing parent/child and ex-spouse relationships in a new context;
2. To develop new relationship patterns so that the household progresses from the initial stages in which there is little connectedness between the individuals (Figure 2) to a sense of trust between them that brings with it the recognition that the household has constructed a solid identity as a family unit (Figure 3).

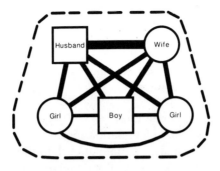

Figure 1. Nuclear Family

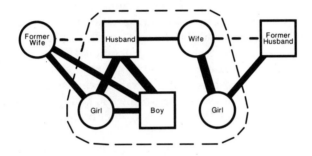

Figure 2. New Stepfamily

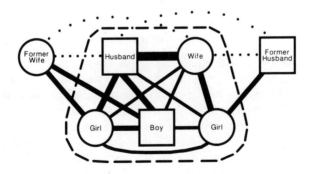

Figure 3. Mature Stepfamily

In the effort to fulfill this basic task, present information suggests that satisfactory achievement of the following goals leads to individual happiness and good stepfamily integration:

1. There is a good couple relationship.
2. There are warm parent/child relationships.
3. There are mutually satisfying steprelationships (there can be wide variations in the degree of closeness in these relationships).
4. Children are not cut off from a biological parent.
5. The adults in the children's households are able to cooperate in connection with the children.

Working toward these goals can be a lengthy process because individuals in stepfamilies do not start from a neutral position in their effort to develop mutually satisfying family patterns. Instead, children and adults come together with built-in alliances, problematic generational boundaries, a locus of influence outside of the household, and little if any family history or loyalty. Theirs is a struggle to move from disintegrative to integrative patterns and to establish themselves as a viable and worthwhile family unit, albeit a family system connected through the children to other households, thus creating a "suprafamily system" (Sager et al., 1983).

The transformation of stepfamily disequilibrium and complexity into equilibrium and richness requires patience, humor, and tolerance for ambiguity. However, it also has many rewards: it clarifies productive and unproductive coalitions and alliances; it outlines what is necessary for development and maintenance of relationships; it makes conscious and visible what is necessary for family satisfaction and happiness.

STEPFAMILY NORMS

There is a tendency to evaluate stepfamilies by normative impressions that apply to biological families rather than using suitable norms that apply to stepfamilies. Nuclear (or biological) families are idealized and other types of families are compared negatively with them, thus creating a "deficit model" for other than nuclear family structures (Ganong & Coleman, 1984). The use of this model for stepfamilies is both inaccurate and damaging; stepfamilies need to be evaluated by use of their own norms (Anderson & White, 1986). This is very important since an essential ingredient in happiness is self-esteem and a feeling of self-worth; when individuals (or families) are compared, or compare themselves, with unsuitable and unrealistic positive standards, they become disillusioned and discouraged.

A. General Stepfamily Characteristics

Our list of general stepfamily characteristics contains 15 normative standards, most of which have been addressed by both researchers and clinicians. All of them are important and contribute, particularly initially, to the "make-believe" ambience of the household in which individuals may pretend they belong, while in fact they feel disconnected from one another and from their environment. The first eight items tend to remain somewhat constant over time, while the last seven change as a stepfamily develops and grows.

1. Stepfamilies have a complex structure. There are many possible relationships, each of which can cause problems, particularly at first (Visher & Visher, 1982; White & Booth, 1985). It is helpful to think in suprafamily system terms, since there may be connections to other households, with decision-making involving more than one household. There are usually a large number of people with whom relationships may be established.

2. There are different and unique structural characteristics (Bernard, 1956; Sager et al., 1983; Wald, 1981; Visher & Visher, 1979). A set of characteristics which distinguish stepfamilies from nuclear families is given in Table 1. While the tasks arising from these characteristics change over time, the basic structure does not. It is important to recognize that their special structure does not make stepfamilies *better* or *worse* than nuclear families; they are simply *different.*

3. Stepfamilies have more stress than nuclear families (Pasley & Ihinger-Tallman, 1982). We believe much of this is caused by stepfamily ambiguity (Boss & Greenberg, 1984), complexity, and the "lack of fit" with cultural norms of an "ideal" family. Since the complexity remains, so does the stress, although this lessens considerably as children become independent and leave home. It is important to note that stress cannot be equated automatically with dissatisfaction since many sought-after situations involve stress.

4. Satisfactory stepfamily integration generally takes years rather than months to achieve. Age and sex of children, as well as type of stepfamily (i.e., stepmother or stepfather family, complex stepfamily structure) can affect the integration time. The minimum seems to be about two years (Stern, 1978).

5. *Very often there are cut-off relationships.* In a random sample of divorced couples, 75% of the children had no contact with their fathers (Furstenberg & Nord, 1985). There may be partial cut-offs when siblings live in two different households. These may not change over time, although when children reach adulthood they may seek to find their absent parent.

6. *There may be continual transitions.* Messinger et al. (1978; 1981) speak of the necessity for "permeable boundaries" so that children who see both of their biological parents can move easily between households. The necessity for such permeability remains even when the children have grown. For example, imagine the task of juggling four families at Christmas or Hanukkah if each adult in the couple has parents who are divorced or remarried. You need a computer!

7. *There is less cohesiveness in stepfamilies than in nuclear or single-parent households.* We do not know of a study that has looked at this directly, but it follows from the need for permeable boundaries. Research reviewed by Ganong & Coleman (1984) finds that stepchildren feel less close to stepparents than they do to biological parents and they do not wish to be like their stepparents when they grow up. (To us, this implies less family cohesiveness.) Clinically, there are many retrospective reports by grown children saying, in effect, "I didn't like my stepparent when I was growing up, even though now we're the best of friends." As children become adults, other situations arise which suggest less cohesiveness, such as the importance of inheritance issues (Visher & Visher, 1979).

8. *There is a great variety in the patterns in stepfamily households (Bradt & Bradt, 1986; White & Booth, 1985).* In addition to patterns related to children from previous relationships, there are diverse custody and residential arrangements. Moreover, a stepfamily formed after a death may be significantly different than one formed following a divorce. Within the household, the "expected" ways a family operates may not apply. When one stepfamily with children from two former families found it beneficial to the family for the children to eat separately from the adults and for the adults to spend Saturdays doing something without the children, they were labeled a "bad" stepfamily.

Creativity and flexibility seem to be a must in stepfamilies as they seek out the many creative solutions which allow them the time and space, both physical and psychological, that they need to develop and grow. Creativity and variety may be needed less frequently over time, but situations continue to arise (weddings, births, deaths, holidays) that may call for unusual solutions and arrangements.

9. There are many unrealistic expectations and a lack of realistic norma-tive information (Coleman & Ganong, 1987; Schulman, 1972; Visher & Visher, 1979). This is changing as normative patterns become more widely known. Therapy can provide corrective information and education.

10. There is no past history of homeostasis (Goldner, 1982; Visher & Visher, 1979). The new stepfamily is a group of individuals who need to work out interactional patterns; it is not a family with repetitive interactional cycles.

11. Previous "givens" are no longer givens (Goldner, 1982; Visher & Visher, 1979). New stepfamily individuals often speak of "culture shock." A self-consciousness of their own behavior and an acute awareness of the behavior of others in the household create the feeling of an unfamiliar, at times alien, environment. Seemingly trivial things can become important and need to be respected by others.

12. There is no shared family history (Goldner, 1982). Initially, there can be no history as a family. Sharing individual histories and creating stepfamily memories can be helpful. Too great an expectation of intimate family togeth-erness too early only increases the new family's discomfort.

13. Steprelationships have no solid foundation of understanding so the relationship is measured by what is happening at the moment. Unlike biolog-ically "given" relationships, steprelationships have no foundation of under-standing and caring. For parent/child and other biologically related individuals, the ups and downs of the moment are superimposed on a largely uncon-scious foundation of shared experience and caring. For steprelatives, even direct communication is more difficult because they do not have understand-ing, built up over time, of nonverbal cues and the implications of verbal communications. There is a need to "learn each other's language." The older the children at the time of stepfamily formation, the longer and more difficult this process may be. Therapists can be helpful by acknowledging this area of difficulty and having steprelatives clarify their messages.

14. There are many loyalty conflicts (Anderson & White, 1986; Keshet, 1980; Sager et al., 1983; Visher & Visher, 1979). While loyalty issues occur in other types of families, the loyalty conflicts in stepfamilies are more promi-nent because of stepfamily structure. According to Keshet (1980), "The stepfamily will always have strongly bounded subsystems to which members remain loyal" (p. 530). However, if the family does not achieve a satisfactory resolution, the integration of the family will be incomplete.

15. Roles in the stepfamily are ambiguous. Much has been written on this subject and considerable empirical research has examined the stepparent role (Hetherington, 1985; Mills, 1984; Stern, 1982). A positive aspect of ambiguity is that it provides freedom of choice. A variety of roles with different children is possible. Therapists are providing invaluable assistance to stepfamilies by helping parents to take active parenting roles and enabling stepparents to stand back and support the parents' efforts to do so. (Limit-setting issues are discussed at more length in Chapter 11.)

These normative characteristics have often been labeled as dysfunctional. Our premise is that they can be expected, even anticipated. Indeed, in that acceptance lie the seeds of change where change is possible, and the ability to find happiness within those parameters of stepfamily life where change is not possible.

B. Specific Stepfamily Characteristics

Clinical impressions of stepfamilies and the ways in which they can enhance their development and functioning are important guidelines for therapists. In the past few years, many of these therapeutic observations and assumptions have been tested empirically. In a number of areas, research is supporting clinical impressions, while at other times it is opening new lines of inquiry. In still other areas, there are contradictory findings which need to be clarified. With education and changes in the expectations of society, normative data can change over time. What follows are specific characteristics where present research findings are consistent and have important implications for therapy. In most of the studies, children are included only when they reside in the household at least 50% of the time.

1. The marital relationship. Helpful to therapists is the clear message that marital satisfaction in a stepfamily does not ensure family satisfaction. Put another way, stepfamily dysfunction does not necessarily signify a poor couple relationship (Anderson & White, 1986; Brand & Clingempeel, 1987; Crosbie-Burnett, 1984; White & Booth, 1985).

Forming a solid couple relationship does not mean that stepparent/stepchild relationships will necessarily be positive. Steprelationships will need to be developed independently of the couple relationship. We see interdependency between the marital relationship and stepparent/stepchild relationships. However, because of the lack of identity as a family unit, we believe that forming a good couple relationship comes before therapeutic concentration on the stepparent/stepchild relationship. The couple needs to have adequate bonding in order for the stepfamily unit to remain together to develop satisfactory steprelationships. In addition, there is more motivation initially to work on this relationship. One man put it succinctly when he said, "We married each other because we loved each other, not because we loved the kids and couldn't wait to be their parents."

If the remarried parent does not have satisfactory emotional bonding to his/her new spouse, it is unlikely that the parent would be able to relinquish enough emotional connection with the child to allow the stepparent to form a relationship with that child. However, even though there is marital satisfaction, research is indicating that often families do not stay together when positive stepparent/stepchild relationships are not developed (White & Booth, 1985). Dynamically, this is quite different from first marriages.

2. Stepparenting. Bernard (1956) has said that parenting in a stepfamily is "one of the most difficult of all human assignments" (p. 14). Recent studies continue to support this statement (Duberman, 1975; Fast & Cain, 1966; Furstenberg, 1987; Giles-Sims, 1984). While this is not an easy task both for stepmothers and stepfathers, there is strong evidence that stepmothers have much more difficulty than do stepfathers (Adams, 1982; Ahrons & Wallisch, 1987; Nadler, 1976). We believe this may be rooted in expectations that women are the ones who are primarily responsible for the ambience of the home and the care of the children, including stepchildren. In fact, many women still derive much of their self-esteem from their role as parents. This, in turn, may contribute to the finding that there is more tension between the mother and stepmother than between a child's father and stepfather, the more negative repercussions of which can affect particularly the acceptance of the stepmother.

While boys exhibit more problems than girls following divorce, girls have greater difficulty than do boys following a remarriage (Clingempeel, Brand, & Ievoli, 1984; Hess & Camara, 1979; Santrock et al., 1982; Wallerstein & Kelly, 1980), with the stepmother/stepdaughter relationship being the most difficult relationship to develop (Clingempeel et al., 1984; Ferri, 1984). In fact, Adams (1982) found that having all female stepchildren was the best predictor of stepmother unhappiness, regardless of whether or not she was a residential or a nonresidential stepmother.

3. Adolescent stepchildren. Clinicians and researchers report that adolescents have a particularly difficult time in new stepfamilies (Peterson & Zill, 1986; Visher & Visher, 1979), especially in the area of discipline (Lutz, 1983), and when there is differential treatment of stepsiblings within the household

(Ihinger-Tallman, 1985, 1987). In fact, adolescents tend to leave their stepfamilies to live on their own at an earlier age than they do in biological families (White & Booth, 1985).

4. Stepfather families. Stepfather families are stepfamilies in which the man is the stepparent. Studies indicate that this type of stepfamily tends to have less stress than the other types of stepfamilies (Clingempeel et al., 1984; Crosbie-Burnett, 1985; Visher & Visher, 1979). Boys in particular respond favorably to having a stepfather join the household (Santrock et al., 1982), and many develop satisfying relationships with their stepfathers (Bohannan & Yahraes, 1979). Having contact with their biological fathers tends to enhance the ability of boys to form good relationships with their stepfathers. From the perspective of stepfathers, having no children other than stepchildren increases the stepfather's ability to bond with his stepchildren (Furstenburg & Spanier, 1984).

5. Stepmother families. Stepmother families are families in which the woman is the stepparent. These families exhibit much more stress than do stepfather families (Clingempeel et al., 1984; Hetherington, 1987; Santrock & Sitterle, 1987; White & Booth, 1985). Not only do stepmothers report high stress levels, but the children as well experience higher stress when they are living with their father and stepmother than when they are living with their mother and stepfather (Jacobson, 1987).

These are consistent findings which we feel are important because they indicate that, whatever the personality clashes or individual psychology within the stepfamily, there are strong situational dynamics at work which create special relationship problems for stepmother families. Since stepmother families are usually defined as stepfamilies in which the father has custody of at least one of his children, it may be that disturbances in mother/child bonds, particularly mother/daughter bonding, are more upsetting to children than disturbances in the father/child bonds during and after divorce. Difficulty between the children's mother and stepmother has been mentioned previously as a possible contribution to the difficulty in stepmother families.

We wonder if another of the factors which account for these differences has to do with the identification children have with their same-sex parent and the different parental living arrangements after a divorce and remarriage (e.g. fathers, as a rule, move out after a divorce, and boys lose the person with whom they identify; after a remarriage, children, as a rule, live with a stepfather, so that boys have an important male figure again, while girls become competitive with their mothers). These are important questions for further clinical observation and empirical research.

The implication for therapy appears to us to be that stepparents, particularly stepmothers, may need considerable support from the therapist as new stepfamily relationships are forming.

6. Complex stepfamilies. Complex stepfamilies are families in which *both* adults have children from a previous marriage. The greatest difficulties reported by stepfamilies have been problems connected with the children (Messinger et al., 1978). This perception is validated by several investigations, all of which find that the presence of stepchildren increase the chances that a remarriage will end in divorce (Becker et al., 1977; Cherlin, 1978; McCarthy, 1978; White & Booth, 1985). In fact, White & Booth (1985) find that the greatest likelihood of divorce is in complex stepfamilies. Thus, in a stepfamily, complaints about difficulties concerning the children can be considered valid and do not necessarily signal marital problems, although they may cause tension between the couple.

It may be that divorce and stress are not highly correlated. While White & Booth (1985) find the highest divorce rate to be in complex stepfamilies, clinically we find stepmother families to be overrepresented in therapy and to be the type of stepfamily that seems to exhibit the greatest amount of stress (Visher & Visher, 1979).* It may be that these stepmothers are less likely to divorce than are stepmothers/mothers in complex stepfamilies who have the support of their children and the recognition that they can function on their own, after divorce. We hope researchers will address this question.

STEPFAMILY TASKS

Achieving an Identity

Stepfamilies have before them basic goals of "blending and becoming" (Wald, 1981). We conceptualize it as creating a new family culture. They have the need to develop a strong sense of family self, a positive identity as a worthwhile family unit. Achieving this goal is difficult for many remarried family units. In fact, many of the specific problems raised by stepfamily individuals tend to arise from their struggle to feel like a "real" family. As Goldner (1982) says: "Crises that paralyze remarried families are ultimately rooted in fundamental questions of family identity that can be traced back to fundamental problems with family development" (p. 201). The unifying thread running through this book is that there are common challenges that arise for stepfamilies as they attempt to accomplish the tasks necessary for

---

*Stepfamily Association of America supports this observation. A sampling of calls and letters revealed that an overwhelming majority of inquiries come from stepmothers with no children of their own (Mullen, 1987).

achieving a sense of stepfamily legitimacy, and there are ways in which therapists can help families with this complicated process.

It is because of their basic structure that stepfamilies have tasks with which they need to deal before they can attain a solid family identity. In fact, adults and children in stepfamilies come together suddenly with little connectedness or trust. As they work to gain their equilibrium, it is not that the homeostasis of the family has broken down; rather, new stepfamily groups have never had stability. Achieving this stability is their basic task.

Specific Tasks

Table 1 (p. 10) lists the major structural characteristics of stepfamilies which we consider important and the specific tasks arising from these characteristics. Accomplishing these tasks requires considerable time. Papernow (1984) has studied the emotional stages experienced by adults as they attempt to structure their new family units.* Remarried parents and stepparents are often bewildered by the array and strength of emotions they are feeling. Learning more about these predictable stages can often help them immeasurably because they no longer feel that there is something the matter with them because they are experiencing such feelings as jealousy, rejection and anger. In addition they can see how far they have come and that there is "light at the end of the tunnel," even though it may be a long tunnel. (A description of our adaptation of these stages appears in Chapter 4 because we consider that the emotional stage of the adults in the family is an important determinant of whom it is productive to see together in therapy. Please refer to Table 3, p. 65.)

We have found it helpful to conceptualize into eight general areas the difficulties commonly encountered by stepfamilies in their attempts to develop a satisfying and solid family identity. We realize that the divisions are interrelated and overlapping. However, they can be used as organizing principles:

Coping with loss and change	Power issues
Unrealistic beliefs	Loyalty conflicts
Life cycle discrepancies	Boundary problems
Insiders/outsiders	Closeness/distance

---

*We are using the term "structure" rather than the usual "restructure" because we consider that while former relationships are being *restructured*, this is the initial *structuring* of the stepfamily unit.

Table 2 summarizes our thoughts regarding the integrative tasks of step-families, the major areas of difficulty found in accomplishing each task, and the major intervention strategies we find we use in dealing with each area. (While all interventions can apply to all areas, enhancing self-esteem and the reduction of tension appeared to us to be too general to include separately.) Later chapters expand on these intervention strategies and areas of difficulty.

Therapeutic Needs of Stepfamilies

A. Validation. The very act of coming to therapy signals the reality of the stepfamily as a unit and offers the opportunity of participation in a project which produces shared experiences. It can often mark the beginning of the family's history together and, therefore, of its very existence. All too often, stepfamilies feel invisible, as though they are seen simply as dismembered parts of original "real" families who are occupying a common space. Even when only individuals or subgroups are actively involved in therapy, the viability of the stepfamily is validated as the therapist becomes the mirror reflecting back from the outside the visibility of the new family configuration.

The basic therapeutic task is to assist the family to move from the fragmented family system of Figure 2 (page 13) to the more cohesive system of Figure 3 (page 13) with important new relationships, a sense of stability, and satisfaction with and loyalty to the stepfamily unit as a significant entity in the suprafamily system.

Complicating the process of developing a positive sense of family are a number of important constraints: personal characteristics of the individuals, the amount of time the children are in the household, and the attitude of friends, relatives, and the general community. Steprelationships are more difficult to form and take a longer time when the members of the family are together intermittently, say only two days every two weeks, with parent/child relationships typically somewhat strained and superficial (Furstenberg & Nord, 1985; Greif, 1982). Added to this are the difficulties that outside individuals and society have in accepting changes in the constellation of families (Cherlin, 1978; Visher & Visher, 1979).

While it is indeed necessary to incorporate memories and experiences of prior family units into the present, the stepfamily is a new entity, separate and distinct from former family constellations. Too often, legal and social institutions (and sometimes grandparents and other kin) consider "stepparents as added appendages to the nuclear family" (Visher & Visher, 1978) so that the first marriage family becomes the only "real" family. Under such conditions it is understandable why many stepfamilies attempt, to their detriment, to

TABLE 2

Tasks*	Major Areas of Difficulty	Especially Important Intervention Strategies
1. Deal with losses and changes	Coping with loss & change Unrealistic belief systems	Relate past family experiences to present Make educational comments Use genograms Use accurate language
2. Negotiate different developmental needs	Life cycle discrepancies Power issues	Restructure/reframe Teach negotiation
3. Establish new traditions	Unrealistic belief systems Insiders/outsiders Closeness/distance	Teach negotiation Make educational comments
4. Develop solid couple bond	Insiders/outsiders Loyalty conflicts Boundary problems Power issues	Use genograms Relate past family experiences to present Teach negotiation Make educational comments Reduce a sense of helplessness

5. Form new relationships	Unrealistic belief systems Insiders/outsiders Loyalty conflicts Closeness/distance	Fill in past histories Encourage dyadic relationships Separate feelings & behavior Make educational comments
6. Create parenting coalition	Loyalty issues Unrealistic belief systems Power issues Dealing with losses & changes	Relate past family experiences to present Make educational comments Restructure/reframe
7. Accept continual shifts	Boundary problems Closeness/distance Unrealistic belief systems	Use genograms Reduce sense of helplessness Make educational comments Make specific suggestions
8. Risk involvement despite little societal support	Closeness/distance Dealing with losses & changes	Encourage dyadic relationships Make educational comments

*See Table 1 on p. 10.

masquerade as nuclear families. If stepfamilies can escape from their present negative stereotype (Bryan et al., 1986), their integrative tasks will become much easier. Outside of their households they need to find recognition and acceptance. Then, within their households their goal of integration as family units can become a more personally rewarding pursuit.

In summary, stepfamilies need internal and external validation that they exist. Therapists can provide an important source of such validation. This will help families progress from a stage of disequilibrium as the givens of the past come under conscious questioning and there is acute awareness of who says what to whom, through stages where the family balance seems as fragile as an eggshell, to an emotionally satisfying equilibrium in which the family sees itself "as a 'real' family that has dignity, worth, and value in its own right" (Wald, 1981, p. 193).

B. Supportive therapeutic climate. Sometime ago, we were impressed at the answer given by a panel of teenagers to the question, "What do you think makes a therapist a good therapist for stepfamilies?" These adolescents were siblings, the wife's children in a complex stepfamily in which both adults had children from a previous marriage. The couple had been married for eight years and had seen a number of therapists during this period. When the teenagers commented that some therapists had been helpful and shook their heads as they thought about the others, they were asked if they could identify what made a good therapist for stepfamilies. They responded without hesitation:

1. When you walk into their office, you know whether or not this is a person you would trust with your deepest secrets. What matters is whether they are warm or not. They need to be warm.
2. They need to have been there (in a stepfamily), gone through it themselves, so they know what you're talking about.
3. It's not helpful to take one person off from the rest and see that person alone. You need to see everyone, and not say it's one person's fault.

It seems to us that these young people succinctly and directly touched the basic core of therapy—warmth, knowledge, and understanding, along with a perspective that does not overlook the interpersonal milieu in which people are living. Stepfamilies, we believe, have a heightened awareness of these elements.

The importance of a friendly and warm therapy environment is well known. In studies of the effects of various types of therapy, a major finding has been that positive therapeutic outcome is more related to the warmth of the therapist than to the therapist's training and theoretical approach (Luborsky et al., 1985). For individuals in stepfamilies this is especially crucial since many stepfamilies feel that theirs is a "second-rate," "not-as-good" kind of family. Unfortunately, much of their experience may have reinforced this negative identity so that they often come to therapy with very low self-esteem, not only as individuals but also as members of a type of family considered inferior. Even as they look ahead to making things better, changing may be seen only as creating shifts to make the negative less painful. This is illustrated by the fact that often they are apologetic about the fact that they are in a stepfamily situation. It is difficult to reveal what seems personally negative, so at times stepfamily status is not even acknowledged for fear that the therapist will have a negative reaction.

As was discussed in Chapter 1, therapists and counselors frequently need to reevaluate their concepts of remarried families so that they will both consciously and unconsciously create a positive and validating therapeutic environment. To us this seems crucial since we believe that for families, as well as for individuals, liking your identity and feeling worthwhile as a family are fundamental to the optimal functioning of the unit.

The individuals in stepfamilies typically come together as partial strangers with no history as family groups and yet expecting themselves, and being expected by others, to exude confidence and quickly know what they are about as families. In actuality, even when the individuals exhibit good self-esteem, we do not believe that the sense of a solid identity as a stepfamily unit can exist until roles and rules have been negotiated, relationships formed and transformed, and enough time has elapsed for the stepfamily to develop its own traditions and create a firm foundation built on positive shared memories. The search, then, is for a solid and satisfactory identity.

If the vision of a functioning stepfamily is colored with dark overtones, then the goal can seem unworthy of the work involved. Relinquishing the "deficit model" for stepfamilies seems to us to be extremely important for individuals in remarried families and for professionals who are in a position to validate them and help them feel the warmth of acceptance.

To the teenagers referred to above, it seemed essential that stepfamily therapists have the experience of stepfamily living. This is a comment about the counselor or therapist often made by stepfamily members who have had an unsuccessful therapeutic contact. Such comments can occur in therapy in general and give therapists the opportunity to explore the negative feelings being expressed, as well as assess their reactions to and understanding of the person being seen. In the case of stepfamilies, not all of us have the luxury of getting married, having children, divorcing, and finding a suitable second partner prior to seeing stepfamilies in therapy! While it is true that life experiences can lead to therapeutic sensitivities, empathy is basically the result of professional training and knowledge of specific areas of interest. We are hopeful that this book will provide helpful information for those working with members of stepfamilies.

As we see it, the third issue raised by the teenage panel is concerned with a basic perspective of therapists, namely: Whom or what do they see as being central to the difficulties encountered by those with whom they work? While individuals bring their own emotions and reactions to every situation they encounter, we consider that interpersonal interactions and contextual and structural elements interact with these personal elements. We believe, then, even when working with a single individual, that the situational and inter-personal matrix of that person needs to be kept in mind as contributing to the difficulties encountered by the individual. This inclusive perception tends to be transmitted by the therapist so that the feeling is generated that one person alone is not responsible for the problems. In this way one individual is not "sep-arated off from the rest because it's their fault," as the teen panel commented.

C. Suprafamily system context. We believe it is necessary to conceptualize stepfamily systems in terms of the remarried family's suprafamily system. This includes, at a minimum, the members of the two households in which the parents of the children now reside. When both of the adults have children from a previous marriage, there can be at least three important households where stepsiblings are relating to each other. Many times the grandparents also play important roles in the suprafamily system drama, while aunts, uncles, and cousins can be important as well.

Because of continuing links to other households through the children, stepfamilies lack the distinct boundaries of nuclear families. Thus it is important to think in terms of a suprafamily system with a multitude of relationships, numerous subsystems, and the presence of more than two parenting adults. In place of two parents whose ability to work together affects the development of their children, there may be three or four adults whose ability to cooperate can affect the growth and happiness of the children.

We find the development of a "parenting coalition" to be a useful concept. A coalition may be defined as "a temporary alliance of discrete entities for the purpose of accomplishing a project." Each adult is separate, with different role expectations, but all are involved with the growing children. The specif-ic roles adopted by the parents and stepparents in the suprafamily unit can be extremely varied, depending on the needs of the children and the needs of the adults. Indeed, it has been found that a steprelationship offers many possibilities, from supporting the remarried parent or being an adult friend to the children to taking on a traditional parent role. The important element is that the role be satisfactory to the particular stepparent and stepchild (Crosbie-Burnett, 1984; Mills, 1984).

CONCLUSION

It can be challenging and rewarding to work with stepfamilies! A counselor or therapist is helping families develop skills, often at their birth; families not bounded by the constraints of nuclear families, which have fewer individuals to carry out necessary family tasks. Theirs is a complex structure, making possible many rewarding relationships, personal richness, and diversity.

When stepfamilies are successful, boundaries tend to be more open than those of other families; creativity and flexibility become valued personal attributes; a rich web of relationships have been forged; and individuals experience deep satisfaction and pride in their accomplishments. A 17-year-old says, "I know I can adjust to a million more situations because of what I've gone through. That's really a good feeling." An adult comments, "I can feel that we've moved. Not easily, because it's been a pain in the ass. But I feel very clear that our family works. That is resolved. It's been proven over the years that we could do it and we're doing it. We're happy for the most part. There's a lot of love. You can feel that the family is working" (Papernow, 1980, p. 204).

CHAPTER 3

Intervention Strategies

It's really great to find we're on track!

—Stepfamily adult to therapist

There are many theoretical approaches to working with families. In our experience, regardless of the therapist's theoretical orientation, the common element in working successfully with stepfamilies is the perception we have outlined that the family's first task is one of dealing with the changes inherent in the transition to a new family culture. No matter who in the family system is being seen, helping stepfamily members view many of their problems as difficulties that are inherent in their situation rather than in the personal characteristics of the players can help restore self-esteem and start them on their way to coping more effectively with their challenges. In this chapter we will discuss strategies which we consider can be of particular importance in working with stepfamilies and relate common dynamics of remarriage families to each intervention.

A. ENHANCE SELF-ESTEEM

An important goal of psychotherapy is the enhancement of self-esteem (Coopersmith, 1967). The lower our self-concept, the less able we are to cope adequately with the challenges of living. Individuals in stepfamilies confront powerful myths and negative community attitudes which frequently interfere with stepfamily integration and lessen the self-esteem of the individual stepfamily members (Schulman, 1972; Visher, 1984). For example, adults in stepfamilies usually expect that the new household will settle down quickly and that close relationships between stepparents and stepchildren will develop almost instantly. Characteristically, when this does not happen, stepparents are likely to feel that there is something wrong with them and that they have failed. They may feel guilty that they do not love their stepchildren and become angry and resentful because of the rejection they receive from their stepchildren.

The remarried parent, on the other hand, may feel guilty about the psychological trauma the children experienced at the time of the divorce or death of their other parent. He/she may also be frustrated and angry because the new family arrangement is not bringing happiness to either the children or the adults in the stepfamily. In this situation, children often feel responsible for causing tension, and consider they are bad or unloveable.

Frequently, guilt, anger, and disappointment result in anxiety and low self-esteem. It is very difficult to give emotional support to others when you are feeling empty and in turmoil. Since everyone in a new stepfamily may be experiencing considerable emotional pain at the same instant, there tends to be little support and validation available within the family system. In such instances, stepfamily growth often begins following implicit and explicit therapeutic messages that these reactions are to be expected in such situations and do not mean that there is something wrong with the individuals experiencing them.

A study by Papernow (1980) emphasized the importance of therapeutic support. She found that emotional support was necessary to achieve satisfactory integration of a stepparent with no children of his or her own. In 7 of the 9 families she studied in depth, this needed support came not from the spouse, but instead in most instances from a therapist, counselor, or friend. According to Papernow, external support was an essential ingredient in the success of the new stepfamily unit. The support of a therapist often can be the essential external support to restore a sense of worth to stepfamily adults.

The "countertransference" feelings of therapists may markedly affect their ability to be supportive to all members of the stepfamily. For example, therapists are generally able to quickly understand children who fear abandonment or have experienced relationship losses and may be having emotional reactions to these situations. We have all lived through similar feelings in childhood. The reaction of a parent who has remarried may also seem understandable to a therapist who is a parent, but empathy with and understanding of the feelings of stepparents may not be as easy for therapists who have not been stepparents or become familiar with the emotions experienced by individuals in this role. The stepparent is an outsider joining a subgroup composed of a parent and children. If the therapist is unable to identify and empathize with the feelings of the stepparent, stepfamily integration may be impeded, since the stepparent will be excluded from the new subgroup, which now includes the therapist and the other family members.

One therapist was unable to understand a stepmother's wish to have the couple's bedroom be off limits to the children after 9:30 p.m. He could, however, understand the children's wish for their accustomed unlimited access to their father, and their father's wish to please his children by not setting a time limit for their freedom of access. A coalition thus formed between the father, the children, and the therapist. The result was a further lowering of self-esteem and personal validity for the wife/stepmother. She felt guilty about her wish for exclusive husband-wife time together and angry about not being supported by the rest of the family and the therapist. As a consequence, the entire household gradually became more upset and soon broke away from therapy.

On the other hand, when a therapist is a stepparent, there can be danger of overidentification with a stepparent so that the therapist-stepparent alliance prevents the therapy from continuing on a smooth course. A therapist who was herself a stepmother found herself identified with a new stepmother whose husband would not include her in any of his outings with his three young children. The couple was seen conjointly, and the therapist's identification with the feelings of rejection experienced by the stepmother led the husband to feel that he was not being understood by the therapist. As a result, he began to withdraw from the therapy. Fortunately, the therapist began to ask about the husband's personal background. It soon became clear that his experiences with the divorce of his parents when he was a child led him to behave in a manner which tended to exclude his new wife from his relationship with his children. This clarification enabled the therapist to become supportive of both adults so that they could then work out more satisfactory arrangements for the children as well as for the participation of their stepmother.

When therapists are not able to understand stepfamily feelings and experiences, they may produce remarks such as the one made by a stepfamily adult who said, "I didn't need to have more guilt piled on." This type of comment usually stems from the lack of awareness by the therapist of stepfamily differences as he/she attempts to fit the stepfamily into a biological family mold. When this occurs, stepparents are not integrated into the family, emotional validation is not experienced, and there is little growth within the new family system. Therapeutic support, on the other hand, can reverse these trends, sometimes with surprising rapidity.

Tania, a stepmother with no children of her own, sought help because her stepdaughter's teacher reported that Lisa had begun failing in school since her father's remarriage. The counselor asked Lisa's new stepmother, "How often do you hug your stepdaughter?" When Tania replied that she did not show much physical affection to Lisa, the counselor commented on the importance to children of physical affection and attention. Tania felt even more guilty than she had previously, and when she got home she tried to hug Lisa, but Lisa pulled away. Instead of making the situation better, the counselor's advice had created even greater difficulties within the household.

Tania did need help adjusting to her new situation and she went to see a therapist who knew that it would take time to build a relationship between Tania and her stepdaughter. Improvement followed when Tania learned about the need to create a friendship bond before physical affection would be appropriate.

It was also helpful for Tania to have some positive recognition of her own strengths. At one point the therapist remarked, "Lisa is lucky to have a stepmother who is willing to drive her to school when it is raining and take her shopping for new school clothes." Tania began to like herself again and the situation improved between her and Lisa. A few meetings with all three members of the stepfamily supported their commitment to creating a new family unit, and they decided that they were "on track" when compared to other stepfamilies at a similar point in their history. This therapeutic enhancement of self-esteem can be of particular importance to stepfamily members because of lack of validation and support on the cultural level.

B. USE GENOGRAMS

The use of genograms can provide important data when working with any type of family. The longer we have worked with stepfamilies, the more we have come to value them. We have found that drawing a genogram at the beginning of therapy can be especially helpful as it provides information about previous marriages, the length of the single-parent household phases, and details about the shifts in the living arrangements of the children. It gives a picture of where family members have been and the direction in which they need to go. Most important of all, the complexity of the suprafamily system frequently becomes obvious to all. This promotes new understanding of underlying reasons for feeling overwhelmed, confused, and under stress. The construction of the genogram also signals to everyone present that all individuals in this complicated family system can be talked about.

Drawing a genogram may help virtual strangers who have come together to form a new family unit to overcome their general reluctance to reveal themselves to one another. Communication channels are opened, and historical backgrounds are filled in. It gives the family a specific task on which to work together, while at the same time providing the therapist with a great deal of important information.

Awareness of comments and nonverbal behavior can often highlight sensitive areas and dynamics of the family. For example when his children were present in the session, one husband supplied information that his first wife had been killed in an automobile accident. The children reacted visibly and the therapist immediately recognized the potentially painful area.

In another instance, a wife pointed out that the genogram did not include "two important members of our family, an accountant and an attorney!" The therapist thus quickly learned that there had been a great deal of legal sparring with one of the ex-spouses and that there was also a great deal of bitterness and anger on the part of several family members.

A study of the family's genogram can often suggest to the therapist what some of the major difficulties may be. Checking these hunches can shorten the length of the initial evaluation phase of therapy either because of the correctness of the interpretations or by the elimination of material no longer considered relevant.

We follow the standardized method of genogram construction described by McGoldrick and Gerson (1985). Genogram 1 along with its sections (Section 1-Section 8) and the symbol key illustrate the basic principles.

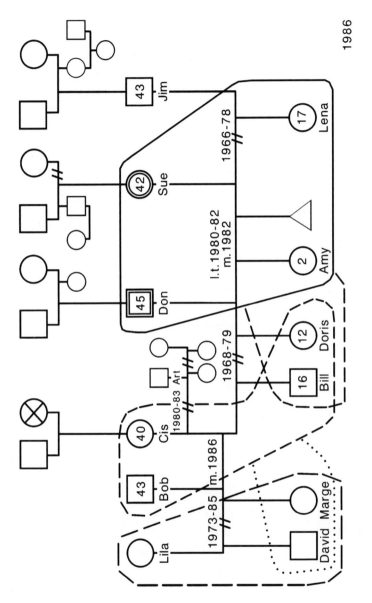

1986

Genogram 1

35

KEY

male

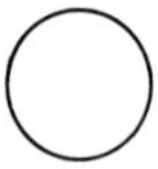

female

pregnancy

central individuals

marriage connection

living together

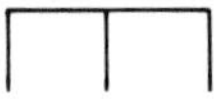

children

separated

divorced

deceased—year

m.   married—year
l.t. living together—year
d.   divorced—year
s.   separated—year

The date in the lower right is the year in which the genogram was drawn. The individuals and the recorded information indicate what the situation is at the time of drawing the genogram.

Relationship lines are drawn diagonally (see McGoldrick and Gerson, 1985). We do not generally include these lines; instead we note it in writing.

36

Living arrangements. The more solid the line the greater the duration of time spent by the children in the household. For example:

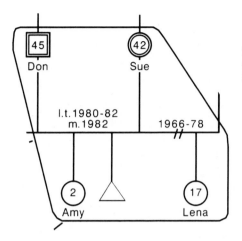

Don, Sue, Amy and Lena are together 100% of the time (Lena is cut off from her father, Jim).

Section 1

Children (Bill and Doris) live with Cis and Bob 50% of the time, and in Don and Sue's household 50% of the time. When there are two or more different living arrangements in the same household, we draw the group living together the most as the primary boundary (Don, Sue, Amy and Lena), and join the other lines to this line (Bill and Doris).

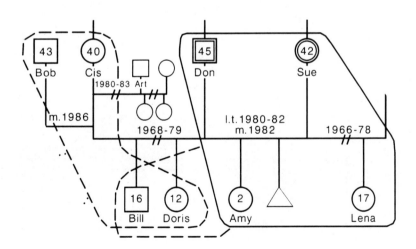

Section 2

37

Multiple marriages. To the extent feasible it is useful to draw all marriages. At times this becomes more complicated than is helpful and secondary marriages are not included.

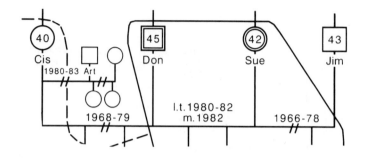

The marriages of the central couple are all on the same marriage line. The husband is drawn on the left.

Section 3

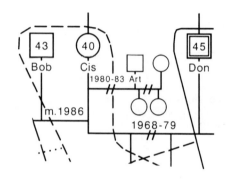

When the former spouses of the central couple have remarried, the remarriage line is drawn slightly above the major marriage line (Cis and Bob).

Section 4

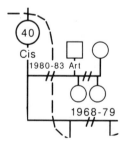

When less important, secondary marriages can be drawn in miniature and significantly above the major marriage line (Cis and Art).

Section 5

Children. Children are drawn below the marriage line with the oldest child on the left (Bill, Doris, Amy, her mother's pregnancy, and Lena).

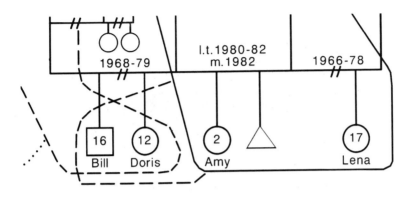

Section 6

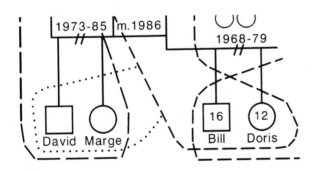

When there are children in a remarriage that are important to include, they are drawn on the same plane as the other children even though the marriage line may be drawn above the central line (David and Marge).

Section 7

Relatives. Each major horizontal plane represents a separate generation. Brothers and sisters of the central adults are represented in miniature (Don and Sue's parents and siblings—oldest to the left).

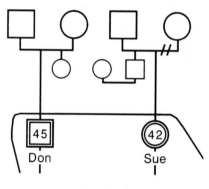

Section 8

For other symbols and more complete presentation, see McGoldrick and Gerson (1985).

Families are often more complicated than illustrated here and therapists have the opportunity to use their creativity! As McGoldrick & Gerson (1985) say ". . . there are limits to what the genogram can show, particularly regarding multiple marriages. Sometimes, in order to highlight certain points, the arrangement of the genogram structure is reorganized" (p. 25).

Genogram 2 is an example of a genogram that was helpful to the family in understanding what they were experiencing. Pam and Paul had come to therapy with a prominent issue before them: Pam's feelings of isolation and her sense of not being a part of her new stepfamily. When all five members of the household were seen together, the genogram was drawn. Paul looked at it and exclaimed, "No wonder Pam feels so alone! There's nobody over on her side of the family, and we've got all these people on our side."

Even when a genogram has been previously prepared by the couple, it can still be important to cover the essential features with other family members when they are part of a subsequent therapy session.

C. MAKE EDUCATIONAL COMMENTS

Although the need for education about stepfamilies is not as crucial as it was a few years ago before the publication of many books on stepfamily life,

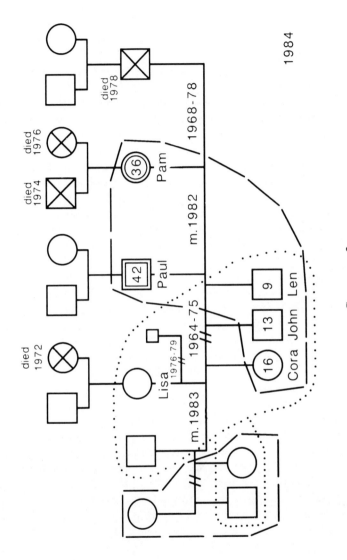

Genogram 2

we find that there is still a great deal of information about stepfamilies which therapists can supply. As we have noted, the basic concept of the nature of family life is derived from the model of the nuclear family, and this type of family is still considered the "ideal" or "model" even by those who have grown up in stepfamilies.

It is difficult for many of the stepfamily members who come for help to shift their thinking about families from patterns learned both consciously and unconsciously from childhood experiences. However, the popular media and professional literature are providing us with a new set of norms which can be taught directly or indirectly through therapeutic interactions. We believe that the specific guidelines, normative data, and general background presented in this book can be used as a basis for helpful educational comments. For stepfamilies who are not familiar with popular books, a lending library or at least the names of several stepfamily books can provide them with a foundation of knowledge (see reference list in Appendix B). However, because stepfamily norms have not been part of most people's childhoods, appropriate statements by the therapist and discussion of stepfamily norms often do much to relieve tension.

It is sometimes difficult to believe that those in stepfamilies do not understand their situation even in intellectual terms. They often keep their status secret from friends, anticipating critical remarks or attitudes. They struggle on in their isolation, unaware of and unable to utilize resources that might help them to understand their situation and thus deal with it more effectively.

An example of the helpfulness of information and education provided by their therapist is the situation of Marv and Esther:

Marv and Esther, with his two children and her two children, were talking with a family therapist during an initial appointment. Adults and children alike complained about the family's lack of closeness and the uneasiness they felt with one another. When the therapist pointed out that they had been living together only for six months and that they seemed further along in their integration process than is usual for six-month-old stepfamilies, the family relaxed and began to talk comfortably together about their progress during the time they had known each other. Their increased comfort with one another in turn led them toward ever-increasing family satisfaction. In order to feel good about their progress, they needed a normative guide with which to compare their progress with other families.

In another instance, Barbara, a stepmother to two teenage boys, was distraught because the boys did not share her values regarding health habits and maintaining a positive outlook on life. Her anxiety was greatly diminished when the therapist suggested that she had given herself the task of "finishing someone else's artwork." The therapist pointed out that the picture produced would be necessarily different from the one she might have painted if she had started with a blank canvas. After that Barbara no longer thought of herself as a person who carried total responsibility for the lives of her two stepsons. The boys' biological parents had played an important part; while she might have much influence on their growth and development, their basic personalities had been formed long before she knew them. For Barbara, the "letting go" that followed this therapeutic work paved the way to less intense and more constructive relationships between her and her stepsons.

Many stepparents mistakenly see their stepchildren as blank canvases or "unfinished masterpieces" which require much effort to complete during the few remaining years before they leave home. Effort is expended to try to "shape them up," an effort which is usually met with anger and resistance on the part of the children, followed by frustration and anger on the part of the stepparent. When therapists suggest at appropriate times the futility of expecting major personality changes, this perspective can be immensely relieving to all concerned.

Knowing what to expect leads to less stress and to a greater ability to handle situations. It is likely that before the era of Dr. Spock the negativism of two-year-olds kept many parents awake at night wondering what was wrong with their parenting and worrying about what to do. After Dr. Spock, the same two-year-old behavior could be understood by a parent as a passing phase of "the terrible twos." Similarly, a therapist who points out the "predictable consequences" (Schulman, 1972) of stepfamily characteristics which are causing anxiety to the individual or stepfamily can reframe a situation from a problem to a passing phase or a manageable challenge.

We find that such specific knowledge is particularly helpful initially, and then plays a less important role as therapy proceeds because the first exposure to a new concept is likely to be more accepted by families than one which occurs later on. Second, information can be presented as a tentative observation originally, without suggesting that the therapist is expressing a definite opinion or taking sides. Later, when the beliefs and positions of the individuals in therapy are known, the therapist who provides information may be seen as aligning him- or herself with the family member whose thinking most closely resembles the information offered. What could be seen initially as "neutral insight" has become personal contradiction or support.

D. FILL IN PAST HISTORIES

Helping stepfamily members "become acquainted" with one another can be important since a new stepfamily is a family with no history. A number of individuals who do not know each other are suddenly living together under one roof and are expected to act like "a family." Except for the couple bond, there are frequently no characteristic family feelings because there has been no time for other interpersonal relationships to develop. Unfortunately, many stepparent-stepchild relationships suffer because the only contact they make with one another is in connection with limit-setting and polite conversation. It is true that living together will yield shared memories over time, but if one relies on time alone, even minimal integration usually takes longer than is comfortable. In addition, if the memories are uncomfortable and superficial, positive bonding is not likely to occur.

When strangers meet, the time it takes them to form a warm relationship usually depends upon their willingness to share personal information about their past histories. If they learn little about one another and the topics of conversation remain personally distant, then emotional bonding between them does not take place. Stepfamily "strangers" need to develop relationships, and at times it takes the assistance of a therapist to start or encourage this process.

One therapist learned during the initial hour with a stepfamily that there was one teenage boy who had remained with grandparents for a three-year-period after his father died and before his mother remarried a man with three younger children. The family was seeking help because the young man had announced suddenly that he wanted to return to his grandparents' home to live. Although the stepfamily unit had been together for two years, the therapist discovered that no one had discussed the boy's experiences during the three previous years in which he had lived with his grandparents, and he in turn knew little about his mother's life during this period. The mother and stepfather felt distant from him, and the stepsiblings also felt detached and strange in his presence. No one had thought to build a relationship by filling in the past for one another. The major portion of the first therapeutic session was devoted to encouraging the exchange of historical information between the family members.

The most emotionally difficult relationship was between the mother and her son, and the therapist intervened by saying, "It sounds as though the two of you have not talked together about how it was for you during the period when you did not live together. Perhaps you would like to share a bit about that time now." The mother began to talk about her pain during the separation. She had felt that she could not work and take care of her son alone.

As the session progressed, the young man was able to open up more. Then the therapist shifted the focus to sharing between the stepfather and stepson, and between pairs of stepsiblings. The sharing of past histories continued for several sessions while current family difficulties were also discussed. As bonds developed between the members of the stepfamily, household regulations were discussed and decisions made. The teenager felt more a part of the family unit and decided to continue to live there while continuing to visit from time to time with his grandparents who had meant so much to him during a critical period of his life.

As Goldner (1982) has said, ". . . the impact of this [exchanging past memories] seemingly mild intervention is often unexpectedly powerful (p. 202)."

E. REDUCE A SENSE OF HELPLESSNESS

A stepfamily is forever scrambling to maintain some semblance of equilibrium. There is an ever-present ambiguity and sense of confusion. . . . Will Johnnie's father return him on time so that his stepfather, mother, half-sister, and Johnnie can catch the plane for their Florida vacation? Will Suzy's mother send a party dress and clean shoes with Suzy so that she will be appropriately dressed for a neighborhood birthday party? The ambiguity, the lack of control, and the inability to predict stir deep feelings of helplessness more constantly and more acutely than would occur in a nuclear family. (Visher & Visher, 1978, p. 155)

A stepfamily household is but one subgroup of a larger suprafamily system with many decisions which cannot be made unilaterally by one household because of the connections which exist when children have two parents who live in two different homes. When animosity exists and dictates the behavior of ex-spouses, there is likely to be little desire to be cooperative. In these instances the sense of helplessness is extremely acute and power struggles may ensue. If both households agree to come to therapy together, a more amicable relationship often can be achieved. There are, however, many instances where the two households will not work together. In such situations, the therapist can assist the family to understand the realistic nature of their helpless feelings and work with them to delineate the areas of control that do exist for that particular household.

Just as our human tendency is to want the other person to change when we are upset, adults in one stepfamily household may see change in the other household as the only solution to a problem. Recognizing and accepting that they cannot control the other household can lead to fewer feelings of impotence and to more effective situational changes. This point is illustrated by the case of the Larson family.

Jim and Sue Larson had been married for two years. Sue had two children from a previous marriage—Stephen, age seven, and Arlene, age nine. When the children's father, Scott, came to pick them up every other weekend, he expected them to be clean and dressed in clothing suitable for a weekend in a fashionable setting—no torn jeans or faded T-shirts. Sue did not mind having the children dressed appropriately. The problem was that the children's father did not arrive to pick them up until much later than he had said. Sometimes he would be as much as three hours late. The children, who had been called in from playing with their friends in order to get dressed, had been sitting waiting for their father for a long time and were getting restless and irritable. Sue and Jim would feel frustrated and angry. Sometimes they had planned to go out together and had to cancel their own plans because of the father's lateness.

Sue and Jim had spoken to the children's father and tried to persuade him to be on time or to call if he was going to be late. This approach had not worked. Sue and Jim discussed the matter with their therapist and began to see what they could do to change their situation. They formulated a plan which they could control themselves. After letting Scott know what they had decided, they agreed to call the children in from play only *after* their father arrived, even though Scott might have to wait in the car or return in 15 or 20 minutes when Stephen and Arlene were clean and dressed. If Sue and Jim needed to leave before Scott arrived, they arranged with a teenager in the neighborhood to be "on call" until Scott arrived.

Coping with their situation in this manner worked well for the adults and children in this household: Sue and Jim no longer felt helpless and angry, and Arlene and Stephen ran out to join their father with smiles instead of scowls. Scott began to find that he could arrive on time more frequently since he, and not Sue, was inconvenienced when he was late. After a few months, the children began to be ready when Scott arrived because he could be counted on to arrive very close to the arranged time.

Within the household as well, adults and children frequently experience a lack of control because the other stepfamily members' ways of doing things seem strange and disconcerting and little seems familiar. One way of increasing the feeling of mastery and control on the part of the adults is to suggest they decide on the three changes most necessary for their emotional well-being, and then concentrate on those areas while letting the others go, at least for the time being. One couple, for example, agreed that in their stepfamily household the three most important concerns were:

1. No TV until homework was done.
2. Personal belongings to be removed from the common areas of the house.
3. Stereos and radios to be turned off at 10:30 on school nights.

By working with their teenagers on these areas and dropping the nagging about dirty jeans, gum chewing, sloppy table manners, and noisy friends, this family was able to adjust to one another's differences and slowly explore and negotiate other changes in a climate of positive rather than negative energy.

While children often talk as though they want full control, it usually turns out that they still want adults to be in charge; they simply want to be heard on the issues under discussion. Giving children some control over their lives (which may have seemed to them very chaotic and disrupted) may include such simple things as choosing their own breakfast menu or determining their own dress code in accord with the styles current with their friends. Children, as they grow older, can begin to have more input in deciding which of their households to live in, or what arrangements work best for being with their other parent. The rule seems to be to allow children age-appropriate responsibility to control their own lives to the extent that they are able, while being appropriately considerate of others.

F. RELATE PAST FAMILY EXPERIENCES TO PRESENT SITUATIONS

In all families, it can be important to understand the connections between early family experiences and present attitudes and behaviors. While many elements in our past contribute to our experience of the present, we have found four major areas that can lead to difficulties in the present for stepfamily members. Exploring these areas may be necessary for the achieving of stepfamily integration.

1. Losses

Those who have experienced many previous losses appear to have the greatest difficulty with stepfamily losses. Those with few previous losses frequently have an optimistic outlook so that they are more able to cope productively with their new loss experiences.

Adults and children who have experienced many losses tend to fear interpersonal commitment. Adults find it hard to form an emotionally vulnerable couple relationship and children withdraw from developing close ties to stepparents. In such instances, children may also move away from emotional involvement with their own parents. As one teenager said, "I'm going to be totally independent. I'm not ever going to put myself in a position again with another adult where I might be hurt." Learning to trust again can be a necessary yet lengthy therapeutic task. A continuing and reliable contact with a therapist provides an essential ingredient for such learning.

2. Couple and Parent-Child Relationships in the Adult's Family of Origin

The family of origin serves as a model of a couple relationship and of parent-child relationships for the children as they grow and form their own family. In a stepfamily, the parent-child bonds predate the couple relationship, and these bonds may be very strong. If both adults have come from families in which the couple relationship and the parent-child relationships were good, they seem better equipped to handle the complicated stepfamily relationships in a productive way. If, however, the pattern in the family of origin of one or both of the adults has modeled a strong parent-child relationship and a weak couple relationship, those adults may find that forming a primary couple bond in the stepfamily may seem contrary to the way it "ought to be." They may, therefore, fail to establish satisfactory adult-adult bonds in their new stepfamily situation.

Making conscious the bonding patterns experienced by the adults in their families of origin can help a great deal in the alleviation of stress caused by a weak couple bond in a stepfamily. Exploring these elements in their pasts, preferably together, can help the couple understand and depersonalize their situation to some extent. Most people accept the strong influence exerted by childhood models. When they realize the type of relationships they and their partners experienced as children, they are frequently able to alter noncon-structive patterns in their stepfamily.

When Mary was 30 years old, she married Douglas, a man of 38 who had two children from a previous marriage. After three years of marriage Mary sought help because she was depressed and felt she was "on the bottom of the totem pole," a position in Douglas' affection beneath that of his two children and his ex-wife. Douglas was willing to attend Mary's therapy sessions "so that he could let the therapist know how he saw the situation in the household."

By the third session Douglas, as well as Mary, seemed comfortable with the therapist. During this session the therapist explored the inter-personal relationship patterns in their families of origin with both Mary and Douglas. Using the genogram drawn during the first session as a guide, the historical background differences between the two of them became apparent to each.

Mary had grown up in a loving family in which she experienced warm relationships between herself and her sister, between the girls and each parent, and between her mother and father. In fact she had at times envied the closeness she perceived between her parents and looked forward to having a close relationship with her husband when she got married.

Although Douglas had experienced a close mother-son relationship, he had neither experienced nor observed a good couple relationship. Douglas was an only child whose father and mother had divorced when he was six. He had continued to live with his mother, who did not remarry, and he lost contact with his father who moved to another state.

For Douglas, a close couple relationship was an unknown; the parent-child bond was the one that would endure regardless of other family changes. After his divorce and remarriage, Douglas had felt it necessary to placate his former wife to ensure his continued contact with his children. Mary felt that he saw his former wife's needs and his children's needs as more important than hers. As they shared the information about their families of origin with one another, Douglas and Mary suddenly saw clearly the source of much of their unhappiness together. They learned to be more tolerant of their differences, and Douglas accepted the importance of developing a strong and deep relationship with Mary in order to provide his children with a model of a stable family house-hold. He overcame his guilt that developing a strong marital bond would be "betraying my children" and the couple slowly established a mutually satisfying relationship, at the same time as Douglas maintained and Mary developed solid bonds with the children.

3. Child-rearing in the Family of Origin

Stepfamilies do not have the luxury of time that first-marriage families have. The adults are suddenly "faced with situations they did not even know were problems." Rules and ways of doing things must be decided quickly. The adults who have been parents previously have worked out their parental behaviors using their family of origin as a model (which they often wish to either emulate or reject) so that by the time they remarry they have become "set" in their approach to child-rearing. Frequently there are significant differences between the values of the two adults, and therapists are expected to act as judges.

An important intervention in such situations is to have the adults (preferably in conjoint therapy sessions) explore their perceptions of child-rearing in their families of origin. Often this leads them to have more tolerance for their individual differences, thus allowing them to escape from their Right/Wrong positions. When this happens the way is paved for negotiation of situations they consider to be the most important. As the couple is able to work together, it may be important to include the children in the sessions so that mutual understanding is possible and children and adults can work together to improve the functioning of the household.

Sometimes a major cause of tension in the couple relationship stems from the perception of one (or both) that his or her children are upset with the child-rearing practices of the other. Frequently the therapist needs to check this by seeing the group together, or by meeting with the children alone if a joint session might be unproductive and split the household. If the household is not seen together, the therapist will need permission from the children to discuss their feelings in specific areas with the adults. It is our experience that parents frequently misjudge their children's reactions and are unjustly critical of the stepparent.

The child-rearing area is of major importance in stepfamilies. Initially, the position of the children's biological parent is of prime importance (Mills, 1984), and household changes need to be made slowly. If the two adults are not able to resolve their differences, participation in some type of stepfamily group can be an effective adjunct to therapy.

4. Past Marriage Experiences

The influence of former marriages on a stepfamily is often underestimated. Former spousal expectations and behavior affect the expectations of the new spouse, while lack of psychological separation from a former partner usually produces serious difficulties for the new couple. Understanding the impact of these earlier experiences can be important in the resolution of present difficulties.

A 40-year-old woman, Lucy, remarried for two years, entered therapy because of difficulty with a 14-year-old stepson. Lucy had had children of her own, had enjoyed being a parent, and was warm and outgoing. Her stepson, Bill, was moody and withdrawn and would not relate to his stepmother. Bill's mother had died after a long illness and his father had remarried Lucy within the year. The therapist realized there were many difficult emotional relationships within the family and decided to see them together for several sessions. Then Lucy requested a separate appointment and talked about her continued unhappiness with her stepson. In exploring Lucy's strong reaction to Bill's "not having a smiling face," it came out that Lucy's first husband had been very moody and unhappy, and she revealed for the first time that his death had been a suicide. Suddenly Lucy and the therapist could both understand the strength of her feelings about Bill's apparent depression. Further work with the family allowed Lucy to see Bill as a person separate from her former husband, and as a boy who had not been given the opportunity to mourn the death of his mother. While some other situations took longer to resolve, Lucy and Bill began to support and enjoy one another.

G. TEACH NEGOTIATION

While at times agreement or resolution of differences may occur without deliberate efforts, in most instances active negotiation is necessary. This is especially true for stepfamilies where individuals have come together from a variety of backgrounds, carrying with them sets of beliefs and values that have never been questioned previously or even thought about consciously. After a remarriage, the unconscious suddenly becomes conscious! "THEY eat their dinner in front of the TV. WE carry on a civilized conversation around the dining room table. HE wants the children in bed by 8:30 and MY children are used to staying up until 10:00. THEY want the brine left on their corned beef, but I have always soaked it off before cooking." Initially in a stepfamily, there is an assault on family members' views of the world every hour or so (Visher & Visher, 1979). You can feel like an outsider, deposited in the middle of an alien culture.

We have found that one area that lends itself well to teaching negotiation in therapy is that of household chores. In stepfamilies, "who does what" has not developed slowly; in most instances, neither the couple nor the family have realized the importance of working out these specific living arrangements. One job may have two people who think of it as their responsibility, while another duty goes unattended. There may be expectations that have not been verbalized, or a lack of awareness that household jobs alter as children move back and forth between households.

An illustration of an "overlap" problem was the situation of one couple who came together after a number of years as heads of two single-parent households. Both enjoyed cooking and both enjoyed shopping, one espoused plain American food and the other insisted on a health food diet. After their marriage, the husband had taken charge of the shopping and cooking and his wife had grown more and more upset as she felt her authority slipping away in this and other areas of household management. During the second session this matter of food preparation arose:

Josephine: I used to do all the shopping and cooking for my daughter and myself, and now Ronald is doing it and I feel as though he is taking over everything.

Ronald: I was divorced 12 years ago and for 10 years I cooked for myself and my children when they were with me. I like to shop and I like to cook, and I thought I was helping Josephine by doing it.

Therapist: (*to Josephine*) You look upset. I take it that it doesn't feel like caring to you.

Josephine: No, it doesn't. We cook different things and I get the feeling that Ronald doesn't approve of what I give us to eat.

Therapist: Can you tell me more about what you mean?

Josephine: Ronald is what I call a health food faddist, and I'm a meat and potatoes and gravy person. My daughter is used to that kind of food too.

Ronald: She's right, I think that red meat and all that fat is very bad for you.

It was becoming clear that below the surface were many emotions making for the couple's difficulty in finding a solution. The feelings were explored during a 1½-hour session. By the next appointment, using the ideas outlined in the Stepfamily Association of America's *Learning to Step Together* manual (Currier, 1982), they sat down together in the therapists office and:

1. Stated how each felt about shopping and cooking—avoiding a "Right" or "Wrong" evaluation of their differences.
2. Brainstormed the different ways that might work for them.
3. Settled on an acceptable solution.

In this instance the couple decided to alternate by weeks, one shopping and cooking for a week, and then the other doing the same, each having the freedom to set the menus for that week. As their hurt and anger subsided, both volunteered that they felt that a satisfactory diet lay somewhere between Mom's apple pie and a vegetarian plate. A daily source of tension and misunderstanding had been removed.

In another example, the Tracy family had come for therapy with many complaints. The children did not help, the relationship between the couple was often explosive, and the new stepsiblings were constantly fighting whenever they were together. Tom Tracy had two children—Margaret, age 15, and Mike, age 12—who were in the household every other weekend. Beth Tracy had three children—June, age 13, Bob, age 10, and Rachel, age 8—who lived in the household all the time except for Christmas vacation and a month in the summer. Both adults worked outside the home.

After drawing a genogram and listening to the complaints of the adults for a few minutes, the therapist asked about the household functioning. On this there was agreement! There was little satisfaction with the manner in which the family operated at home when all were together or when only three of the five children were there. The family group accepted the therapist's suggestion that it might be helpful to focus on the details of living together. This task moved them away from bitter complaining to working together in a constructive manner, while teaching them negotiation skills which they began to use at home.

First, the family made a list of all the household chores they could think of, in no particular order. Next, individuals volunteered for certain tasks. The family decided that on the weekends when Margaret and Mike were there they all would take an hour on Friday afternoon or Saturday to work in the yard and bathe the dog, since these tasks did not have to be done on a daily basis. At one point the adults looked at each other in disbelief when the two older children said that they felt the couple ought not to wash dishes on the weekends. The few remaining chores were negotiated or assigned by the adults on a monthly rotational basis.

We find that asking one of the children to be in charge of keeping the list of tasks stimulates an interest on his/her part. We have not had negative responses from families in which the therapist asked one child to take the responsibility when none volunteered. In one case when a third grader volunteered, the family cohesiveness grew quickly as the others helped him to spell some of the words.

It often seems that stepcouples are so busy attempting to make everything work smoothly that they lose sight of the fact that having input into family management decisions is important for children, particularly teenagers. Indeed, such input often produces a feeling of participation and cohesiveness.

H. SEPARATE FEELINGS AND BEHAVIOR

The separation of feelings and behavior is of particular importance in stepfamilies. While we have little control over our feelings, we often lose sight of the fact that ordinarily we have a great deal of control over our actions—what we do about our feelings. Clarification of this principle, for example, might be relieving for a stepfather who might then realize that he need not carry an extra load of guilt for his negative feelings about a stepdaughter or stepson, thus reducing his anxiety to a more manageable level. In addition, if he ceases to concern himself about formerly "unacceptable" feelings, he will have more emotional energy to put into deciding how he wishes to *behave* towards his stepchildren. He can give them a cheery "hello" when he sees them after work; he can drive them to basketball practice; and/or he can give them birthday presents which are comparable to those he gives his biological children.

For Enid and Karl one area of tension centered around Little League baseball. Karl had two young sons who played, while their stepmother, Enid, had no children and did not enjoy baseball. However, she was willing to attend the weekly Little League games at least twice a month. The children were pleased when Enid attended a number of their games, but Karl was critical of his wife because she did not jump up and down with excitement at the matches the way he did. In a biological family, Enid's lack of enthusiasm might well have been scarcely noticed by her husband, but in this stepfamily arrangement Karl was constantly assessing Enid's feelings about his sons. Baseball was an important area for Karl because he had a strong need to recreate the situation in his growing-up years when his parents had immersed themselves in his athletic activities. It took considerable time in therapy for Karl to accept that Enid's feelings about baseball might be different from his and were not a measure of her caring about her stepsons. What was important were her actions—attending the Little League games.

We have found that many stepparents and stepgrandparents assume that it is hypocritical to behave similarly towards children and stepchildren or grandchildren and stepgrandchildren when there is a basic difference in their underlying feelings about them. It often needs to be pointed out that we separate our feelings and behavior frequently in the interest of maintaining personal relationships. For example, there was nothing "wrong" with Enid— she did not need to "like" baseball to attend the Little League games.

In another instance, the therapist suggested that the stepmother behave towards her stepdaughter "as if" the girl liked her stepmother (the opposite of the way the stepmother had been feeling and reacting). To the woman's surprise, shifting her behavior in this manner resulted in a positive change in her stepdaughter's behavior—and the stepfamily ambience changed dramatically.

I. RESTRUCTURE AND REFRAME

Therapists have many opportunities to reframe situations in stepfamilies because of the lack of understanding that people have about stepfamily interactions and dynamics. Reframing can turn a "problem" into a "challenge."

One new stepmother was upset because her five-year-old stepson pushed himself between her and her husband whenever all three of them were walking together. "He's always trying to come between us," was her complaint to the therapist. Another stepmother in the discussion group to which they both belonged had a different reaction: "I had the same situation, but I discovered that the child was not trying to come between us but was simply unsure of where he fitted into the new family pattern and was afraid of being left out." Her restructuring of the situation allowed the new stepmother to respond to her stepson with empathy rather than with anger.

A stepfather and a 14-year-old stepdaughter got into a heated argument in therapy over his demand for a curfew hour. She felt that he was being mean and restrictive. He talked about her homework, her safety, and her need for rest. As the tension built between them, the therapist stepped in and commented that it was clear that the stepfather cared about his stepdaughter. The girl asked the therapist for an explanation, and the therapist pointed out that her stepfather was showing how much he really cared about her well-being. The girl's anger quickly subsided and the stepfather felt better about himself and his need to be protective. With the reduction in tension, both could go on to work out bedtime guidelines that were mutually acceptable.

J. MAKE SPECIFIC SUGGESTIONS

Anxiety frequently produces an inability to see alternatives. In general, the anxiety level in stepfamilies is higher than in other types of families (Nadler, 1976; Wald, 1981), with the result that individuals in such families frequently get locked into patterns that are ineffectual and unsatisfactory. It is as though their automatic pilot is on and they do not have the energy to do more than keep going in the programmed direction. In a therapy setting, the offering of specific suggestions can be most helpful in reducing anxiety. With less upset feelings and the modeling that there are alternative ways to deal with stressful situations, stepfamily individuals can then begin to formulate their own alternatives when confronted with challenges.

In one stepfamily there were two "resident" teenage boys, and three sons of the husband who were in the household on weekends. These weekends were frequently chaotic. There was continual fighting among the boys and the couple spent much time trying to settle the arguments. Many times, angry feelings were expressed by the adults to each other. Each expressed frustration with "your boys." Drawing a genogram in the therapeutic session revealed that two of the husband's sons were similar in age to the wife's, while the third son, age nine, was four years younger than the youngest teenager. A review of the details of a typical weekend appeared to pinpoint a major difficulty: the four older boys did not want to include the younger one in their activities, and the nine-year-old continued to interfere with the activities of his older brothers and stepbrothers.

A simple suggestion was made by the therapist. Since the husband's sons did not know other boys in the neighborhood, as they attended a school near their other household, they depended on the household unit for their companionship when they were all together. The youngest boy, however, was a misfit as he had no friends his own age when he was at his father and stepmother's house. The therapist suggested to the adults that the weekend might work better for him if he brought one of his friends with him. The adults accepted this idea and were amazed at the positive transformation which took place. Now the nine-year-old had a friend to play with, while the older boys could carry on their activities without interference from a younger child.

In another stepfamily with somewhat similiar weekend difficulties, there were young children in the neighborhood and the solution lay in suggesting to the couple that they take an active role in helping the nine-year-old girl feel comfortable with two neighbor girls. This was accomplished by planning a backyard barbecue and inviting them. On the next weekend, the adults planned a visit to the zoo for the same group. After this, when no particular event was planned, the nine-year-old felt secure enough to seek out one or both of her "new friends" on the street.

At times the inability to find reasonable alternatives lies in a belief in the "rightness" of a narrow range of behavior. For example, one young mother of three children was about to be remarried. The relationship between her and her former husband had been somewhat rocky since the divorce, but for a number of months the two of them had been able to work together relatively smoothly in planning for the children. However, Jody became very anxious when confronted with the necessity of informing her ex-husband of her impending marriage. In a discussion with her, the therapist wondered if she might feel less anxious communicating with her ex-husband in writing. In response, Jody shared the following feelings:

1. She feared her ex-husband would be upset that she was going to remarry.
2. She believed he would find it easier to receive the information through a letter rather than by a telephone call or in person because he would have time to digest the news.
3. She felt much more comfortable writing about her plans since this would give her time to consider how she wished to express herself.
4. The only "right" way to inform her ex-husband was by talking to him in person—a very strong belief that was in conflict with her other feelings.

Exploring Jody's reasons for these beliefs led her to accept the seemingly superior alternative of writing to her former husband. This proved to be a good decision. Using this situation as a model, she began to use this means of communication with her ex-husband in other emotionally loaded situations. She also became much less committed to the idea that events "should" be handled in a certain manner.

K. ENCOURAGE DYADIC RELATIONSHIPS

The events of today become the memories of tomorrow, and the patterns of the present become the traditions of the future. Within this structure, individual relationships grow and mature through dyadic interactions. Therapists can help the family develop these bonds by encouraging direct communication between family members, since frequently the necessity for one-to-one time is overlooked by stepfamily members. Couples need to plan consciously to have pleasurable times together even though they may feel guilty because they consider that they are "deserting the children." While they may be temporarily separating themselves from the rest of the family over the protests of the children, in the long run they may be ensuring needed family stability.

In many instances during the single-parent household phase, children will have had a great deal of "alone" time with a parent. When the parent remarries, the loss of the parent's attention is keenly felt. The impact is less if the children continue to have times alone with their parent at the same time that they build relationships with the new people in their stepfamily. Learning that she still had a direct line to her father allowed one young girl to stop her destructive behavior and "settle in" to her stepfamily. In another instance, a therapist was able to help a newly remarried mother understand her son's depression and plan to have some quality time alone with him. In the flush of her new relationship, the mother had overlooked the extent to which she had withdrawn from her son.

When there are several children, remarried parents and stepparents sometimes see spending time with only one child as an impossibility. They need to recognize that such contacts need not be daily, nor for lengthy intervals. Perhaps it would be possible to take a child to the store when the adult has some shopping to do, or drive with the child to a soccer game, or help with homework, or talk together while cooking an evening meal, or read a bedtime story.

Because of prior parent-child bonding, it is understandable that new stepparent-stepchild relationships can often develop more easily in the absence of the more familiar biological parent. In one stepfamily, the stepparent and stepchildren were together without the biological parent early in the history of the family when the biological parent had to be away for awhile. The stepfather said, "All of a sudden the two kids and I had to fend for ourselves. We sat down and figured out together how we would manage to get the shopping and the cooking done. We set aside Saturday morning to clean the house and do the laundry. By the time my wife returned, my relationship with the girls was pretty good. I think we all had a feeling of working something out together, just the three of us. We really got to know one another in a hurry!"

While the mother in this situation was delighted with the formation of the new steprelationships in her family, many remarried parents are conflicted and may need help to understand their dilemma. Consciously, they long for good relationships between their spouse and their children, while unconsciously they sabotage the formation of these relationships by being unable to let go of a bit of their closeness with the child so that there will be room for the stepparent to form a good relationship with the child. Letting go brings with it sadness. The understanding and support of a therapist enables many remarried parents to make these necessary shifts in their relationships with their children so that warm stepparent/stepchild bonds have room to develop.

L. REDUCE THERAPEUTIC TENSION

Minuchin & Barcai (1972) characterize the belief of many family therapists when they say:

Because crisis requires change, at least temporarily, a period of crisis may be an optimum time for establishing the foundation of permanent therapeutically indicated change. . . . As family therapists, we frequently induce and capitalize upon crisis induction. (p. 322-323)

In a biological family there is a family loyalty that allows the family to remain intact in the midst of chaos and upset. Since the structure of stepfamilies is such (see Chapter 2) that family loyalty tends to be very weak or even nonexistent until integration has occurred and a sense of "we-ness" has developed, we believe that this lack of family loyalty creates a fragile family system that cannot tolerate the same degree of tension as can a biological family. Without the binding force of biological loyalty, chaos and tension can more readily fragment stepfamilies, splitting them along biological lines. Indeed, they often come to therapy complete with their own crisis which requires no therapeutic induction. In fact it is necessary to frequently reduce anxiety and tension in therapeutic sessions.

The Brown family had been together for eight years; however, a sense of family unity and cohesiveness seemed almost totally absent. It was as though they had moved in together within the last several months. Kathy Brown had three children from a previous marriage: Jack, 12, Bert, 10, and Lola, 8. Charles Brown had not been previously married. The tension in the family was extreme, and during the therapy hours the therapist found himself using a number of techniques to reduce the chaos.

When the emotional climate appeared to be escalating to a psychologically destructive point, the therapist encouraged the communication in the session to go through him rather than encouraging the direct confrontation that was producing the unacceptable tension. This reduced the emotional impact, created a little distance and objectivity, and allowed the therapist to reframe where helpful.

Tasks were a help and led to a dramatic shift in the family. When the adults were seen together as a couple, their anger and blaming of each other continued unproductively. They accepted the "homework" task of each writing down two lists without sharing them—one containing five specific things he/she wanted the other to change, and the other five things he/she was willing to change. Kathy and Charles returned a week later, shared their lists, discussed them, and for the first time began taking some personal responsibility for the chaotic family situation. In further sessions, they referred back to their lists, seeing this task as the turning point in their therapy.

The use of a tape recorder during the sessions also reduced the tension level and had an added impact when one or both reviewed particular sessions together at home. The children did not participate in reviewing tapes of sessions in which only the couple participated.

Throughout the sessions, the therapist continued to make it clear that while he felt he could be helpful, he could not change the family interactions. Only the members of the family could do that. Slowly a trust developed between the adults, and then between the other members of the family group.

While therapy helped this stepfamily to become integrated, as with any group of families there are those stepfamilies who are not able to achieve a satisfactory integration, even with therapeutic assistance. Sometimes, as with any family, the divisive forces are too strong and cannot be successfully overcome in therapy.

M. USE ACCURATE LANGUAGE

"Language is both a reflection of and a determinant of beliefs" (Lewis, 1980, p. 6). The language used by therapists working with stepfamily members has great significance because of the messages it conveys about the concepts of "family" held by the therapist. The English language does not contain comfortable terms, or any terms, for many stepfamily relationships, and unrealistic beliefs held by stepfamily members can be reinforced by inaccurate terms.

Often the adults in a stepfamily are attempting to force their family unit into a biological family mold. If a therapist refers to a stepparent as "your new mother" or "your new father," unrealistic beliefs are fostered in the "reconstituted biological family." This can produce even greater stress in a stepfamily where the adults may be pushing the children to think of a stepparent as a "parent." A therapist who refers to a stepfather as a "father" risks losing the trust and confidence of the stepfamily members, particularly the children, since the stepparent's role is different from that of the biological parent and not interchangeable with it.

According to Lewis (1980), "The therapist's job is to help families find words that feel congruent with their own family situation. . . . Often families have created unnecessary problems for themselves, either by skipping over the very important language decisions required, or by making unrealistic demands of one another about the words they will use" (pp. 7-8). One stepmother was unable to take an active role with her husband until the therapist introduced the term "household" rather than "family." It had not *felt* to her like a family, and therefore she had felt she did not deserve to have her needs considered. A father/stepfather felt depressed because he had children who "visited" him. It felt accurate when he talked of children "living" with him on weekends and for vacations. With the use of that term, his tenseness disappeared and his ability to deal successfully with his stepfamily role increased dramatically.

SUMMARY

In our experience, there are a number of intervention strategies that are of particular importance when working with stepfamilies because of certain specific characteristics and common dynamic patterns associated with the integration process.

We have been asked if there is a hierarchy to the list we have included. Except for our belief in the basic need of individuals who come for therapy to gain or regain good self-esteem and a sense of mastery, we see no order to the remaining interventions. None are mutually exclusive or related to a specific situation. All can be important and their use is dictated by the particular circumstances of the individuals and the family. We, as well as a number of therapists with whom we have talked, have realized that these strategies can make a significant impact on the functioning of the family.

CHAPTER 4

Whom to See

You mean you want to see my ex-husband and his new wife together with us? Gee you must be brave.
> —Remarried mother to therapist

Therapists differ widely in their ideas about whom to include in therapy of stepfamilies, with their opinions seemingly affected by their views of stepfamily dynamics and systems.

Isaacs (1986) considers "turf" to be a major therapeutic issue and begins therapy by seeing the adults, first together as a couple, and then individually. If the presenting problems are child-centered, and an agreement is made to continue with therapy, she then sees the children to assess the situation from their point of view. Isaacs continues to work primarily with the couple, including other suprafamily members later if it seems desirable.

In contrast, Ahrons & Perlmutter (1982) attempt to include the entire "bi-nuclear" family unit for the first meeting (all parents, stepparents, and children). Following the initial session, various appropriate subgroups are seen rather than the entire suprasystem. Whenever possible, the entire group is brought together for the final meeting.

Sager et al. (1983) also begin by seeing a larger group, followed by appointments with appropriate subgroups. For them the "suprasystem" is the basic unit, and they include in that group grandparents and other important relatives. However, if the presenting problem appears to be a couple issue which does not involve a child, only the couple is seen. When a child is involved, a larger group is seen, at least initially. Their families are in a clinic setting, and sometimes different members of the family unit have individual therapists within the agency. When the suprasystem group meets, the individual therapists also attend. At times a senior therapist is in charge at these sessions. Since it is considered vitally important to involve as many as possible of the family unit, telephone screening is done in an effort to persuade reluctant suprasystem members to come to the sessions.

We certainly agree with those who believe that the feelings and actions of grandparents, parents, stepparents, and children intimately affect each person across households because all are linked through the children. It is, therefore, important to keep the concept of the suprasystem in mind at all times. However, we suggest that there are a number of additional factors to be considered in determining whom to see in therapy, and the remainder of this chapter will be devoted to a detailed discussion of each:

A. Emotional Stage of the Stepfamily
B. Locus of Major Difficulties
C. Individual Ego Strength
D. Age of the Children
E. Comfort of the Therapist
F. Therapeutic Balance

A. EMOTIONAL STAGE OF THE STEPFAMILY

We have previously written about working with different stepfamily individuals and subgroups, depending upon the issues and the functioning of the unit (Visher & Visher, 1979). We have long been unwilling to see the children in the household together with the adults until the bonding between the couple appears to be strong enough to enable the adults to work together and withstand the emotional pulling towards the past that often occurs when stepfamily adults and children meet together in therapy. Our clinical impressions match closely the work of Papernow (1984) and are in agreement with her statement that it is important to assess the alliances in a stepfamily to determine whom to see in therapy. Table 3 lists the stages of emotional development in stepfamilies as we have adapted them from Papernow, correlating these with their common characteristics and with the individuals or groups we believe can make productive use of therapy when seen together.

These alliances form a basis for a progression from individual to couple to household to suprasystem. The decision of whom to see is not necessariliy related to the length of time the household has been together, because many individual factors determine the length of time it takes for a couple to form a solid relationship and for new steprelations to develop. We have not found it difficult to add the children to the therapy after the couple has been seen for a time. If former spouses and new partners are included after a therapeutic

TABLE 3
Stages of Emotional Development*

Stage	Characteristics	Whom to See
Fantasy	Adults expect instant love and adjustment. Children try to ignore stepparent in hopes that he/she will go away and biological parents will be reunited.	Individual. Couple. Stepfamily household (unlikely to see anyone except for education).
Pseudo-assimilation	Attempts to realize fantasies. Vague sense that things are not going well. Increasing negativity. Splits along biological lines. Stepparents feel something is wrong with them.	Individual. Couple. Older children if disturbed.
Awareness	Growing awareness of family pressures. Stepparent begins to perceive what changes are needed. Parent feels pulled between needs of children and of new spouse. Groups divide along biological lines. Children may observe and exploit differences between couple.	Couple seen individually and/or conjointly. Children if need help.
Mobilization	Strong emotions begin to be expressed, often leading to arguments between couple. Stepparent clear on need for change. Parent fears change will bring loss. Sharp division between biological groups. Stepparent with no children is in isolated position and lacks support.	Couple seen individually and/or conjointly. Children if need help.
Action	Couple begins working together in attempts to find solutions. Family structure changes. Boundaries are clarified. Children may resist changes.	Emphasis on couple. Appropriate subgroups. Suprasystem subgroup combinations.
Contact	Couple working well together. Closer bonding between stepparent-stepchild and other steprelations. Stepparent has definite role with stepchildren. Boundaries clear. More ability to deal with suprasystem issues.	Any suprasystem grouping (depends on issues).
Resolution	Stepfamily identity secure. When difficulties arise family may regress to earlier stages, but moves ahead quickly. Usual difficulties are around nodal family events involving the suprasystem.	Any suprasystem grouping (unlikely to come in now).

*Stages adapted from Papernow (1984). From *Stepfamily Workshop Manual* (Visher & Visher, 1985b) distributed by Stepfamily Association of America. Copyright 1985 by E.B. Visher and J.S. Visher.

alliance has been developed with individuals in the household, it may be necessary for the "other household" members to meet with their own therapist and for both therapists to be present when individuals or subgroups from both households meet together. In our experience, shared by other therapists with whom we have talked, seeing the entire household unit too early can cause stepfamily disintegration rather than having an integrative effect because of the strong emotional pulls that exist along biological lines.

Of course, these stages are not discrete entities with a sudden passage through a threshold. Instead, there is a general progression from one phase to another, with overlapping and blending together as one stage gives way to the next. Similarly, the ability to profit from therapy does not suddenly change from one day to the next. Nevertheless, we believe it is helpful to be aware of the emotional stages of stepfamilies as outlined in Table 3 and described in more detail below.

1. Fantasy: "It won't happen to us."

This is a period in which the adults are "on a pink cloud" and are not able to imagine having difficulties structuring the new household unit, even when they have been exposed to information and education concerning realistic stepfamily expectations. Because of the feeling that "it won't happen that way to us," it is unlikely that therapists will see many stepfamilies during this initial stage.

During this early phase, adults who read stepfamily literature or attend educational stepfamily classes find these experiences helpful in several ways:

1. They learn of guidelines which they can use to develop rewarding stepfamily experiences and to plan for their new families. It is like having a road map before you start a journey into an unfamiliar area.
2. When difficulties arise, the adults do not experience lowered self-esteem because they recognize that the problem is familiar and does not reflect on them. As one stepmother said, "I never expected I would feel jealous of my stepdaughter, but I do, and it makes me act just the way it said in the book. So I've come (to therapy) because I want to figure out what to do about it. It's a big help to know I'm not alone and that there's not something wrong with me. That made it easier for me to come here for help."
3. Individuals, couples, or households can benefit from available stepfamily information and education. Prior therapeutic contacts may be continued during this fantasy period, as well as later on, but therapy content at this

time is usually related more to the divorce or death and the single-parent household phase than to the remarriage. For children, the death or divorce and the remarriage become blurred together.

2. Pseudo-Assimilation: "Of course we're one big happy family."

During this period there is a growing sense that things are not working as well as had been anticipated. Emotional eruptions occur within the household, and parents and their biological children draw together as steprelationships grow more prickly. The adults begin to feel upset with one another. Children who expected the stepfamily to provide them with an effortless "new beginning" are tense. Stepparents with no children of their own feel increasingly isolated and begin to wonder what is wrong with them.

Although there are shifts within society, women are still given the responsibility for the emotional functioning of the family. Perhaps as a consequence, women are more apt to seek therapeutic help than are men. As a result, it is predominantly stepmothers who seek therapy at this time.

Frequently, stepparents come to therapy during this stage because they are unclear about what is going on with them, and they feel responsible for the tension in the household. They often need to be seen in individual therapy at this point. Whether or not to see the couple together or individually, given a willingness of both to be involved, depends on such factors as ego strength, the amount of hostility between the couple, and an assessment of the support systems available for each individual. Appointments may alternate between individual sessions and conjoint sessions with the couple. As a rule, an equal number of individual appointments for both husband and wife gives the nonverbal message that the therapist is not assigning responsibility for the family stress to any one individual.

If one member of the couple is being seen more than the other, it is important to give careful consideration to ego-enhancing ways to frame this imbalance. For example: (To new stepmother with no children of her own) "Since you have not been a parent before, you are in the position of needing to learn how to be a parenting figure as well as coping with all the adjustments of being a spouse. How about making a few appointments for yourself so that we can have more time to talk about that?"

We do not advocate seeing the children and adults together at this time. If there are older children who are upset, they can be seen separately from the adults. Young children usually respond quickly to adult changes, so unless they have been highly disturbed for some time they may not need to be seen.

The household is typically dividing along biological lines at this stage. As a result, if adults and children are seen together the division may be heightened and emphasized rather than reduced.

3. Awareness: "I can see what's bothering me but I don't dare tell you."

The couple is not yet working well together and the household often is divided, so that it continues to seem important to see the adults separately. Stepparents are becoming clear about what is bothering them. They are beginning to see ways in which their household needs to be restructured, at the same time that biological parents are feeling increasingly stressed and fearful of disturbing the status quo with their children. Remarried parents feel pulled emotionally between the needs of their children and the needs of their new spouse; stepparents continue to question their feelings and often feel embarrassed by them. As a rule, spouses are not sharing their feelings with one another.

During this phase, stepmothers in particular feel responsible for the family's upset; their husbands are very often in full agreement with this appraisal. Stepfathers often see their stepchildren as the problem, and therapists are presented with that assessment during the initial interview. Some push is needed to get adults to accept their feelings, assess their validity, and begin talking together about possible solutions. Sometimes this motivation comes from therapy; at other times, some other external intervention occurs.

In the case of Ursula and Miles, Ursula knew that she was very upset when her husband's children came for the weekends. She had no children of her own and felt that her stepchildren ignored her. They would telephone their mother several times on Saturday and Sunday. Ursula also felt cut off from Miles because he became a full-time "activities director" for the children when they were there. Ursula felt very selfish because she wanted to have some time alone with her husband on the weekends; since both she and Miles worked at demanding jobs, she longed to go out to dinner or to the movies without the children. Miles felt the pressure from his wife and he also felt pressure to make the weekends special for his children, "to make up for the fact that I don't see them during the week."

When Ursula sought therapy, she considered that she had no right to ask Miles for couple time alone. Her self-esteem was so low that the therapist did not feel she had sufficient ego strength in her relationship with her husband for them both to be seen conjointly. She was not strong enough to speak up for herself. After four or five appointments, Ursula was willing to talk with her husband about her needs.

Miles was willing to meet alone with the therapist. They spent two sessions identifying Miles' sense of helplessness and restructuring the situation so that he could see that he was in a powerful rather than helpless position because of his membership in both the spousal subsystem and the parent/child subsystem. He agreed at this point that it would be helpful to talk with Ursula about the tension that arose when his children were with them. Following this, the couple were primarily seen together, although there were still times when one or the other would be seen individually.

4. Mobilization: "You're wrong, that's not the way it is."

Ursula and Miles also illustrate this stage. As they shared their feelings, they began to argue constantly. Ursula said they had no weekend time together; Miles said that wasn't true. Miles said the children really liked Ursula and didn't leave her out of their conversation; Ursula disagreed.

The mobilization stage is critical for stepfamilies as their dissatisfactions come to the surface and they begin to talk with one another. As one stepfather said, "I can feel my anger oozing out under the door, and we can't talk about it without raising our voices." Emotions may become expressed explosively, and during this stage a separation or divorce is a distinct possibility.

One goal of therapy at this juncture is to help the couple listen to one another and not judge one another's feelings as right or wrong. Becoming tolerant of individual differences, separating feelings from behavior, and negotiating ways of satisfying different needs become a major focus of therapy. Individual appointments become less necessary during this period, and the couple are often seen together to help them to confront their issues and to search for satisfactory solutions. Children can be seen separately, if advisable. However, having both children and adults present in the therapy situation during the mobilization stage usually enhances divisiveness rather than enhancing the efforts of the adults to respect one another's perceptions of the needs of the family.

The words of Clara, a woman whose three stepchildren were with her and her husband every other weekend, illustrate very well the progression of their stepfamily from the mobilization stage to the action stage:

I struggled for a year to tell him I wanted some time alone with him while they were here. The weekend was our only time together. He would tell me I was being selfish, and then I'd withdraw and get depressed. Finally, it occurred to me to ask him what it was like *for him* when I asked for time alone. He said he felt incredibly hurt. That he wanted us to be a family, that he had so little time with his kids, and that it felt like I was asking him to disown his children, that I had time with him during the week and why couldn't I let go of him during the weekend?

Instead of defending myself, for once I *repeated back* what he said to me: that he felt really hurt and maybe scared. You know he started to cry! Something changed after that. It was like we were more on the same team trying to figure out a hard problem: how to give him the time he needed with his kids and still give me and us time alone, together. We came up with this neat idea that the Thursday night before weekends when the kids come, we would have a *date*. When we were poor, it was pizza and watching *Hill Street Blues*. Now we go out to a nice restaurant. We also take at least one walk together while the kids are here. It makes such a difference! (Papernow, 1987, p. 78)

5. Action: "It's hard but we'll work it out together."

At this stage the couple has become a unit and is working reasonably well together in their attempts to solve the problems that arise in the household. Even when a couple has reached the action stage quickly, working out major challenges takes a number of months. Often it takes couples three to four years to reach the action stage and then one to three years to work out the new relationships, create necessary and satisfactory boundaries, carve out productive roles, and feel a solid sense of family.

This is the point at which it can be most helpful to see all members of the household together to help them with their communication and their understanding of one another. Unlike a biological family, they have not yet settled into a recognizable family pattern. Developing a "family feeling" and a suitable household structure is an important task, the accomplishment of which can be facilitated by therapeutic assistance.

When households first meet together, drawing genograms and modelling family meetings can be very helpful. Topics of discussion can range from plans for vacations to complaints about who will feed the parrot and jealousy among the stepsiblings who feel that they are not being treated fairly by their stepparent. Any type of family can benefit from family meetings, but stepfamilies in particular have a great deal to gain because there are so many new situations for individuals who hardly know each other. "You are in the middle of a problem before you even knew one existed," said one remarried father.

The families benefit from having an experienced guide (the therapist), to show them how to have a family meeting which is a productive problem-solving situation and not a "dumping ground." The feelings and opinions of all members, young and old, are equally important and valid, even though adults have the task of guiding the family along realistic lines and are responsible for letting the children know what ideas are outside the limits of realistic possibilities. Wanting to take a trip to the Bahamas for three weeks may not be a possible solution to the question of where to go for a vacation!

We suggest to families that they have two containers in some convenient spot at home: one for things that are bothersome and one for things that they have liked and appreciated. Between family meetings, slips with comments are placed in the containers. At the family meeting the discussions can center around the thorny issues that have been dropped into the "complaint" container, followed by acknowledgment of the items in the "appreciation" container. In this way, positive as well as negative interactions and events will be recognized and acknowledged. Too often we take for granted the many comfortable things, while the annoyances grab at us with a moment or more of anger or displeasure. We tend to remember these longer.

> Joan and her stepdaughter, Caroline, found such meetings very produc-
> tive. For example, putting off a discussion of the fact that Caroline
> forgot to return her stepmother's red sweater after borrowing it for the
> school picnic made it possible to discuss the matter more productively.
> Joan knew it would be worked out, so at the time it happened she put a
> note in the box and "let go" of some of her feelings about it; by the time
> of the meeting her more acute emotional reactions had been tempered
> by time.

We heard of one family that had had professional help in communicating in this way. However, the children never enjoyed sitting down and working out situations, so that when the adults would comment that a discussion would need to be scheduled, the children took care of the matter at once to avoid the need for a "family council." Not the orthodox way in which to use this type of negotiation, but effective for this household.

For families who are not able to get together and talk productively outside the therapist's office, the suggestion of an "appreciation" container only can be a remarkably effective way in which to shift the ambience of a household. One warring family devised their own rule: "You must say three positive things about another person in the family before you can say something negative." In the frantic search to make positive comments so that the desired negative statement could be made, the emotional climate in the household changed from sour negativity to an astonished neutral and even positive atmosphere.

Beginning in the action stage, various subgroups can have productive therapeutic sessions—the couple, the children, all the adults in the children's households. The types of subgroups we feel seldom are appropriate to see together are biological parent and children, former spouses, or both biological parents and their children. If such combinations are to be seen, the permission of new spouses seems essential.

The dynamic nature of relationships needs to be acknowledged, albeit nonverbally. New units and new subgroups now exist (Keshet, 1980). Now parent and stepparent are responsible for caring for the children in their household. Four adults may be parenting three children who go back and forth between two households. Stepsiblings share living space and emotional space with one another. Grandparents/stepgrandparents interact with their grandchildren/stepgrandchildren at "family" events. As we said earlier, the shifts in group membership are not always acknowledged by society, and this hinders the development of a stepfamily's "identity." A therapist can assist a stepfamily's search for identity by verbally and nonverbally validating the existence of the new subgroups.

If the present couple does not feel supported as a unit by the therapist, it will be difficult to persuade the individuals to work cooperatively with the adult or adults in the children's other household. It takes a strong sense of self before one can interact productively with others. Similarly, the new couple needs to feel secure as a couple before constructive contact with the children's other household can take place.

We find that there are several important considerations to keep in mind when working with former spouses:

1. Make direct contact with each parent. Do not send a message to a former spouse. You can control the message and the interaction by calling the person directly.
2. Inform the person in the other household during the initial contact of the specific purpose for meeting together.
3. Clarify the monetary responsibilities; otherwise, you may get caught in the hostility between former spouses. We feel that *if at all possible,* each household should pay for its appointments and split the cost evenly between households for joint sessions. With these arrangements, the adults come

as equals who share in the caring for their children, not as one person or couple coming to help the other.

4. Keep joint sessions focused on the present. Do not try to resolve past difficulties which arose because of former relationships.

5. Meet together when *all the scheduled adults* are present. Very often an adult, a stepparent especially, needs the message that he/she is an important person in the stepfamily household and will not be left out of the therapy session.

Six-year old Matthew's transition from preschool to first grade precipitated a conflict for his two households. The four meetings that focused on where Matthew was going to attend school illustrate many of the foregoing points. Genogram 3 shows those who were involved.

Cindy and Dale had been married for six years and had one son, Matthew. At the time of their divorce, Matthew was three years old. A year later, Dale married Linda, and the following year Cindy married Don. Until the time of the initial therapeutic contact, Matthew had spent alternate months with each parent and had attended a nursery school situated geographically midway between the two households. Now Matthew would be leaving the nursery school and going into first grade. The anticipated change had created severe tension between the households.

Cindy made an appointment with a therapist, stating that she and

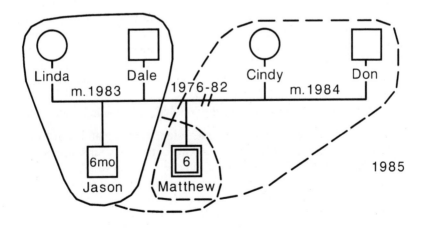

Genogram 3

Dale had met together during the previous years following their divorce whenever a situation with Matthew needed negotiation. This time, however, their meeting had been hostile and fruitless and she didn't know what to do. She had thought of going back to court, but wanted to think it through first. In response to the therapist's inquiry, Cindy said that her husband Don would be willing to come to an appointment with her.

Appointment 1 (one hour). Cindy and Don were present. There was evidence that they cared deeply for one another. Matthew had gone between his two households with relative ease until recently when he cried as he left his mother and stepfather. He also seemed unhappy when he talked with them on the telephone or came over for a meal. Originally, Matthew had not had contact with the other household when he went back and forth, but this was altered because, as Cindy said, "Matthew taught us by his behavior that he needed contact with his other parent during the month he was away from that person."

Matthew's recent unhappiness was of concern, but the major issue was the matter of his school. The crux of the problem was that Matthew's two biological parents did not live in the same school district. This meant that if the six-year-old went to a public school, it would be either to a school in his mother and stepfather's neighborhood or to a school in his father and stepmother's neighborhood. If he went to a private school, he would be at some distance from both households, and he would not have school friends close to where he lived.

Cindy wanted her son to go to school at the public school near her home. Both she and Don talked of household rules that they did not approve of in Matthew's other household, and they thought that the new baby's arrival in Matthew's father's home had distracted Dale and Linda from giving Matthew the attention that he needed. Cindy was willing to have the therapist meet with Dale and Linda in preparation for a meeting with all four adults.

The therapist called Dale and the following interchange occurred:

Therapist: I am calling because I understand that you and your former wife, Cindy, are having difficulty working out where your son, Matthew, will be going to school this fall. Cindy and Don have talked with me once about the situation, and Cindy gave me permission to call you. It is clear to me that you are very interested in the welfare of your son, and I think it could be most helpful to Matthew if you and your wife would be willing to talk with me so that I will know what your ideas are.

Dale: Yes, Linda and I have gotten nowhere with this one. I'd like to talk to Linda about seeing you. I'll call you back in a little while. (A little later he called and made an appointment.)

Appointment 2 (one hour). Dale and Linda were present. As a couple, they, too, demonstrated a caring, supportive relationship. During the session they talked of their discomfort with some of the rules in Matthew's other household, and their concerns if Matthew went to school in that neighborhood. They were afraid of a loss of contact with Matthew and the resultant diminishing of their influence in his life. Dale was thinking of two private schools and was in favor of one of them rather than the public school in either of their two school districts.

Towards the close of the session, the therapist asked if Dale and Linda would be willing to meet with Cindy and Don to discuss the school decision:

Dale: Are you suggesting that the four of us would get together here and tell you what we think ought to happen with Matthew next year, and you'll listen and then make a recommendation of the school that you think Matthew ought to go to?

Therapist: No, that's not how I see my role at all. This is something that involves the four of you. It will work out better for all of you and Matthew if you can figure out the best solution for everyone. I think it could be helpful for all of you to talk together and I will do my best to help facilitate your discussion.

Dale: O.K. We'll come.

Following are the therapist's considerations:

1. Both couples indicated that their relationship was solid and caring. Therefore it seemed likely that they could meet together productively.
2. Since Matthew was six, not 16, if the adults could make a decision about where he went to school to their satisfaction, Matthew would be free to enjoy the school he attended. At his age, having the adults feel comfortable with the choice of school seemed to be the most important element; it did not seem advisable to include Matthew.
3. Stepparents as well as parents needed to be included because all four were parenting Matthew.
4. Meeting with each couple alone allowed them to talk freely about their school choice for Matthew and to express negative feelings about the other household.

5. Meeting only once with each couple kept the balance so that it was less likely that either couple would feel that an alliance had been formed between the therapist and the other couple. When it is not possible to maintain this balance, or one couple suspects an alliance with the other couple and the therapist, we believe this can be defused by acknowledging and talking openly about these feelings as soon as possible. If an alliance *has* been formed, more than one therapist may be indicated—one for each of the two subgroups, for example.

Appointment 3 (one and a half hours). Cindy, Don, Linda and Dale were all present. After the therapist made some positive remarks about their willingness to meet together because of their caring for Matthew, Cindy started by saying that there were two things that she felt they needed to talk about, Matthew's school and the fact that he cried now before going to his father's house. The group decided to talk about the crying first.

Cindy and Don were concerned about Matthew's crying and why it had begun lately. Linda and Dale had also noticed a change and had wondered why Matthew would be playing happily, talk to his mother on the telephone in a sad and unhappy manner, and then become relaxed and happy again very shortly after hanging up.

Thinking that the change might have coincided with the birth of the new baby, Jason, the therapist asked when the new behavior had begun. The response by all four was that the crying had begun five-to-six weeks earlier. Since Jason was six months old, the change had apparently not occurred at the time of Jason's birth.

At one point during this discussion, Dale and Cindy began to bristle at one another and become emotionally upset. The therapist did not need to do anything to calm the situation because Linda reached over and patted her husband, Dale, while Don, sitting close to Cindy, stroked her on the shoulder. Both Cindy and Dale relaxed quickly.

Both couples talked together quite openly about Matthew's behavior. As they talked, the therapist began to see the pattern of Cindy's unhappiness when Matthew left to be with his father and stepmother. It seemed to be related to the beginning of the struggle over where Matthew would go to school. Perhaps Matthew was responding to his mother's present insecurity. The following interaction identified Matthew's problem and offered a solution without placing any person in an uncomfortable position:

Therapist: (to Cindy) What kinds of things are you apt to say to Matthew when he's leaving, or when you're talking to him on the telephone?

Cindy: I tell him how much I love him and how much I'll miss him when he's gone.

Therapist: (to Dale and Linda) When Matthew leaves, what do you say to him?

Dale: It depends on what we've done. We say good-bye and tell him we've had a lot of fun and we'll look forward to doing such and such a thing when he's with us next time.

Therapist: (to Dale and Linda) Do you think that since you've had Jason, Matthew knows that when he leaves you have Jason there, so you are not lonely? (And to Cindy) When Matthew leaves your house, there is no child there, so you may be lonely. He may think of you as not having any fun at all when he's gone, so he feels sad and upset because he loves you and doesn't want you to be unhappy.

There was agreement that this seemed to fit what was happening. The couples recalled things that Matthew had said which tended to confirm this interpretation.

Therapist: (to Cindy) Do you have a good time when Matthew is not with you?

Cindy: Oh yes, of course.

Therapist: (to Cindy) It is certainly important for Matthew to hear you say that you love him, but perhaps he would feel more comfortable about not being with you if he knew you had good times *with* him and also good times when he wasn't there.

Cindy: That makes sense. I think I need to let him know the things Don and I do when he's not there that are fun, as well as tell him I'll be looking forward to seeing him when he comes back. I think maybe I've been overdoing the "missing him" part.

The couples decided they could now address the school decision. Since there was no time to do this during the current appointment, they agreed to meet again in two weeks. The therapist commented on the billing arrangements that had been discussed previously with each couple: that the charge for the joint sessions would be split evenly between each household.

Appointment 4 (one and a half hours). Linda and Dale and Cindy were present at the scheduled time. Cindy said that Don had called to say that he was very busy at work and to please go ahead without him. The therapist said that it was important for all four to be present since the school decision would affect all of them. Perhaps they could find another time when all could be present. Cindy called Don and another appointment was arranged for the same day. (In this instance, the therapist let the couples know that there would be no added charge for the "unused" time. Had more appointments been made, a clear understanding would have been necessary in regard to the financial arrangements for missed appointments.)

At the beginning of the session with all present, the couples informed the therapist that Matthew had gone from his mother's house to his father's house without being upset and had been happy when he talked to his Mom on the telephone. Cindy was very pleased with what she had been saying to Matthew prior to his departure, and all four adults decided that this difficulty was one they could handle if it arose again.

Perhaps linked to the ease with which Cindy had been able to alter her behavior, with positive results, she and Dale had talked together several times on the telephone and had arrived at a mutually satisfactory decision that Matthew would attend the public school in his mother and stepfather's neighborhood. He would spend Monday night through Thursday night with Cindy and Don, and Friday through Sunday night with Linda and Dale, who would pick him up at school on Friday afternoon and return him to school on Monday morning. Vacation times and some special weekend times would be worked out in the future, with Matthew's input, after he had settled in to the new school.

The major portion of this appointment was devoted to a discussion of something special for Matthew at his father and stepmother's home. All agreed that since Matthew would have school friends in his mother's neighborhood he would need something special at his other household so that he would still enjoy and value being there. Eventually Dale talked of his son's interest in sports and the fact that he'd seen the neighborhood children playing soccer. Matthew knew the children because he had played with them when he was with Dale and Linda, and Dale mused aloud about his willingness to take an active role in seeing that Matthew would have soccer as an activity at his house. In fact, Dale said that he would see about helping the other parents in the neighborhood to organize and run the soccer program. Cindy and Don agreed with Dale that Matthew was interested in this activity and that they would leave this as a special area for father and son.

At this point, Linda talked about her wish to be an active participant in raising Matthew and being an important part of his life. Don, who had been relatively quiet during this session, spoke up and said that he, too, wanted to play an active role with Matthew. The two stepparents talked to each other for a few moments as they empathized with one another in this important area.

No further sessions were scheduled. The therapist felt that the meetings had defused a potentially explosive situation to the satisfaction of the adults, and to the benefit of Matthew. We have noted that frequently, as with these couples, meeting together with a therapist, or even the prospect of all meeting together, enables the adults to work outside the therapist's office to solve problems involving the child and his or her two households. It is likely that these adults will now be able to more easily work out future situations affecting both households. As Matthew grows older, he will need increasing input on his part into decisions affecting his life, and the interchange between all four parenting adults may create a base from which all five can work together if it is necessary to do so.

6. Contact: "We're all getting closer."

At this point in stepfamily development, boundaries between households are clear, children go back and forth more easily and can accept the benefits of having more adults in their lives to nurture and care for them. Stepsiblings may have become important role models or close peers. Steprelationships are growing deeper and the stepfamily unit is able to solve its day-to-day problems. At times, situations arise that once again split the household along old biological lines, but now the couple soon comes together again and works to resolve the problem.

If a thorny situation arises that sends the family for therapeutic help, there is a cohesion and solidity to the unit that was not present in the early stages of emotional development. Because of this, any group from a dyad to the entire suprasystem may be able to work productively to solve the problem. Whom to include will depend primarily on the nature of the disturbing situation.

7. Resolution: "It's different and it's O.K."

This final stage is marked by an acceptance of the family for itself. It is not a copy of a first marriage family: there may be children coming and going every few days or every few weeks; a child may have moved far away either geographically or emotionally; and at transition times such as graduations, weddings, christenings, holidays, and funerals the complexity of diverse households, linked through the children once again creates situations that require more than the average amount of understanding and flexibility.

As a rule families do not seek help once the resolution stage is solid. Stepfamily identity is secure. At times, individuals may wish help mourning a loss of dreams or of relationships with children. Once in a while, situations arise that tax the strength of the family, but the relationships are now solid and caring, and the problem situation will basically dictate whom to see.

B. LOCUS OF MAJOR DIFFICULTIES

Assessment of the individuals involved in the difficulties can be important in determining whom to see, and we tend to make this assessment during an interview with the couple. Two case examples will help to illustrate this point:

Elsa Townsend called to say that she was having a terrible time coping with her nine-year-old stepdaughter, Amy. Elsa and her husband had been married for eight months and Amy was with them most of the time. Elsa had not been previously married and she said, "Being a stepparent is the hardest thing I've ever done. I'm not doing a good job of it. My husband and I get along OK except where Amy's concerned. But Amy and I can hardly talk to one another."

While Elsa was describing a poor relationship with Amy, she gave no indication that Amy was outwardly depressed. She was doing well in school, had a number of friends, and chattered "like a magpie" when her father was home. The difficulty appeared to be within the household, with a lack of cohesion between the adults where Amy was involved. Apparently the couple had not yet solidified their relationship sufficiently to be working together on the situation (not yet at the action stage), and therefore the therapist asked to see the couple. It did not appear to be necessary to arrange for Amy to be seen immediately, nor for members of Amy's other household to be interviewed.

Elsa believed that her husband, Richard, would be willing to come with her and agreed to call for an appointment after she had talked to him and knew what times they would both be available. An initial appointment was made with the couple, following which the therapist continued to see them together for three months. Each was seen twice individually. The therapist helped Richard to be supportive of his wife and to work together with her as a couple. Richard helped his wife become a part of the household, thus increasing her power within the family unit. In turn, Elsa became more realistic in her expectations of Amy and of herself, and she felt she had more control within her home. Her relationship with Amy gradually improved. The couple reported that Amy now brought her friends home to play and talked easily with her stepmother most of the time.

As in many such situations, Amy was not seen in therapy. The couple had been validated and became much more emotionally close as they worked together on their stepfamily situation. Amy saw her mother and stepfather every other weekend. Now that the relationships within her primary household were comfortable, Amy's time with her mother and stepfather seemed to flow easily. As a result only the couple was seen by the therapist.

In contrast, Roger and Marilyn made an appointment to talk about Marilyn's two sons. During the initial appointment, it became clear that although the couple had been married only six months they were working well together in trying to determine what had happened to cause 13-year-old Carl to strike his mother. After Carl's emotional explosion, he had been living with his father. Now, whenever he came back, he fought with his 10-year-old brother, Robert. Now Robert, as well as Carl, was emotionally on edge.

If the couple had had little "glue" between them, they might have needed to be seen separately from the boys. In this instance, Carl and Robert were very upset and needed therapy. Since the couple were working well together, the therapist made an appointment for all four of them to come together. Roger demurred at first, saying that he thought the problem was between Marilyn and her sons. He was, nevertheless, willing to come too when the therapist pointed out that the household was certainly upset when his stepson, Carl, was there, and that as a stepfather he was a part of the household.

The family members were in pain and open to emotional sharing. Important dynamics emerged and were discussed during the family sessions. Carl had felt a need to separate from his close dependence on his mother and instead of verbalizing his wish to be with his father he had acted out in such a manner that he behaviorally brought about what he was afraid to ask. The change, however, was not an easy one for anyone and Carl's ambivalence led him to fight with his brother Robert when he was with him. This had become Carl's way to strengthen his resolve to live apart from his brother ("See how awful it is when we're together") as well as to cover his sadness at their separation. Rooted in the same ambivalence, Carl continued to abuse his mother verbally, while he and his stepfather maintained a distant and strained relationship.

As family members began to understand their hidden emotions and talk more directly and poignantly with one another, the tension subsided and the household settled down to an expected level of tension for new stepfamilies. At this point, intimacy issues surfaced between the couple and they continued in couples therapy, the issues alternating between their individual reactions to closeness and their stepfamily difficulties. From time to time, when they were unable to resolve tense family interactions, the four met together in family sessions. Very slowly the family inched towards stepfamily contact and resolution.

C. INDIVIDUAL EGO STRENGTH

Much has been written about working with families with severely disturbed members. When there is a psychotic or highly disturbed member in a stepfamily, the usual difficulties are magnified because of the added structural and emotional complexity of this type of family. At times, the added complexity may have contributed to the psychotic decompensation of a child or adult who has been able to cope with a less complicated type of family. Once again we believe that the acceptance of the complex nature of the family system and the transition being encountered can lead to more satisfactory treatment plans.

In the T. family (see Genogram 4), 15-year-old Toby had had "emotional problems" for some time and was unable to cope with his mother's remarriage to James. He became destructive in the household to the point that he required hospitalization. Roberta's former husband would have nothing to do with either of his children, while Candy saw her father, James, frequently. The grandparents did not live in the area and had little contact with the others in the family suprasystem. There were several aunts and uncles, but they too were uninvolved.

In this stepfamily, Toby had played the role of "man of the house" before his mother's remarriage, and he felt totally displaced by his stepfather. In addition, Toby directed his anger at his father, Dick, onto James, his stepfather. His sister, Judy, on the other hand, while angry at the disappearance of her father, accepted the new situation halfheartedly. James felt guilty about his divorce from his wife, and feared loss of contact with his daughter. Roberta, in turn, felt caught between her husband and her son, while James considered that he was being asked by his wife to give up his relationship with his daughter.

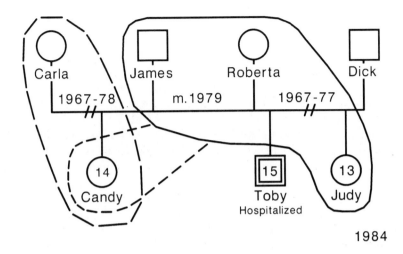

Genogram 4

Toby's ego strength was not great enough, at first, for him to be seen productively with other members of the family. As he was being seen individually, the couple was seen by another member of the hospital staff. Although James and Roberta had been married for five years, the anger at one another that had built up quickly after their remarriage had prevented them from forming a solid relationship. Indeed, Toby's aberrant behavior had helped to split the couple.

In therapy, James and Roberta realized that they needed to form a functional unit so that they could deal together with the tensions in the family. When Toby felt more secure and had worked through much of his anger at his own father, Dick, he was seen with James and Roberta with both therapists present. At first, Roberta and James had difficulty maintaining their newfound unity, but slowly the relationships improved. Sensing the solidity, Toby began to accept the remarriage as he had not done previously. In sessions with James, Roberta, and the three young people, family difficulties were worked out. Toby left the hospital and lived for several months with friends. Then he gradually rejoined the family.

In this situation, the therapists were cognizant of the interplay between Toby's longstanding emotional problems and the social stresses caused by the more involved stepfamily structure. They were clear that Toby was operating in a stepfamily context and the therapy addressed the salient issues. Dick was not willing to make any contact with the hospital or with his children.

Elinor Davidson illustrates a very different pattern. She could hardly talk on the telephone when she made an appointment, and when she came to her first session she carried a shopping bag with a large bath towel protruding from it. During the hour, Elinor talked of wondering what rights she had as a second wife to Raymond, who had a 17-year-old daughter, Cissy. Elinor had no children and was attempting to form a relationship with her stepdaughter who was with Elinor and Raymond for short periods several times a week. According to Elinor, her husband insisted that Cissy could do just as she pleased when she was with them. Elinor was upset with much of Cissy's behavior but felt that any mention of this to her husband would result in verbal abuse from him.

The event that precipitated Elinor's call had occurred during Cissy's most recent visit. Cissy had driven her car through a mud puddle on the way to her father and stepmother's. When she arrived, she turned the garden hose on her car and then dried it with a fancy bath towel that Elinor had just purchased. Cissy's father had seen what she was doing and had said nothing. As she talked, Elinor pulled the stained bath towel from her bag to show the therapist, as though she expected she would not be believed.

Clearly Elinor needed support from her husband, and the therapist suggested that the two of them come together for the next appointment. Elinor agreed, but then called to break the appointment. In retrospect, the therapist considered that she had rushed too fast to include Raymond before Elinor was psychologically strong enough to deal with a conjoint session. The therapist now considered that before being seen with her husband, Elinor needed to sense her own worth and believe that her needs were important. Until she valued herself, she could not negotiate successfully for what she needed.

D. AGE OF THE CHILDREN

In stepfamilies, children come with past family experiences, not just the "in utero" experiences of children joining a nuclear family. Naturally, the older the children, the stronger the emotional bonds between parents and children, and the more certain the children are about how a family "ought" to operate. Because the younger children are "less formed" and also are more dependent upon their parents and stepparents than are older children, changes instituted by the adults tend to influence them more. For this reason we consider that in most situations working with the adults alone can bring about necessary changes for younger children. As children reach latency age, 6-12 years, this becomes less true, and during the teen years most adolescents need to be active participants in the therapeutic process if the situation involves them directly.*

> In one family, a father, Joel, called for an appointment for him and his second wife, Sara, to discuss the change of custody of his 14-year-old daughter, Alisha. The couple had been married for six years, and recently his daughter had come to live with them and had requested a change of custody. She had been living with her mother since she was two years old and now wished to move from her mother and stepfather's to live with her father and stepmother. The change had been worked out amicably by the adults, and the hearing for the legal change of custody had been set.
>
> Since living with her father and stepmother, Alisha was behaving in an "obnoxious" way towards her stepmother and was refusing to participate in family activities with her father and stepmother. The father was panicked, and he and his wife roared into the initial therapeutic session and gave the therapist "nine days to turn the household around!"

The therapist divested herself of the responsibility for the family, but did clarify that she might be able to help the three of them with the situation if they had more time to work it out. The therapist asked if there was any reason the court date had to be in nine days. The father looked surprised and said that it probably could be changed. In their panic, neither he nor his wife had been able to consider other alternatives.

The court date was reset for nine months in the future. During the first two sessions, the therapist helped Joel and Sara make more "psychological space" for Alisha in their home, relaxing their expectations that Alisha would spend considerable time with them, allowing her to play the music she had been used to and enjoyed, and letting her have girlfriends over on weekends. Next, Alisha and her father and stepmother were seen together. Several combinations were scheduled, depending on what appeared to be most needed at the time—Alisha alone, all three, Joel and Sara, and once Sara and Alisha, at Sara's request.

As has been mentioned previously, in stepfamilies a good relationship between the couple does not ensure good steprelationships (Crosbie-Burnett, 1984). With teenagers, the stepparent/stepchild relationship

---

*Laws differ on the permission needed to include children in stepfamily therapy. However, this is governed in most states by the consideration of "the best interests of the child" (Victor, 1986).

can be a difficult one to develop. In this family, Joel and Sara were a close couple who worked hard to meet Alisha's needs. However, no matter what they did, Alisha continued to be uncooperative in the household and unpleasant to her stepmother. In her individual therapy hours, Alisha made it clear that she wanted her stepmother to "disappear." Then came a few crucial appointments, the major elements of which are outlined below:

Appointment A. Joel and Sara. In desperation, Joel said, "The situation is still not satisfactory. Alisha continues to 'bad-mouth' Sara, and refuses to eat dinner with us. These two behaviors are unacceptable. If Alisha does not change them, she will have to return to live primarily with her mother and stepfather."

Therapist: (to Joel) Have you told Alisha about these feelings of yours?
Joel: No, I haven't.
Therapist: I think Alisha needs to know what you are thinking because this is very important information for her to have. Let's all get together next week so that you can let her know.
Joel and Sara: Yes, that's probably a good idea. We're getting so discouraged.

Appointment B. Joel, Sara and Alisha. Joel was not an emotional man, but during this hour, with the tears rolling down his cheeks, he said to his daughter, "Things are not working out, and if they don't go better and I have to choose, I'm going to need to choose my wife and you will have to go back to live with your mother and stepfather. I don't want that to happen, but I can't see anything else to do."

Therapist: (to Alisha) Did you know your father was feeling this way?
Alisha: No.
Therapist: (to Alisha) I think you have some decisions to make.
Alisha: I have no decisions to make. It's all decided.
Therapist: (to Alisha) I'm not so sure about that. Why don't you come by yourself next time and we can talk about it.

Appointment C. Alisha.

Therapist: Where do you really want to live?
Alisha: Where I am now, with my father and stepmother.
Therapist: Then you know what you need to do to make that happen.
Alisha: What do you mean? My Dad's decided I have to leave.

Therapist: I think you know what you need to do. From what your Dad
  was saying, I have a hunch that if you do not talk back to Sara, and if
  you will eat dinner with them, you will be able to stay.
Alisha: Well, perhaps.

Alisha did make the decision to change her behavior and the relationships
in the household improved steadily. The custody was changed and Joel, Sara
and Alisha were all pleased to be with each other much of the time.

In many stepfamilies there is more than one household that can be the
primary home for children. Teenagers, in particular, can usually manage to
work it out so that they live in the one that looks the best to them. At times, a
change to another household is brought about by the young person consciously or unconsciously behaving in an unacceptable manner in one
household so that he/she will be sent to live in the other household. For this
reason, the therapist needed to clarify Alisha's wishes, since she had *said* she
wanted to be in her present household, while her behavior was suggesting
something else.

The responsibility for family functioning is shared by children as well as
adults. For children, this can be a positive message since it means that there
are many ways in which they have control over their lives. In this family,
Alisha changed her behavior in the two major areas important to Joel and
Sara. Immediately the atmosphere in the household improved. Alisha and
Sara began to like one another and develop their relationship, and the
ambience became positive rather than negative. Alisha had learned what the
consequences of certain behaviors would be, and she chose to behave so as
to produce the consequences she wanted. The four adults involved with
Alisha had worked out the residential and custody changes among themselves and were not all included in therapy.

The behavior of preschool children is much more dependent on the
behavior of adults, and the inclusion in therapy of elementary school children, we believe, depends on the specific situation. One seven-year-old
changed his uncooperative and surly morning behavior when his father and
stepmother gave him a choice of what he wanted for breakfast, what clothes
he'd wear to school, and what he wanted to have in his lunch pail.

On the other hand, another seven-year-old was included in the therapeutic
process because he continued to run away even when the adults altered their
behavior. In this family, after the boy had developed some comfort with
therapy, it was explained to him what would happen if he ran away another
time. He did not like the stated consequences and did not run away again.

E. COMFORT OF THE THERAPIST

We believe that an important element in deciding whom to see in stepfamilies is the comfort of the therapist. Anxiety in small, or even medium, doses can be productive and mind-stretching, but too great a tension in the therapist can lead to unproductive therapy sessions. The setting where therapy takes place—in agency or private practice—can make a difference in this regard, both logistically and psychologically.

In general, stepfamily suprasystems are more chaotic than other family systems. In the remarriage system, there are usually more members than in nuclear family systems. While these individuals are "related" they may have little or no "relationship" as yet. Also, new or nonfunctioning stepfamily households do not have a sense of family loyalty. Even within the household there is a feeling of fragility, "as though the whole group could explode and fly apart at any time."

When members of other households in the suprasystem are included in therapy, the coming together in a therapy session can produce extreme tensions for members with much anger and bitterness, who may have little ability to cope with their feelings. Even in an initial evaluation interview, working with this type of family system can feel overwhelming for therapists not used to working with large family groups.

Sometimes "enlightened" members of a suprafamily system inform the therapist that they all wish to come in together. Once again, we believe that the therapist must assess his or her comfort with this arrangement before accepting such a request. An example is the following case:

Jonathan Brown telephoned a therapist to say that there were some visitation difficulties arising between his stepchildren's two households. Jonathan and his wife had been married for two years. He had not been married before. With this marriage, he had become the stepfather of two young children. The children's father had not remarried.

Jonathan stated that the three adults could talk together easily and that it was perfectly fine for them and the two children to all come together; in fact, they had done this before. The therapist had worked with a few nuclear families and had read a good deal about the advantages of seeing stepfamily groups together. Because of this, she agreed to meet with all five.

During the one-and-a-half hour appointment, the children seemed distressed and often clung to their mother. The father and stepfather smiled stiffly at one another once or twice and avoided all eye contact at other times. The former spouses interacted very self-consciously a few times during the appointment. Jonathan did most of the talking and seemed quite open about his distress over the breakdown in visitation arrangements and the many personal adjustments he felt he was being asked to make. The others were extremely quiet.

The therapist identified strongly with the children's discomfort and felt her own anxiety mounting. The tension in the room increased, and the therapist found herself unable to address the process taking place. Constructive discussion did not occur. A second appointment was scheduled for the group, but the following day Jonathan called to say that they had decided to see someone else because they did not feel comfortable with what had taken place during their appointment the day before. The therapist felt discouraged at the prospect of ever learning how to work with this type of family situation.

While remarriage with children from previous relationships is producing a very complex system of interrelationships that challenge us to stretch and develop our professional skills, we believe that therapists need to make more gradual and studied shifts in their way of practicing. The anxiety that can accompany a quick plunge into unfamiliar therapeutic waters can discourage therapists, as well as prove ineffective or even detrimental to the stepfamilies they see. When it is practical, one solution is for cotherapists to work together with the entire group or with subgroups each has seen in therapy at other times.

There are many ways of being helpful to people in stepfamilies who seek therapy. Understanding and validating feelings and dynamics are important for any family. For stepfamilies, it is perhaps the most important aspect of successful therapy, and this can take place regardless of whether or not one person or many people are being seen, since a change in any part of the system can produce change in other related parts.

F. THERAPEUTIC BALANCE

When different households are involved in therapy, we have found that "balance" is important. If one of the former spouses has not remarried and does not now have a significant relationship with another adult, there could be three stepfamily adults involved in a therapy session and the one without a partner usually feels in a "one down" position. We have talked with a number of therapists about this issue, and it seems that therapists may not be in a position to even out this imbalance; as a result, the therapy is frequently not successful. An exception appears to be in situations where the unmarried adult has been seeing a therapist and a decision is made for the adult plus the former spouse and his or her new partner to meet together with this therapist. In this situation, the unmarried person does feel a "balance" because of the prior alliance with the therapist.

When this special situation does not apply, there are several ways therapists have found to be effective in equalizing the power structure:

1. Involve two therapists, one for the couple and one for the single adult. Even though there is still an "odd" number of people, the adults in each of the two households feel that there is a therapist there for them.
2. Include an important person related to the single adult, such as a close sibling, a grandparent of the children, or a good friend.
3. Include a larger number of suprasystem individuals provided other considerations indicate the possibility of a productive interchange.

Without this balance, it is easy to understand the "structural" problems arising in the therapy sessions.

SUMMARY

We have outlined what we consider to be major determinants in deciding whom to see in therapy when working with stepfamilies. We find the most important consideration to be the emotional stage of development reached by the stepfamily, and we have described and illustrated this in detail. For us, the locus of the major difficulties and the ego strength of the individuals are important, as are the age of the children, the comfort of the therapist, and the therapeutic balance.

While working with suprafamily systems can be more complicated than working with less complex families, the increase in the number of people involved does give the therapist more choice. If one member refuses to participate, there may be others who are less resistant with whom one can work. Therapeutic flexibility can become a good model for stepfamily creativity!

CHAPTER 5

Change and Loss

When I'm with my mother I cry because I miss my father. Then I go to my father's house and I cry because I miss my mother. You just have to go with the pain. Don't fight it. Just accept it so you don't miss out on seeing both of your parents.

—Teenager to other stepfamily teenagers

All changes, wished for or not, involve loss. Very rarely are changes a relinquishing only of negative situations and relationships. Even when we move towards something that is desired, we leave behind people, experiences, places that have meant a great deal to us. For stepfamily members, the changes and the losses that they experience are more in number and of much greater magnitude than typically occur in the early years of first marriage families. Indeed, we sometimes say that a stepfamily is a family born of loss. This chapter will discuss various types of losses experienced by those in stepfamilies, together with examples of interventions designed to assist people to deal more effectively with them.

A. RELATIONSHIP LOSSES

The formation of a stepfamily occurs because there has been a divorce or the death of a parent. Regardless of the age of those involved, there is a tearing apart of parent/child relationships and of the marital relationship. What is produced are difficult changes and interpersonal losses for children and adults that may require therapeutic help to enable them to move on with their lives.

Not infrequently, a parent has remarried without adequately mourning the loss of a shattered marriage, grandparents are cut off from their grandchildren,

91

and children have lost full-time contact with one or both parents. They wonder where they will fit in and whether they will continue to see the parent they feel is being "replaced" by a stepparent.

We have found that it is often necessary to help adults mourn the loss of their previous marriage relationship in individual sessions rather than with their new partner. If both have been married previously and have developed a secure relationship with one another, they may be able to share their feelings of loss. However, it seems to us that it is close to "asking the impossible" to expect a new spouse, particularly a person who has not been married before, to sit quietly while his or her partner explores the sadness felt subsequent to the death of the former marriage relationship! When the new marriage is 10 months old, and the former marriage lasted 10 years, insecurity derives from the fact that in comparison to the first marriage the new couple as yet has had very few shared memories and experiences. A type of loss that can be shared is the loss of friends and a familiar neighborhood necessitated by a move. It is our experience that adults, especially, tend to overlook the losses that accompany change, especially when the new situation is one desired and happily anticipated.

Jack was unhappy in his first marriage and was the one to seek a divorce. He felt relieved to be away from the tensions of the marital relationship. After some time he married Lena. Soon after the marriage, Jack began to criticize his wife's household management and her reactions to his children. Lena made an appointment for them both, and also for his children. As the therapist listened to Jack, she sensed that he had rushed into a second marriage "on the rebound" from his unsatisfactory first marriage. Lena had not been previously married and was feeling that she had failed her husband in some way. The new couple relationship was severely strained. Since it appeared that exploring Jack's reactions to his past marriage had the potential to harm rather than help Jack and Lena's relationship at this point, the therapist made a decision to see the adults individually at the beginning of therapy.

In his session with Jack, the therapist commented that along with the relief that comes after the severing of an unhappy relationship there can also be sadness on remembering pleasant times as well as sadness at the loss of one's dream of a happy marriage. Jack began to talk about some of the positive elements in his first marriage, particularly those that occurred in the early years. Tears filled his eyes and for the first time Jack could recognize and mourn what he had lost.

As Jack realized the source of some of his emotional turmoil, he became able to "let go" of his unconscious expectations that Lena would in some way remove the hurts and losses of his past. With the therapist's help, Lena's sense of personal adequacy began to increase, and she and Jack began to work together more. Now the couple was seen conjointly to begin to work on their own relationship.

At the time of the remarriage we find that the emotions of the adults and of the children are often as far apart as they ever will be. The adults are on a pink cloud of anticipation, while the children, in marked contrast, are unhappy because they are faced with many losses. They now will need to share their parent who is marrying with another adult; perhaps there will be other children with whom it will be necessary to share. Children may fear they will not continue to see their other parent as much as before and may be insecure because they do not know how they are going to fit into the new family system.

Children tend to act out their feelings rather than verbalize them, but the adults often do not understand the message, particularly when their own emotions are very different. When all family members are being seen together, we have found that the therapist can lead children to a recognition and expression of their feelings so that their parent and stepparent can understand what they are experiencing. Then the adults are better able to clarify plans, be reassuring about future contact with the other parent, and discuss with the children ways in which losses can be minimized. If only the adults are being seen in the sessions, the therapist can translate the children's behavior for the adults and help them to understand and ease the pain of loss for the children.

As we have mentioned earlier, we have found it can often be easier to identify with the relationship losses of children than with the losses of the adults since we adults can usually remember times when we were children and felt abandoned or angry and unhappy about changes over which we had no control. As a result, it may seem easier to work compassionately with children who have experienced parental death or divorce. Yet it is often difficult to fully appreciate children's anger and upset at the addition of a stepparent in their lives. For most children, the new person initially brings losses rather than gains into their lives. The remarriage is a behavioral statement that dashes their hopes that their biological parents will get back together again. It also means that they now must share a parent who has married with a new adult and, perhaps, with other children. One young woman, recalling her early teen years, described her feelings very well:

At the time, I knew I was being awful but my behavior seemed out of my control. Now I suspect I was reacting to a deep sense of displacement. Not only was I beginning a slow, gradual, steady loss of my relationship with my father, but I was experiencing a loss of actual and fantasied closeness with my mother.

It had been my expectation, once I had acknowledged to myself the reality of my parents' divorce, that my mother and I would be like sisters, that I would help her find another man, almost as if we would hold joint interviews of the candidates. And here she had gone out and on her own brought home not only a man who would take a lot of her attention away from me, but also four children who would, I was sure, take all her remaining attention, for she seemed so eager for them to like her. (Visher & Visher, 1980, p. 51)

Other children may be reacting to a very different type of loss: their rejection by one of their parents, either through emotional withdrawal or through the actual physical disappearance of that parent. In many instances, when a parent disappears it is not because he/she does not love the child; it is rather the adult's reaction to the pain of separation from the child, or a cut-off instigated by the custodial parent, sometimes because of the belief that children will be able to accept a stepparent more readily if the biological parent withdraws. Present research, however, indicates that this belief is not well founded (Crosbie-Burnett, 1984; Hetherington, Cox & Cox, 1985; Lutz, 1983; Wallerstein, 1985). It appears that the reality is that children do not respond positively to a stepparent when they are being asked to give up a biological parent.

When children are young, therapists are often in a position to assist them through the adults by helping the adults to understand their children's sadness and depression that may have resulted from the loss of contact with one of their parents. When this has happened, children need to hear that their rejection has to do with something going on in their parent's head rather than being based on the child's own behavior or "unloveability." Unless this message can be conveyed to the child, he/she may suffer a severe loss of self-esteem.

Except in situations where it is judged to be physically or emotionally detrimental for children to see their other parent, a cut-off tends to work against rather than for the stepfamily unit. Frequently the children construct a fantasy parent who is never cross, always giving, and a paragon of virtue. When this happens, the remaining parent or the stepparent can never compete with this idealized image. Therapists can help by working with the adults or the children to examine the fantasy so that reality predominates.

Another technique which is helpful with children who are trying to deal with their loss is to use books which have been written for children their own age. The child can then identify with the book's characters who are having similar experiences and are managing to deal with their losses and changes. (See Appendix for list of books for children.)

When children are experiencing emotional rejection by a parent, they frequently deny it to themselves and others. Misbehavior, depression, and delinquency are common responses. The case of Carlos illustrates an all too common situation:

Carlos, age 15, was referred to a therapist by the school because he was withdrawing from his friends and a suicide note had been found on the floor after he had dropped some books by his desk.

Carlos's parents had divorced eight years ago when he was seven years old. His father had remarried two years later, and his mother remarried two years after that, when Carlos was 11. Carlos and his sister had continued to live with their mother after the divorce, but friction between Carlos and his mother escalated to the point where it was arranged for Carlos to move into his father and stepmother's home. Carlos was discouraged and depressed but told the therapist that he really didn't know why. Nothing had changed lately, although he was finding it very hard to get along with his younger stepbrother.

Carlos was now a junior in high school. He had found it difficult to change schools in the middle of his sophomore year when he came to live in his present home. He visited occasionally with his mother and stepfather, and saw his sister then and when she came to visit for weekends with her father and stepmother. Carlos did not want the therapist to talk with his parents and stepparents; since he was mature for his age, the therapist respected his wishes that she wait until later to include the others.

Carlos felt that he was somehow different from the other students in his school. He was depressed that he could no longer play soccer because his new school had no soccer team. In his previous school he had been one of the best soccer players on the team. Carlos did not talk of any anger towards his parents or stepparents.

After a few sessions, Carlos talked about his suicidal feelings. He was willing to talk with his father and stepmother about this and the three of them had two very important therapy sessions together, in which the adults were able to begin to understand the losses Carlos had experienced. Communication between the three of them was opened, and continued at home. The adults were supportive of Carlos and came in alone to talk more about how to help Carlos. Also, outside of therapy the three of them planned to do more fun things together. Carlos became more cheerful and reported that he no longer felt that suicide was an answer to his frustrations. However, at school Carlos was still withdrawn and continued to deprecate himself. During one therapy session the following interchange took place:

Therapist: You say you and your mother didn't get along very well. Have you any idea why?

Carlos: I don't know. She used to like me before the divorce. She thinks my sister is the good one and I'm the bad one.

Therapist: What makes her say that?

Carlos: I think it's because I argue with her and she doesn't like that. She and my Dad used to fight and she sometimes says to me, "You're just like your father."

Therapist: Are you and your sister very different?

Carlos: Yes, we certainly are. She's a little prissy miss, and my mother thinks I'm a mess. I don't look the way she'd like.

Therapist: Do you look like any one else in your family?

Carlos: Yeah. I look like my Dad.

Therapist: Your mother was pretty mad at your dad when he wanted to get divorced, wasn't she?

Carlos: Yes, she sure was.

Therapist: Do you think that maybe she gets mad at you because you remind her of him?

Carlos: (long pause) Maybe. I'd never thought of that.

The remainder of the session was devoted to a discussion of this possibility.

Following this appointment, Carlos's sense of himself improved and he began to make friends at school. However he continued to resist his father and stepmother in many ways. A sudden shift in this behavior came soon after a therapy hour in which the therapist had suggested that he might be feeling mad that his parents had divorced, that he'd changed schools, and that he no longer could play soccer. Carlos erupted in anger and was startled at the strength, even the existence, of his feelings.

The resulting change was swift. By the following week Carlos's complaints had diminished, he had decided to go out for basketball, and his conversation was enthusiastic and animated. He also reported that he was seeing his mother much more often, not arguing with her, and having a really good time when he visited.

During the next month, Carlos and his father and stepmother came for a session together, and later Carlos decided that he wanted to "try his wings."

During his final appointment after 10 months of therapy, Carlos summed things up by saying: "It's not what happens to you that matters but how you think about it—that's important and makes a difference. I hope I can remember that."

Carlos's case illustrates several important postdivorce dynamics:

1. The adults do not recognize the many losses the child has sustained. Many times this is due to the guilt the adults feel at seeking their own happiness. They have a need to deny the child's unhappiness.
2. A parent rejects a child because of the child's similarity to the former spouse.
3. Children act out their anger rather than expressing it directly.

For example, when the adults with whom Carlos lived most of the time recognized the many losses with which he had to deal, they became supportive rather than concentrating on his "misbehavior," and the three of them began to develop a closer relationship. At first their guilt at having caused unhappiness for Carlos as they sought their own happiness made it impossible for the two adults to listen to Carlos talk about his sadness and many losses. The therapist was able to help the stepfamily unit to see the negative effects of the adult guilt and the need to accept Carlos's feelings so they could all work to create a satisfying present and future together.

Carlos's self-esteem could shift in positive directions when he could understand his mother's sudden rejection of him. Carlos realized that she did not reject him as a person, and understood her behavior as a reaction to the fact that he had facial characteristics and behavior that reminded her of his father, whom she continued to dislike. When working with the adult, the counterpart situation often occurs—the adult's sudden recognition that his/her anger at a particular child is rooted in feelings about the ex-spouse and the child's similarity in certain respects to that adult.

When a child's behavior is indirectly expressing negative feelings, it can be destructive, or at least unproductive, for the child. Until Carlos was able to recognize and accept his anger at the adults in his life he was caught in behavior patterns that were harmful to himself. In this case, a shift came very quickly. More typically, the therapy deals for a number of sessions with the young person's hostility and the resolution of his/her anger.

Many losses may not be recognized as such by the individuals affected. Understanding and mourning the losses can be important to the successful integration of the stepfamily, and often are an important task of therapy. In fact, many stepchildren have said in retrospect that they consider that they learned to cope effectively with change and loss earlier than children growing up in nuclear families. They consider this to be positive because the experience has given them self-confidence and the conviction that they are able to deal constructively with the changes and losses which inevitably occur in everyone's life. Adults who find themselves able to cope successfully with change are also able to savor the joy of the present once they have said good-bye in emotional terms to their past.

B. LOSS OF MARRIAGE DREAMS

... the common theme of all members of the new stepfamily is one of loss. The exception is being a single person marrying for the first time and becoming a stepparent. (Muller-Paisner, 1983)

Many would agree with this view. In our experience, however, the loss experienced by a spouse who has not been previously married can be very great. As one therapist put it, "No little girl wheels her doll carriage and says to herself, 'Someday I'm going to grow up and be a stepmother.'" Marriage fantasies may be less prominent for men, but it is doubtful that a man envisions being married to a woman with three children who stand behind them during the ceremony, not to mention a former husband who lives across town.

The parents of a previously unmarried adult, the stepgrandparents of the children, also frequently experience profound feelings of loss. They had not imagined that their son or daughter would be marrying someone with children from a previous marriage. One man whose son married a woman slightly older than himself who had five children commented rather poignantly about the wedding reception: "When 5-year-old Jimmie ran up to me and called me 'Grandpop,' I fought him off in my mind. I'm not old enough to be a grandfather."

Frequently the loss of marriage dreams goes unrecognized and acts as a block to satisfactory stepfamily integration. Because these feelings of loss can generally be understood and accepted once they are recognized, a short therapy contact is often all that is required. The case of Ann is illustrative:

Ann contacted a therapist several weeks prior to her marriage to William. Ann had never been married before, while William had been previously married for 10 years and had three young children whom he saw most weekends as well as for special holiday periods.

Ann began by saying that she had done a great deal of reading about stepfamily life. She named the books she had read, and asked for other references she might have overlooked. Her reason for asking quickly became clear.

Ann: I'm to be married in three weeks and lately I've been feeling like crying a lot. I thought my relationship with William was a good one, but now I'm beginning to wonder.

Therapist: Are there situations arising between you and William that bother you?

Ann: I can't really think of any.

Therapist: How would you say it is for you with the children?

Ann: I think that my relationship with them is growing. I know it will take time, but they are really very nice children.

Therapist: Was this the kind of marriage you had expected to have?

Ann: Oh, no. (Ann began to cry) I didn't think of marrying a man who had children and an ex-wife.

Therpist: Perhaps you're feeling sad because of this.

Ann: I hadn't thought of that, but it *is* very different than I'd always expected. I guess I'm sad it isn't going to be the way I thought.

Therapist: It's hard to let something like that go.

Ann: Yes, but it's a help to know what's happening. I was getting pretty anxious. I didn't know why I felt like crying so often. I thought maybe I didn't love William, but I don't think that's it at all. I think I just have to let go of my old dreams.

I think my parents are having the same problem. They keep making remarks about my marriage that hurt me. I think they didn't expect me to marry a man who already had children. I guess it's hard for all of us, but I love William very much and it's worth it.

Ann left the appointment with a feeling of relief and a sadness she now felt she understood. She agreed that she would call again if she continued to be upset or found other things she would like to discuss. She did not call back.

When you consider the differences between a first marriage and a marriage in which children are present from the beginning it is not difficult to become aware of important losses: perhaps no formal "honeymoon" for the couple; no extended honeymoon period which gives time to adjust to one another; no period of months or years in which the couple can freely come and go without thoughts of babysitters, food for dinner, or little league games to attend; and very little time for privacy, even in their own home. The parent who is remarrying is used to living with children and is simply continuing a now familiar pattern. To the person who hasn't had children before, it is like suddenly moving to a foreign country with no plans to return home.

In working therapeutically with adults, one of whom has not been previously married, there are several important tasks that often are overlooked:

1. Acknowledging and supporting the experience of loss sustained by the person with no children.
2. Helping the parent who is remarrying to understand and accept the feelings of loss experienced by the spouse without children.
3. Understanding and assisting all adults to understand and accept the losses experienced by the parents of the person with no children who is marrying a person with children.

C. MAJOR CHANGES FOR CHILDREN

Looking at the stepfamily system even within one household, one sees numerous changes, and therefore losses, for the children. Some of these are discussed in the following pages.

1. A Change in Ordinal Position

As Dennis the Menace says in a recent cartoon, "It's scarey. One day you're an only child and the next day you could have three sisters!" Or perhaps you go from being the youngest in a household of three children to being the middle child in a household of five children. A child's ordinal position in a biological family unit is not something that can be changed except by the birth of a sibling. In stepfamilies, of course, household composition may change every day of the week, so that positions change from day to day.

Certain role expectations tend to accompany your position in the family. If you are the oldest, you are to be the mature and responsible one. If you are the youngest, you are the "baby" of the group, with lowered expectations for performance and higher expectations of being more "cared for" than the older siblings.

In therapy it certainly can help to share with one another the role changes that are anticipated or being experienced. Often, new roles or the continuation of former expectations can be negotiated. Even when desired changes are not possible, being able to talk together and to have the feelings understood and appreciated does a great deal to relieve the stress.

2. Exploding the Fantasy that Biological Parents Will Get Together Again

This is a fantasy held by a large percentage of children, and one that often withstands a remarriage or two. For example, a 55-year-old woman whose parents had separated when she was in her teens spoke of the experience of having her parents marry each other again 40 years later after long marriages to other people: "I always knew they'd get together again some day!"

Even though this fantasy may remain dormant, children do experience a loss as they interpret a remarriage as reducing the likelihood that their biological parents will get back together.

Frequently the adults are acutely aware of the children's fantasy and they attempt to dislodge the fantasy belief by rational explanations. When the subject is raised in therapy, a productive way for the therapist to proceed seems to be to let the adults and the children know that such fantasies are common for children to have in this situation. However, while they are to be expected, it is important for the parents to explain that the parent or parents have moved into new relationships which have created a new reality. This approach allows the children to retain their fantasies even while they know the true situation intellectually, much as children cling to the Santa Claus myth even though they know it is a fairy story. Usually the fantasies diminish over time or vanish entirely.

In some families where the children's fantasy remains vivid, it may be because the remarried parent is not making a solid commitment to his or her new spouse, thus sending a message to the observing children. In such a situation, the therapeutic focus needs to be on helping the adults form a stronger couple bond (Visher & Visher, 1979, pp. 121–140). Then the children's fantasies will no longer be supported by the reality of a poor couple relationship.

3. More Need to Share

We often say that stepfamilies never have enough time, money, or bathrooms. Since in stepfamilies there are a number of individuals from different backgrounds and households, there is frequently the necessity of finding ways to share money, space, and time or attention. Children are usually less aware than are the adults of the fact that available income is now split in more ways than before. They are very aware, however, of the need to share living space and parental time.

4. Sharing Parental Time

Frequently, the subject of sharing a parent arises in therapy. As we have previously discussed in this chapter, many children feel displaced by new stepparents and stepsiblings. It is important to try to deal with these strong feelings of alienation. Usually the suggestion is made that the parenting adults make a point of seeing that each child gets a share of available time on a one-to-one basis. Obviously, the time remains the same in quantity but has to be distributed to a larger number of persons. If this point is clarified and children are told that their turn will come at such-and-such a time, they usually can more easily delay gratification of their needs.

Special attention needs to be paid to making the allocation of time as fair as possible. For example, when a large group is going to a movie together it could be arranged to have people change places midway through the film so that everyone has a chance to sit with the adults. (In the distribution of time and attention, the adults need to be sure to save significant portions of time for themselves. One couple would see the children one by one in the evening to discuss the events of the day or a problem the child might have. But at 9:30 they would close their bedroom door and put up a sign, "Do Not Knock Unless You're Bleeding." They were giving a clear message that the adults needed time together, too.)

Excerpts from a therapy session with Janet, her two sons and her new husband, Roger, will clarify a typical parental time-sharing situation and will illustrate the solution they found. The four had been together for five and a half months. Janet's son, Matt, lived with them most of the time, and Carl lived with his father but visited frequently.

Roger: What I think we need to discuss is the sharing situation — sharing parents, sharing time. Matt and I have talked about this. I always felt I had trouble getting access to Janet. I'm positive we all have been finding it hard to share.

Carl: I have to learn how to share love throughout the family . . . and I have to learn to take what is given to me and say, "Oh, that's good. I know they still love me."

Matt: I thought I didn't have enough of my mother, and then Roger said — 'cause my brother lives with our Dad — I have her for awhile and then Carl comes in and does stuff with her, and then I feel kind of odd because she's not doing it with me like she used to. And then Roger said, "Well, do you think it would be fair if Carl didn't have any time with her?" and I said, "'No!'"

Therapist (to Janet): The other three have talked about the difficulty of sharing and I was wondering if you also have the same kind of feelings?

Janet: No, I don't. I feel I'm being pulled every which way because they all want a piece of me.

Matt: I wasn't used to sharing. The sharing makes you feel kind of funny. It feels as though Mother's not around with you if you're having to share her.

Roger, Matt and Carl were feeling upset at sharing Janet, while Janet was feeling overwhelmed at trying to meet everyone's need to relate to her. During the session, the therapist demonstrated by looking and talking to one person, and then to another, that when two people are relating, the others are inevitably left out. What can make it work out satisfactorily is to be conscious of switching from one person to another so that the same individual or individuals are not left out, and to let each other know that there will be a turn for everyone.

The family unit responded quickly and positively to this approach. Janet expressed relief at realizing it was futile to attempt to satisfy everyone by trying to spread herself, and the others started talking about taking turns doing things together. Janet entered the conversation by saying with obvious relief, "That means that Roger and I can do some things alone, too, without the others."

The family left the appointment beginning to plan for the week ahead. Two weeks later there were other issues they needed to discuss, but the subject of sharing did not come up again.

5. Sharing Space

Adults as well as children are faced with sharing living space on at least a semipermanent basis with individuals who may start out as virtual strangers. For the children, the common situation is the necessity of sharing a bedroom with a stepsibling. Even school roommates separate during vacations and may be exchanged for someone more compatible if necessary. Unfortunately, the adults are not always sensitive to the stresses that can be created when children are asked to share a room with someone they have not chosen.

By comparing the children's experience with an emotionally comparable situation for the adults, parents and stepparents who are originally insensitive to the reactions of the children often can begin to empathize. They may find that by being creative they can change living arrangements—a study can become a bedroom, or furniture arranged to act as a partial divider in the room. Even when no physical changes are possible, the recognition that the adults understand that it is difficult to share bedroom space eases the frustration of the young person.

Sharing a bathroom can be traumatic for an adolescent, and the feelings of intrusion are profound if a teenager is suddenly sharing a bathroom with an opposite-sex stepsibling. The therapist working with a family in which the wife brought a teenage daughter and the husband a teenage son into the house stimulated the couple's "brainstorming" and helped them to make the decision to turn the family room with an adjoining bathroom into a bedroom. The need for privacy is particularly important during the teen years when sexuality and personal identity are developmental issues for adolescents.

Frequently, a major shift in the use of space revolves around the use of the couple's bedroom. During the single-parent household phase preceding the remarriage, children as a rule have free access to the parental bedroom. In many cases they have even slept in the same bed with the parent. The greater the freedom the children have had to share the parent's bedroom, the greater will be their upset when this pattern is no longer acceptable.

If husband and wife both have children who have had freedom to come and go as they choose, or have had similar restrictions, the new arrangements may be worked out relatively easily. When there is considerable difference in the past experience of the children, or when only one adult has children in the house, the situation will be more difficult to resolve.

Cora and Greg had been married for six months. Cora had no children and Greg had custody of 12-year-old twin girls. Cora had become depressed and sought therapeutic help. A major source of stress for her was the lack of privacy and the feeling that she was always surrounded by people. As she said, "There's nowhere I can go in the house to be by myself, and Greg and I are never alone except when we're asleep. The girls are always around. I don't get home from work 'til 5:00 o'clock and the girls are there. There's a TV in the living room but they always want to watch the one in our bedroom. And their Dad says, 'Sure, why not?' I've lived by myself for 10 years and I'm going crazy."

In this family the issue of bedroom privacy took several months to resolve. Initially, Greg could not identify with Cora's feelings. Then, as he saw that he was in a position to help his wife fit into the present family system with greater comfort, he was able to work out several acceptable alternatives with her. The twins were then included in three therapy sessions so that all four family members could make decisions about a number of household situations. With respect to the privacy issue, they arrived at the following compromise:

a. When the adults' bedroom door was open, the twins could come into the room if one of the adults was there.
b. If the adults' bedroom door was closed, this meant that the children were to stay out.
c. Until 8:30 p.m., if the children had an important question or information to give, they could knock on the door if it was closed.
d. After 8:30 p.m., questions and information could wait until the next morning, unless there was a real emergency.
e. If the adults were in another part of the house, the children were to ask permission to use the TV in the bedroom before doing so.
f. The same rules applied to the girls' bedroom. The adults were to knock if the door was closed, and were not to enter without permission.

Shifting from previous patterns when the structure of the family has changed requires clear messages from the parent to his or her children regarding changes in the use of living space. Acknowledging the feelings the changes may bring and accepting them make the shifts more palatable for the children. When older children can be included in the discussion and planning, they respond much more favorably.

6. Loss of Former Role in the Household

After a divorce, many children feel the need to take care of parents. Often without realizing it, the parent puts the child in the role of confidant, and in many ways the child becomes a surrogate spouse. We have been struck by how seriously the caretaking role is taken by very young children as well as by older ones. A teenager looking back put it this way: "My life began when I was four. That's when my Mom got married. She and my father were divorced when I was two. I don't really remember things before I was four. All I remember is taking care of my Mom. I remember her crying a lot, and I took care of her and talked to her. It's hard to be taking care of your mother rather than being taken care of *by* her when you're two or three. It doesn't seem right."

Older children often stay with a parent until that parent remarries, and then move into the other parent's home when it is a more suitable place for them. In such situations, a remarriage of the parent for whom the role of caretaker has been assumed is a welcome relief from much responsibility.

In other situations, the response of the children is different. Two teenage daughters whose mother died took care of their father for two years before he remarried. They did the shopping and cooking and most of the household chores. Barbara, the new wife, moved into the home in which her husband and his daughters had been living and immediately took over all the household responsibilities. She wanted the house to be her house and the kitchen her kitchen. To quote Barbara, "All hell broke loose!"

Even though the daughters might have appreciated being relieved of some of their heavy responsibilities if they had been included in the decision making, they probably would have resented the loss of a certain status in the house. Such changes need to be made slowly and with sensitivity to the feelings of the young people. Issues needed to be negotiated with all concerned. "You can't ask someone to go back to being a child," was the comment of one of the girls. The family worked with a therapist for a number of months to overcome the anger that had been generated between the daughters, their father, and their stepmother, and to work out a household management plan that was tolerable to all.

In another household, the soon-to-be stepfather informed a friend, "My wife's son, John, is 16 and he's had to take on a great deal of responsibility. I look forward to joining the family and returning him to his rightful place of being a child." It is not surprising that the young man reacted very strongly, saying, "Who needs this bull—I can't do at 16 what I had been doing at 12."

The adults attended a Stepfamily Discussion Course and began to get some awareness of the sources of the major difficulty in their household. As a couple they worked well together, and they accepted the group leader's recommendation that they seek family counseling to work out ways in which they could live together more easily.

Cooperation rather than chaos began to be achieved, partly because the adults had sought outside help soon after their marriage, before the reservoir of anger in the household had been filled to overflowing. The therapist was able to intervene by reframing the situation:

a. The stepfather cared about John and was trying to be helpful to him by relieving him of some of the responsibilities he had been carrying.
b. John was rebelling because he felt that he was no longer considered independent and mature for his age, and he was trying to prove that he was, but in a way that wasn't working for him.

Viewing the struggles in this light, all three were able to work out roles that were mutually satisfactory.

D. LOSS OF FORMER TRADITIONS

Satir has said, "The chances of spouses doing at least some things different from one another are just about 100 percent as neither was brought up in the same way" (1972, p. 129). In stepfamilies, the adults are older and have already worked out the ways they want to run their households. In addition, the children know exactly how the meatballs ought to be cooked, and that you eat Christmas Dinner on Christmas Eve. Older children have belonged to other family units for a longer time than younger children, so their beliefs of "right" and "wrong" ways of doing things are stronger and less flexible. Stepfamilies need to instantly solve many interactions that have been established previously at a more gradual pace in several different family units. Indeed, for many stepfamilies the adults are dealing with leftovers from six or more previous households. Being shown this in a graphic form has proven beneficial for a number of families. The scheme in Figure 4 assumes that each adult is a parent and has been married once previously.

The task for the therapist is to shift the family away from "right" and "wrong" to the recognition that there are simply "different" ways of doing things: working with them to move slowly in changing old patterns, combining more than one approach where desired, and being creative in developing important new rituals.

In many instances, even basic household management issues have not been worked out. In one family, each adult had two children, and the six of them were finding many pitfalls in the way of their ability to get along. During a first therapy appointment the therapist asked them if they had any difficulty with the daily tasks of living and running a household.

Wife: Wow, do we! The kids fuss at everything we ask them to do, and
we bicker and fight over it a lot.
Therapist: Have you ever sat down and talked together about how you
want to divide what needs to be done?

All shook their heads as the husband said, "No." With the therapist's
help, the group all responded to the request to make a list of all the
tasks necessary to keep the household running. Cooperation began to
develop. When the list was complete, the therapist asked them to see
who would volunteer for the tasks. Only a few items remained to be
assigned. The family decided to reevaluate in two weeks.

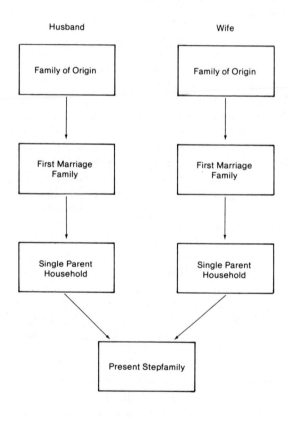

Figure 4

To the amazement of the adults in one family, a 14-year-old boy said, "I'll water the lawn at night, you need to relax when you get home." In another family, a 17-year-old volunteered to do the grocery shopping for the family. He had just received his driver's license and this gave him an opportunity to drive, and he also appreciated being able to go to the refrigerator and find a snack he liked. Unless the family sits down and works out these basic situations, they may not examine the components in terms of their own needs. As a result, assignments may be made that do not fit for the individuals concerned.

Any type of family will, of course, benefit from household management meetings, but the need to solve these "problems of living" becomes acute for stepfamily members who suddenly begin to live together under the same roof. Even when children are coming and going between households, tasks can be worked out on the basis of the composition of the group at given times. Negotiating various roles and tasks brings with it a sense of family membership and identity in addition to the more obvious gain of smoother household functioning.

E. LACK OF AFFIRMATION FROM FORMER SPOUSE

Truman Capote once said, "To lose a good friend is easy, but to lose a good enemy is hard." We often think of that comment when we speak of the fact that many divorced couples find it difficult to separate psychologically, even after a remarriage has taken place. Anger and hostility can tie two people together as effectively as love.

When bitterness and anger continue to hold former spouses together following a divorce, the root of the inability to let go often appears to come from a buried wish for affirmation from that person. Love and appreciation coming from a new spouse do not suffice; the divorced and remarried adult continues to remain tied to the former spouse. At times it is difficult to separate the need for affirmation by the former spouse from the need to maintain contact to insure an ongoing relationship with the children. Often the two needs are closely intertwined.

At times, parents will placate former spouses because of the fear of angering them and being "punished" by not being allowed to see the children. Contact, or even "going along with" the children's other parent to insure seeing the children, is not in itself an indication of the need for approval. The emotion that can surface to alert the therapist to the wish for acceptance and affirmation is a strong need to be thought of as a good or a nice person by the ex-spouse. This need generally goes unrecognized by those involved. If there are hurt and angry feelings still remaining, approval is most unlikely to be forthcoming from the former spouse!

Whether or not the remarried parent was the one who wanted the divorce, the wish for affirmation can remain, although it tends to occur more frequently for the one who has been actively rejected. The person who did not seek the divorce keeps hoping that the former spouse will say, "I really do think you are a very nice person, even though I wasn't able to stay married to you." The one who chose to leave the previous marriage hopes to hear, "I really do think you are a good person, and I understand that you needed to leave." Letting go of this need for a former spouse's approval usually is easier when the adult's self-esteem has risen.

In therapy, individuals can gain needed self-esteem and an awareness of this common and usually unrealistic need. This awareness often allows adults to relinquish the fantasy of affirmation and accept support and appreciation they are getting from those who care for them now—new partners, children, stepchildren, other relatives and friends.

F. CONTINUING TRANSITIONS

In a recent cartoon, a harried father/stepfather is talking to his wife as they head for a holiday celebration. He has a long list of arrangements of who is going to go where, when they are going, and who will pick them up, and he ends by saying triumphantly, "I worked it out on the computer!" In a family unit, as in other groups, when there is a change in membership, there is also an accompanying change in the functioning of the system. In biological families, membership changes are gradual: There is a nine-month waiting period to add each child, camp registration takes place weeks prior to the camper's departure, and there is a built-in expectation that children will leave when they become young adults and are self-supporting, go to college, or get married.

In many stepfamilies there is no similar stability. There is a biological parent elsewhere and children come and go weekly, every other weekend, or two to three months in the summer. Shifts may bring gains, but they also bring losses of time with a child or adult, as well as diminished privacy and alone time for the couple. Complicated logistics underlie these changes and give the uninitiated a feeling of "being in the middle of Grand Central Station."

Papernow (1984) has found that one characteristic of a smoothly functioning stepfamily is that "change is normal." In general, reaching the stage where stepfamilies feel a solid identity and stability in the midst of all these rapid and continuous shifts may take several years, even with professional help.

Just as a child learns "object constancy," the recognition that a parent and the relationship with him/her continue to exist even when that parent is out of sight, so must the individuals in stepfamilies learn to experience family stability concurrent with continual shifting of the household composition. Today there may be two to feed, tomorrow 10; the 15-year-old sweeps the porch on Wednesdays and the twins who are there on weekends take turns doing it on Saturdays. A pattern emerges from a background of many discontinuous strands.

Individuals who have had early experiences of helplessness beyond those commonly encountered may have reacted by developing a strong need to control their environment. For them, the shifts and the ambiguities of stepfamily life are particularly difficult. Marla was such a person. She came into therapy feeling upset and "overwhelmed." In her attempts to control, she was demanding that her children call her each night they were away in the other household. She would call them whenever she was away from them for overnight, and she attempted to make very detailed plans a month in advance. In therapy, Marla came to understand the roots of her anxiety (she had had a dominant and controlling mother who gave her daughter little freedom to make decisions) and to recognize that even though her present household composition fluctuated, there was a "stepfamily constancy" that she could count on.

All too often remarried parents are urged to create stability for their children by lessening or even discontinuing the children's contacts with their other household. Research is indicating that this policy can have negative implications.

For example, Lutz (1983) found that teenagers in stepfamilies perceived not being allowed to visit their other parent as one of the three top stresses in their lives. (Hearing their parents talk negatively about each other and having a parent and stepparent argue were the other leading stresses reported.)

One concern that is expressed is that the children will feel confused and unsettled by constant transitions between two very different households. In our experience, the children prefer to remain in contact with both parents, even after parental remarriages. The alternative of not seeing a parent is seldom acceptable. As a rule, however, very young children need one primary caretaker; preschoolers can adapt to two households, though they do not like to spend more than a week without a contact with their parent in their other household; older children can enjoy living arrangements involving lengthy periods away from a parent.

An important personal characteristic stressed by Huntington (1986) that needs to be considered in making specific plans is the impact of transitions on individual children. Some children adjust quickly to change, while others require more time to shift comfortably. Two brothers, Tim and Josh, illustrate this point. Although they were close in age, Tim being 12 and Josh 10, Tim changed households easily and Josh did not. Their counselor, in calling the attention of the adults to this difference between the boys, and not labeling either adjustment as "good" or "bad," paved the way for the parents to shift schedules so that Tim changed households frequently (weekdays in one household, weekends in the other) while Josh alternated at two-week intervals. When these schedules became routine, it eased much of the tension that had characterized both households prior to the altered arrangements.

We have found that the adults are not always sensitive to the need for reentry time for the children, and also for themselves when the children change from one house to another. Indeed,

One of the initial complaints Claudia and Derek voiced in therapy was that when Claudia's 12-year-old daughter, Jessie, returned from spending weekends with her father and stepmother, the household was extremely tense for two days. This was repeated nearly every week and was producing many arguments between the two adults.

Therapist: What happens when Jessie comes back?

Claudia: I make sure I'm in the living room to greet her. I ask her about her weekend and she often snaps at me.

Derek: Claudia wants me to be there too. If I'm not, she's afraid Jessie will think I don't like her. Sometimes she ignores me or is cross, and I truly just want to stay out of her way.

Therapist: What happens if you are there but are casual with your greeting and continue with your activities?

Claudia: I don't know. We've never done that. I'd be afraid Jessie would think I wasn't glad to see her.

Therapist: When you come home from work, or go to a party at a friend's house, does it take you a little while to adjust to the situation?

Claudia: That's right. I feel strange for a few minutes and then it seems more natural.

Derek: I think I take even longer than Claudia to get comfortable. Are you saying it might be a good idea to give Jessie some time to get used to our house again?

Therapist: I know many children need this period. Then they begin to relate to you again. One boy I know swings in his backyard when he first comes home, and an older girl I've heard about listens to her radio for awhile. It would also give the two of you some time to get used to having Jessie with you.

Too often, adults expect children to run in from being with their other parent and stepparent and immediately start to relate. Reentry time is usually needed. In this case, Claudia was able to give Jessie more psychological space on her return, and Derek also appreciated the opportunity to relax in his interaction with Jessie during transition times. There was a dramatic reduction in the household tension. While a number of important issues required attention, the improvement in household ambience gave Derek and Claudia a success experience that increased their faith that they could find solutions to their other problems.

G. CUSTODY CHANGES: LEGAL OR INFORMAL

Custody agreements are not etched in stone and many situations can change to produce the need for or the desirability of a change in living arrangements. At times there is a legal change of custody while at other times there is simply a change of residence. Frequently, such changes occur when children become teenagers. At this point in their development, children are concerned with identity issues and often choose to live with their other parent to experience that person more intimately than they have in their immediate past. This type of change appears to be especially common for boys who go to live with their fathers when they are adolescents.

Sometimes, adolescents shift residences because they view the other household as more desirable, while in other instances the change is arranged by adults because the child is manifesting serious problems in the primary custodial household. These are very different arrangements than un-thought-out changes coming as angry responses to stepfamily situations.

Whatever the reason for the change the adults who are being "left" usually have feelings of guilt, inadequacy, and/or rejection. While letting go of the young person may be a very loving response to the needs of the individual, it can stir many deep feelings of loss. At times therapists can help by reframing such a change as a positive and caring decision for individuals who have not been viewing their actions this way.

Helping parents and stepparents through these periods of grieving can increase the chances that all members of the suprasystem will deal creatively with the changes. Very frequently a parent and stepparent who have willingly, albeit reluctantly and sadly, supported such a change of living arrangements are rewarded by having a tense relationship slowly replaced by warm and loving responses from the young person.

H. FEAR OF FURTHER LOSS

Because of many previous losses, parents and children in stepfamilies may consciously or unconsciously fear more loss. Children frequently displace anger at their parents onto stepparents to preserve the relationship they have with their parents. Often they may suppress their emotions and their actions in attempts to be "good children" so that they will be wanted by their parents. Since one parent has left the other parent, children sometimes fear that their residential parent could also leave them. Similarly, adults may react by displacing their anger. A common situation occurs when a child has broken a house rule agreed upon by the couple and the parent says nothing to the child (Figure 5).

EXPRESSION OF ANGER

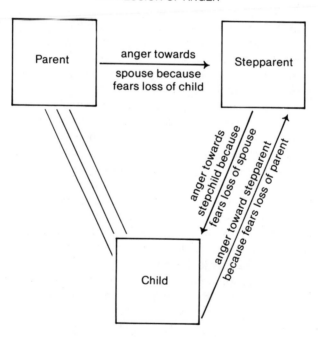

Figure 5. This situation tends to create an alliance
between the parent and child and leaves the
stepparent in a vulnerable, isolated position.

In this instance, stepparents perceive the tight bond between their partner and children and displace their anger at their spouse to the stepchildren, while parents attempt to protect their relationship with their children by displacing their anger on to their new spouse, or at times their former spouse.

In other instances, fathers who have previously taken their relationships with their children for granted now become aware that ongoing contact is no longer a "given," and suddenly their parenting behavior and wish for more contact may increase. Mothers all too often interpret this changed attitude as coming from hostile motivation, and exacerbate an already strained situation by making angry responses. Positive reframing of the father's behavior where appropriate will at times allow mothers to cooperate with the father's new interest in their joint children to the benefit of the children and indirectly to the benefit of all the adults.

We also see fear of further loss as an important element in the negativity that so often arises between the children's two households. Grandparents, stepgrandparents, and their households may also experience angry emotions and react in similar ways. Each fears that the children will want to remain in the other household. The result is that distrust grows between the households until each reacts to the other as an enemy rather than as households involved in the raising of the same children. No "parenting coalition" is formed and adults may experience a great deal of stress.

The more insecure a parent feels in the parent role, the more difficult it is to allow children to enjoy their other household. Before therapists attempt to persuade such a parent to cooperate with the children's other household, they need to validate the importance of that parent to their children and provide a therapeutic atmosphere that will lead to increased self-esteem for that parent. Elizabeth was such a mother:

> In the weeks that followed an appointment with the therapist in which she had gained enough self-confidence to let go of her need for her former husband's approval, Elizabeth found herself allowing her seven-year-old son to be with his father for more and longer periods of time. No longer did she fear that her son would not return home, because her self-esteem no longer depended on winning approval from her former husband. She now believed that her son loved and needed her no matter what opinion her former husband had of her.

Unfortunately, at times the fears between households are based in reality. One parent or a new couple may be attempting unilaterally to alter the living arrangements of the children in a manner which will produce loss for the other household. Therapists are frequently expected to intervene in such situations. Sometimes, therapists are able to reduce interhousehold hostility by clarifying the fears and acknowledging their normalcy. When a parent continues to attempt to undermine the other parent by secretly attempting to persuade a child or children to shift living arrangements, the therapeutic task may be much more difficult. The story of Anita is one such situation:

Anita's father, Perry, and stepmother, Ethel, sought therapy because they did not respect the parenting skills of Anita's mother and stepfather, and they wanted Anita to come to live most of the time with them. Perry kept promoting this plan in subtle ways and, according to the couple, Anita reacted by withdrawal and insolence. Their question to the therapist was, "How can we reduce the tension in the household and how can we persuade Anita she would be better off with us?"

Since the couple had formed a strong unit the therapist made an appointment for all members of the household. At the beginning of this session, the genogram of the family was drawn (Genogram 5), omitting the grandparents who did not live in the area.

Ethel had been divorced for two years before her marriage to Perry, and Perry had been divorced from Fawn for four years before his mar-

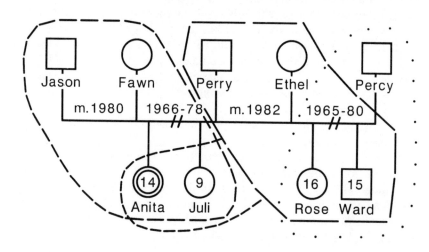

1983

Genogram 5

riage to Ethel. Ethel's two children saw their father infrequently, while Perry's two daughters spent three days a week in his household. Perry wanted Anita to spend at least every other week with him. He had no thought of going to court to force the issue, but he was attempting to get Anita to tell Fawn and Jason that this is what she wanted to do. Perry felt certain that Juli would want to do what her older sister did once her decision had been made.

During the first family session, the therapist was able to facilitate the discussion between Perry and Anita in which Perry verbalized his desire to see Anita more and she responded by saying she wanted to be with her school friends more and didn't want to change living arrangements. Rose and Ward complained that Anita was unpleasant at times and didn't relate to them. Ethel spoke about her upset feelings about the tenseness in the house, while Juli said very little other than that things seemed OK to her.

When the therapist commented that it sounded as though Rose and Ward wanted to know Anita better, they nodded in agreement and Anita began to cry. Anita said she felt very cut off from her father and he was the one she wanted to have time with. As they talked, it was clear that relationships between the stepsiblings had not developed, and that Anita had remained as an outsider in the household and felt alienated from her father.

The next three appointments were with the couple. During this time Ethel and Perry began to understand the isolation Anita felt in their household. They began to accept the ways in which Anita was different from Ethel's children and began to support Anita's wish to listen to rock music and spend more time with her friends. Perry related to Anita differently, playing games with her that they both enjoyed, and not pressuring her to stay longer. He even decided that if the girls didn't choose to come as often as before it didn't mean that he and his daughters would lose touch with one another. Even with these changes, Anita remained withdrawn most of the time when she was in the household—a complete switch from the way she was acknowledged to be in her other household.

A following appointment included Anita, Ethel and Perry, along with Fawn and Jason. The therapist had recommended this meeting since Anita had not changed and appeared caught in negative telephone conversations between her parents, Perry and Fawn. Juli, on the other hand, had shown no signs of stress, and did not enter her parents' heated discussions. This meeting with Anita and the four adults involved in parenting her had taken several weeks to arrange and the contacts had been typical for many such appointments:

1. The therapist obtained Perry and Ethel's permission to contact Fawn and Jason. This contact was for the purpose of asking if they would meet with her, or some other therapist, to work with Anita and Perry and Ethel to help make Anita's household transitions go more smoothly.
2. Perry predicted that Fawn would refuse to come.
3. Fawn reacted to the therapist's phone call by saying that she had asked Perry to go with her to see a mediator about the situation and he had refused, and she was angry at this.
4. The therapist acknowledged that Fawn and Jason might feel reluctant to meet with her since she already knew Anita's other household, and that, of course, they might prefer to meet with a therapist who did not know any of the family members.
5. Fawn said that since the therapist knew the situation she would prefer that they all meet with her. Fawn would ask Jason to see if he would come. Fawn did not think Anita would come.
6. Fawn and Jason declined a preliminary meeting as a couple and chose to come with Perry and Ethel. Fawn still predicted Anita would not join them.
7. Perry backed away, saying that since Anita might not come he didn't think it could be a productive meeting. (Now that Fawn and Jason had accepted, he had to face the reality of such an appointment.) Ethel disagreed with Perry and persuaded him to go ahead with the plans.
8. The therapist was willing to meet only if all four adults were present. She also telephoned Anita to make a direct contact about the meeting and answer her questions about the purpose of the meeting. The therapist let Anita know that she felt it would be important for Anita to include herself so that her feelings would be known; otherwise, the adults might try to guess what her reactions were.

All five appeared for the appointment which was emotionally low key, with Fawn and Perry doing most of the talking. The major theme concerned loss, though it was never clearly stated that way by Perry or Fawn. Fawn and Jason saw Perry and Ethel as trying to persuade Anita to come to live with them, and Fawn, Jason, and Anita thought that the previous therapy contacts were designed to implement this. Perry and Ethel agreed that this had been a wish of theirs, but that they had dropped this idea some weeks before and were surprised that Anita, Fawn and Jason had not recognized their change. Perry and Ethel repeated the message that they were now content with the arrangements for Anita. Fawn hoped this was true and said that she would do nothing to alter the pattern. (Ricci [1980] refers to this type of interchange as "trading assurances.")

The following interchange clarified the dynamics of Anita's refusal to participate in her father and stepmother's household:

Therapist (to Anita): So you've felt that your Dad and Ethel were still trying to have you be with them more?

Anita: Yes, and I didn't want to. I like it the way it is now.

Therapist: Did you think something would happen if you had a good time at your Dad and Ethel's house?

Anita: I guess so. That maybe they'd say, "See, you do have fun here."

Therapist: And then they'd want you to stay longer?

Perry: That makes sense. I can see that. Hey, Anita, that's not true. You can have a good time and I won't think that.

None of the adults accepted the therapist's suggestion that they all meet again in a few weeks to see if things between the households were going more smoothly, so instead the door was left open for more joint meetings if it seemed a good idea in the future.

After this meeting, Anita was able to relax more when she was with her father and stepmother, and the tension lessened in the household. Other structural changes occurred. Rose graduated from high school and took a summer job in another state. This allowed Anita to have a bedroom to herself when she was in the household. The distrust between the households did not totally disappear since Fawn did not accept Perry's continued statements that he was willing to accept his daughter's present schedule. On the other hand, Perry and Ethel understood and became more tolerant of Fawn's fears, and Anita no longer was caught in a crossfire between her two parents.

SUMMARY

A major task of therapy can be to help individuals identify their losses, be able to express their sadness and anger, and then move on to recognizing present gains and potential satisfactions. Adults may remarry without having emotionally resolved their former marriage relationship. Children may not have been allowed to mourn the loss of their parent as a full-time person in their lives. Those never married before often have not recognized the loss of marriage fantasies and dreams of their youth, and those who wanted a divorce have unrealistically expected only relief and happiness, not realizing that they too have lost a dream of what their previous marriage was going to be. Sadness is there, often below the surface or on a deeper level. Therapeutic sensitivity to the pervasiveness of loss can be crucial since stepfamily adults frequently disregard or deny their losses, in an attempt to reassure themselves and their friends and relatives that their actions are "for the best."

Also, adults wishing to comfort and reassure their children often overlook the profound adjustment children must make if they are to deal with the many important losses and changes in their lives. Acknowledging and responding in emotionally appropriate ways to these losses is a first step towards embracing new and realistic expectations and experiencing the gains inherent in new family constellations.

CHAPTER 6

Unrealistic Beliefs

*I think even good therapists don't know what's going on. . . . She [therapist]
kept trying to move the family to a nuclear family, and I'm NOT the
mother. I'm a parental helper.*

— Stepmother of three teenagers

The majority of stepfamilies seem founded on myth—the myth that a
family headed by an adult couple is the family of one's dreams. Since there
are a man, a woman, and one or more children, it must follow that there will
be family cohesiveness and caring. The unrealistic belief of the adults is that
this new group will be "one big happy family," mirroring the attributes of the
ideal nuclear family pictured by the media.

It is important for therapists to be aware of major unrealistic beliefs—
we call them myths—that can impede good stepfamily formation because
this knowledge allows therapists to help stepfamilies form more realistic expectations. In this chapter we will discuss a number of especially prevalent
myths:

Myth 1: Stepfamilies are the same as biological families.
Myth 2: Stepfamily adjustment will be attained quickly.
Myth 3: Love and caring will develop instantaneously.
Myth 4: Working hard prevents the development of a "wicked stepmother."
Myth 5: Withdrawing a child from a biological parent enhances the rela-
tionship with the stepparent of the same sex.
Myth 6: Anything negative that happens is a result of being in a stepfamily.

121

Stepfamilies Are the Same as Biological Families

All families come complete with belief systems concerning how their family "should" be. However, the belief systems of other types of families tend to be more congruent with reality than the beliefs held by stepfamilies, which are often far removed from the reality of stepfamily living.

We have previously written at some length about fundamental ways in which stepfamilies differ structurally from biological families (Visher and Visher, 1979, 1985a). Briefly stated, stepfamilies are families "born of loss," with adults and children coming together at very different places in their life cycles and with a variety of traditions and ways of doing things which may seem incompatible. The parent/child relationships precede the new-couple relationship and children frequently move back and forth between two households since they have a parent in more than one household. Moreover, stepparents in America have little or no legal relationship to their stepchildren. Attempting to fit a stepfamily into a biological family mold under these circumstances does not work, except perhaps in very exceptional circumstances when the children are very young. Even then there can be an upheaval in the family when children become adolescents and seek to know a parent from whom they have been cut off.

Adults frequently consider that their stepfamily will be a reincarnated nuclear family. In fact, when we are asked what is the one thing we consider to be the greatest stumbling block to stepfamily integration, we frequently say, "unrealistic expectations about the kind of family it is."

The following therapeutic contact illustrates the power of this belief and the detrimental effects that it can have on the integration and well-being of a stepfamily:

A stepmother, Carol, called because of tension and upset feelings whenever her stepson was with them. Both she and her husband were willing to come in.

First appointment: The couple came in together. Carol had not been married before; Paul had been married previously and had a son, Johnnie, now four and a half, who visited regularly. Paul and his first wife divorced when Johnnie was only a few weeks old. Carol and Paul had been married four years and now had a young daughter, Julie, who was 14 months old. The following exchange summarizes the feelings expressed during the first hour:

Carol: Johnnie's a real good kid, but my feelings have really become intense since Julie was born. I just don't want Johnnie around at all. I feel like I'm babysitting him.

Paul: In my eyes both children seem the same to me. And I want Johnnie to have the same respect from Carol that she gives Julie. I feel the same for them both. They're both my children—but there's nothing but tenseness when Johnnie comes over.

Second appointment: The couple came in again in about two weeks and reported that the situation was unchanged.

Carol: But Johnnie's coming over tomorrow and we'll have to see if it's any different. What *is* the problem? Do other people feel this way?

Therapist: People often *do* feel the way you two feel. Perhaps part of it has to do with your expectations.

Paul: I'm always optimistic, and I really pushed at first for Johnnie and Carol to like each other. And Carol was angry all the time Johnnie was there. She said, "It's not really Johnnie, yet it *is* Johnnie." I kept trying to figure it out.

Carol: Then my 5-year-old cousin came over to visit, and Paul climbed the walls and she didn't bother me a bit.

Paul: Yes. I could understand then a little more how Carol must feel. I'd wondered why Carol treated the dog better than she treated Johnnie. Then I realized we had *both* chosen the dog. It was *ours,* and Johnnie's an outsider. So now I just hope that maybe it will work out so he's an insider too.

Carol: I don't understand why I have these feelings when Johnnie comes.

Therapist: Do you suppose you had a different idea in your head about what your family would be like?

Carol: That's right. For 18 years I had this bubble of it being just me and my husband and our children.

Therapist: Do you think you get angry to cover up the tears of having to let go of that bubble? You look to me as though you're sad and feel like crying now.

Carol: (in tears) So it's 18 years of conditioning I have to get over. But it really started after Julie was born. I know it did.

Paul: Yes, that's right.

Carol: Why did it start then?

Therapist: Do you think that before Julie was born Johnnie and you two were as close to your bubble family as you could be—and now when Johnnie's not with you, you have that dream family with you and Paul and Julie? Then Johnnie comes and it's not that kind of family anymore?

Carol: (in tears) Yes, that's it. I'm just going to have to take some time working on it.

Paul: I had my own bubble. I wasn't happy in my first marriage and I thought that maybe having a child would help. But as soon as Johnnie was born I knew it wouldn't work. So I left then when he was just a baby so I could find someone else and have that same bubble kind of family. I really pushed hard for that.

The couple decided to think about and work on the situation themselves. They felt that they had begun to grasp what had been taking place and decided not to make another appointment. If things continued to go badly, they would make further contact. A follow-up call two months later revealed that the situation had improved greatly and that they were each feeling satisfied. We believe that the partial resolution attained in the brief period in this instance is unusual since in our experience adults typically do not readily acknowledge such important unconscious expectations. This is, however, a clear example of a major unrealistic expectation.

In a more typical situation, Ginger became distraught and sought therapy because of her relationship with her 12-year-old stepdaughter, Jill. Ginger and her husband, Martin, had a total of three children from previous marriages. The two younger children who were quite young had rather quickly fitted into the new household where they lived most of the time. Jill, however, was refusing to relate warmly to her stepmother.

When Ginger came for help, she talked about how angry she was at an article she had read that said there were fundamental differences between nuclear families and stepfamilies. When the therapist asked her to describe her "ideal" family, Ginger talked about her aunt's family which she had known quite well when she was a child. Her first marriage family had not replicated that ideal family, and Ginger said, "I'm determined this one will."

After several weeks of therapy, Ginger slowly began to accept a new reality. She experienced a week of sadness as she started to relinquish her old beliefs about stepfamilies and began to embrace a new and more realistic concept of stepfamily dynamics and structure. As Ginger relaxed and stopped pushing Jill to relate, to her surprise Jill began to approach her. In time, the family actually became much closer to the family of Ginger's dreams, even with its stepfamily characteristics.

MYTH 2

Stepfamily Adjustment Will Be Attained Quickly

It may be that unrealistic expectations of instant adjustment are more frequently experienced by men than by women. Every man on a panel of five, all in structurally different types of stepfamilies, answered the question, "What surprised you the most about your stepfamily?" by saying he had believed that things would settle down quickly, but this had not happened. One man said he expected the adjustment period to be over in two weeks! This type of unrealistic expectation can lead to discouragement or even to a new divorce.

We find that many families benefit from having specific psychological tasks or "homework" to think about between appointments. Writing down expectations and evaluating which ones seem realistic and which ones do not, can be a revealing and helpful experience in this regard. Indeed it may be the first time individuals have thought about their previously unconscious expectations.

Jan and Charles sought therapeutic help two months following their marriage. They each had children from previous marriages. Their new household was in chaos. During the first session it became clear that they were not working together and were only just beginning to talk about their tensions (Mobilization stage—see Chapter 3). The therapist decided not to include the children at this point in the therapy because the couple relationship was not solid. At the end of the appointment, the therapist asked if each would be willing to write down his/her expectations of the new family unit, evaluate the reasonableness of such expectations, and bring the list to share during their next session. Both agreed to do so.

Second appointment: Charles had his list "in his head" (perhaps reflecting his need to feel independent by not doing *exactly* what was suggested by the therapist) while Jan had hers written down.

Their responses illustrate some other common beliefs of adults forming stepfamilies, in addition to that of instant adjustment.

Charles: I had four expectations, all of them unrealistic:
1. We'd have more time for relaxation, but we don't and we won't.
2. Things would shape up and fall into place immediately. Last week there was a lot of pain for three days and I thought, "If we don't make it, how can I cut my losses?"
3. We'd have more money, but instead we spend it all.
4. There'd be much less household burden, but there isn't, even though Jan does a *lot*.

Jan: I think we all expected that it would be like the "Brady Bunch." And we all thought that whatever had been wrong before would be made right by joining together.

I expected more emotional support from Charles. I think I expected too much, but I'm not willing to give up hoping for more than I'm getting now. I expected I would be a better parent. Now that we're a nuclear family, things *have* to work out. When I was a "single parent," things could slide because it was clear that I didn't have time. I could take the children to the dentist once a year, but I couldn't see that they brushed their teeth twice a day. So if they got cavities, they got cavities, and I'd get them fixed. But now . . .

Charles and Jan were acknowledging and evaluating important beliefs they had held, and this proved to be an important step towards recognizing that theirs was not a "nuclear" family (as Jan had called it) and in deciding together what things they wanted to change in the household. The therapist supported their growing awareness of their situation.

MYTH 3

Love and Caring Will Develop Instantaneously

Another unrealistic belief is that you will automatically and instantly love the children of your partner (Schulman, 1972); because you love the children's parent, you will love the children.

This myth of "instant love" exerts a powerful negative effect on many stepfamilies, directly influencing both the adults and the children who are steprelated. As one teenager put it, "It takes a long time to make a friend at school and here I'm supposed to love my stepmother right off the bat. It makes me mad." Trying to force caring feelings works against rather than for the development of a positive stepparent/stepchild bonding.

Unfortunately, steprelationships frequently are critically evaluated by friends and relatives. At times, therapists can fall into the same trap, using biological parent/child norms as a baseline for comparing and judging steprelationships.

In contrast, one of the most helpful therapeutic interventions can be to give a stepparent permission *not* to love a stepchild by pointing out that it takes time to develop caring feelings. The parent of the child often needs to relinquish these expectations, too—a "letting go" that may be difficult. Stepchildren, on the other hand, can usually understand the unreasonableness of such expectations.

In one such situation, the therapist interrupted the negative interaction between a remarried father and his wife by saying, "I can see that you both very much want a good relationship between Marjorie and her stepson, Peter, but I think you're forgetting how long it takes to get to know and love someone. In fact, at times in stepfamilies when personalities are very different, just getting along is all that occurs. I think if you'll talk to other stepparents you'll find that it happens all the time that the adults try to push for this kind of caring, and they have to cool it and give everyone time."

In another instance, a mother who had remarried had been angry at her husband because he did not love her 10-year-old daughter Cathryn. Paulette and Timothy were arguing about this in therapy:

Paulette: You just don't love Cathryn. You never show her any affection and . . .

Timothy: What do you expect me to do? Hug and kiss her all the time the way you do?

Therapist: (to Timothy) Do you have any time with Cathryn when her mother isn't there?

Timothy: Yes, I drive her to ballet on Thursday when her mother's working.

Paulette: And he sometimes takes her to her friend's house to play when he gets home earlier than I do.

Therapist: Umm. Are there other things Timothy and Cathryn do together?

Timothy: Sometimes I help her do her homework. I'm pretty good at math and she likes me to show her how to do her problems sometimes.

Therapist: (to Timothy) So there are a lot of things you do for Cathryn, (to Paulette) but you've been wanting him to do other things?

Paulette: Well—yes. If you love a child you give them a pat sometimes and hold them on your lap.

Therapist: (to Paulette) Is that what your parents did when you were growing up?

Paulette: Yes, they did, and Cathryn doesn't get it from her father.

Therapist: So that's how you expected Timothy to be with Cathryn if he cared about her?

Paulette: I guess so. Maybe that's not right.

Timothy: I do like Cathryn, but I'm just not the type to do what Paulette finds easy to do. My Dad wasn't affectionate in that way with me.

Paulette: I think maybe Timothy really does like Cathryn but shows it differently.

Therapist: (to Paulette) Do you think you've expected him to be like you and he's shown his caring in other ways?

Paulette: (emotionally) I think I've been so busy looking for what I've expected that I've missed all the caring things he's done.

The therapist helped the couple reframe many of Timothy's actions as caring behavior towards Cathryn, and Paulette began to notice the many times her husband responded positively to Cathryn's needs. She began to accept this type of caring behavior and a positive rather than a negative ambience began to characterize the household.

This is an area in which families can also gain from stepfamily literature and groups, as well as from many of the media stories and presentations dealing with stepfamily living. Love and caring very frequently can and do develop, but attempting to force them to bloom overnight impedes rather than accelerates the growth.

MYTH 4

Working Hard Prevents the Development of a "Wicked Stepmother"

Stepmothers enter the stepfamily with little to recommend them other than the glowing reports of their new husbands. Cinderella is a familiar story, versions of which are found in over 300 ethnic groups around the world.

In an attempt to overcome their negative image, stepmothers frequently try too hard to make everyone in the household happy. Unfortunately, this activity creates tension rather than harmony. One stepmother put it well when she said, "I came in like the cheerleader of the Western World, and it wasn't until I backed away that people began to relax and things started to settle down."

Acknowledgment of the wicked stepmother myth by a therapist and an understanding of a common tendency to "work too hard, so I won't be considered an awful stepmom" can be a first step in helping a stepmother to realize the importance of allowing her new role to develop slowly.

Hugh and Elsie were being seen because they were disturbed by the tension in their household, and they were baffled by the irritating behavior of 10-year-old Mark. During the initial appointment, Hugh commented:

Hugh: I don't understand my son's behavior. He's been a nice child and now he's cheeky, lies to us, and does everything to annoy us.

Therapist: When did you first notice this new behavior?

Hugh: About two months ago. Elsie and I lived together for a year before we got married. Mark would be with us most weekends. We really enjoyed having him. Then we got married and things seemed to change.

Elsie: I don't understand it either. Mark was such a good boy and we seemed to get along well. But now I try so hard and nothing ever seems to be right. Since Hugh and I were married, I've really worked to fix up Mark's room, cook the things he likes . . . but the harder I try, the worse it seems to get.

Therapist: What do you think Mark feels about all the nice things you do for him?

Elsie: I never thought about that. I don't know.

Hugh: He keeps saying he likes it at his Mom's better because she leaves him alone and doesn't bug him.

Therapist: I wonder what he means by that.

Elsie: Maybe he thinks I'm competing with his mother. She really doesn't cook for him. They go out for pizza or hamburgers most of the time I guess.

Hugh: I keep telling him to thank Elsie for all she's doing. I don't think he likes that.

Therapist: It sounds as though you think Mark may be feeling some pressure now . . .

Elsie: . . . to think I'm great and be glad I married his Dad.

Although these realizations were painful at first, in a short time Elsie began to feel better about herself and to take Mark's behavior less personally. Elsie and Hugh both accepted the need for Elsie to reduce her attempts to win Mark's approval and to let the household ride along more casually. They still had discipline and money problems to work out, but reducing the "hot house" atmosphere in their apartment calmed things down considerably.

Withdrawing a Child from a Biological Parent Enhances the
Relationship with the Stepparent of the Same Sex

We have talked in Chapter 2 about research findings indicating that, in stepfather stepfamilies at least, contact with a bio-father tends to enhance a child's ability to form a relationship with the stepfather. Even in stepmother families, while contact with the mother may be more problematic, there is no empirical study to date that addresses the issues of loss of contact with the mother. Clinically, when they are cut off from their mother, children generally reject their stepmother.

The following therapeutic interchange is a good example of the value of dealing directly with such beliefs:

> *Adele (remarried):* My 10-year-old daughter, Julie, is having a very hard time accepting her new stepfather, Bob. My friends tell me that I need to withdraw Julie from her father. She has spent every other weekend with her Dad since the divorce six years ago, and I guess it's very difficult for her to have two men in her life.
>
> I've been planning special weekends so that Julie has seen less of her father the past three months, but it doesn't seem to do any good. In fact, she is ruder to Bob now than she was three months ago. Bob and I have been married for eight months and Julie's treatment of him is creating real problems.
>
> *Therapist:* Do you have any ideas about the reason why the relationship between Julie and Bob is getting worse rather than better?
>
> *Adele:* I've thought about it a lot. Julie talks more now about how great her Dad is and this upsets Bob. She also acts depressed sometimes on the weekends, even when we are going somewhere she used to enjoy. I've been wondering if she is missing her father and is taking it out on Bob. Perhaps having her see her father less is not working. Julie's Dad was willing to step out of the picture to help her adjust, but I know he'd rather see her as he did before. I'm confused.
>
> *Therapist:* I understand what you're describing. There is a belief that children will relate better to a stepparent if they don't have contact with their other parent. However, your experience of the situation getting worse rather than better makes me think about the research findings that children react more positively to a stepfather if they know that they do not have to give up a relationship with their father. This may apply in your situation.

Adele: I'm glad to hear that. I've been feeling mixed up about this and not knowing what to think. Maybe children can love more people than we give them credit for. I'm going to have to think more about this.

Julie's mother decided to ask her ex-husband to return to the former visiting pattern. This shift was made and within six weeks Julie seemed less upset and more responsive to Bob. Bob also worked on accepting the presence of Julie's father in her life, and Bob and Julie's relationship continued to improve.

In this example, Julie's mother gave an indication that she was willing to change an unrealistic belief. As a result, the therapist could be direct and change occurred quickly. However, in many instances when beliefs are more deeply entrenched, they cannot be addressed so directly by the therapist. At such times, change may occur less dramatically over a longer period of time.

MYTH 6

Anything Negative that Happens is a Result of Being in a Stepfamily

Frequently children blame all their problems on the fact that they are stepchildren—their school difficulties, troubles getting along with peers, the personal problems they encounter as they grow up. Even in adulthood some people cling to their own "story" about being a stepchild and how that is responsible for their difficulties with life. The adults, too, attribute unwelcome emotions and behavior of the children to the structure of the family. Adults displace blame onto their stepfamily situation when they are actually feeling responsible and guilty about disrupting their childrens' lives by remarriage.

For children, the myth removes the need to accept responsibility for personal difficulties. Studies have indicated, however, that well-functioning families produce well-functioning children, whether they are nuclear, single-parent, or stepfamily households (Ganong & Coleman, 1984).

Life's experiences do, of course, have concomitant effects, but stepfamily structure per se does not appear to create the lasting negative effects often attributed to it. At times, developmental issues may be the cause of certain behaviors; at other times pressures not related to stepfamily structure may be the precipitants. Blaming stepfamily living for all the family's ills is as unrealistic as expecting that there will be no stresses and strains within the household.

Meg had been divorced for two years before she married Tony. They had been married for eight years and the two adults considered that their stepfamily had done very well. However, Nick, Meg's 15-year-old son, was seeing his father less now because of a heavy soccer schedule, and he was also being very disrespectful of Tony, lashing out at him and calling him "stepfather" for the first time in four or five years. When Tony would ask him to do something, Nick would reply, "I don't have to do what you tell me; you're not my father."

Both adults were devastated; they would get angry and give Nick a long lecture on all the nice things Tony had done for him over the years. But the behavior continued, and Meg made an appointment for the couple to come in to see a therapist. She had begun to feel that they had been fooled and that the stepfamily was not a successful family after all.

The following information came out in the first session:

Nick and his sister Ellen had always enjoyed each other and this had not changed. Nick and Ellen both did well in school and Nick was a leader in his class. However, he was staying away from home more this year and this also concerned his mother and stepfather. Nick would play soccer with his friends after school and get angry if his mother asked him to come home early to help her in the yard. He had always been willing to mow the lawn to earn a little money, but he showed no interest in doing this now. Meg and Tony felt that Nick's true feelings about the divorce and his mother's remarriage were just emerging.

The therapist suggested that Nick's behavior might be due to Nick's stage of personal development rather than to a delayed reaction to the divorce and remarriage. The couple was relieved to hear the therapist's remarks about teenage rebellion and teenagers' need to "stir up" their parents. They left the appointment planning to curb their intense reactions to Nick's new behavior and instead view it as a normal developmental stage. The adults were able to react differently to Nick after this, and many of the tensions in the household subsided.

OTHER IMPORTANT STEPFAMILY MYTHS

There are many more beliefs, held less widely than those we have mentioned, that can be harmful to the individuals and families believing them. For example:

a. *Myth: Love is finite.* "If I love my stepchildren, then I won't have any love to give my own children" (a particular concern of nonresidential fathers). Adults as well as children often need to recognize that loving relationships are not limited in number because of a diminishing supply of love.

b. *Myth: Preparing adequately through classes and reading will prevent the emergence of feelings of jealousy, anger, rejection and guilt.* (When these emotions surface after this preparation, the self-esteem of the individual tends to plummet: "What's wrong with me?")

c. *Myth: Forming a stepfamily after a death is much easier than following a divorce.* (There are differences, but not necessarily on the "easy-hard" continuum.) For example, a deceased former spouse/parent becomes idealized and the surviving adult tends to wish the new family to be the same as the old one; after a divorce, the adults want the new family to be different.

d. *Myth: Being a part-time stepparent is easier than being a full-time stepparent.* (Research suggests that this may even be the opposite of reality [Nadler, 1976].) When the children are in the household less frequently, time necessary to form new stepparent/stepchild bonds is much shorter in duration and the relationship is likely to take longer to develop. In addition, there are many more transitional times.

CONCLUSION

Finding out what are the belief systems of the stepfamily and helping the individuals relinquish unrealistic ones can help the family in many ways. Moos (1978) has delineated the effects on individuals of being in situations in which there are major discrepancies between their expectations and the realities of their situations. One important outcome is an inability to cope effectively with the challenges that are encountered, leading in turn to low self-esteem.

Helping to clarify realistic expectations may do a great deal to improve the mental health of these families so that the integrative challenges become expected and manageable, and they "will learn to perceive the remarried family as different from the idealized nuclear family, but nevertheless as a 'real' family that has dignity, worth, and value in its own right" (Wald, 1981, p. 193).

CHAPTER 7

Insiders/Outsiders

It's all those people. I feel like I'm an alien.
— Woman married to father of two children
with highly involved grandparents

Within families, there are coalitions and alliances of various subgroups held together, as a rule, by a sense of family loyalty. For stepfamilies, there are built-in prior coalitions and alliances between individuals who have come together without a foundation of loyalty to the new group. Indeed, individuals in stepfamilies may differ significantly in whom they perceive to be in the family (Furstenburg, 1987; Pasley, 1987).

It is this lack of basic family loyalty that leads us to weigh carefully whom to see in therapy, and to assess the amount of tension that the group can handle during therapeutic contacts. Papernow's (1984) stages, in effect, chart the subgroup shifts within the stepfamily from disparate individuals and groups to a family held together by a common feeling of belonging. Indeed, "belonging" is a major issue for stepfamilies.

FEELINGS OF ALIENATION

A. *Territoriality*

As Isaacs (1982) has stated, "turf" is a major issue for stepfamilies. If an individual or a parent with children marries and moves into the previous home of the partner, two groups are usually formed: insiders and outsiders. College student "Joanie's room" remains "Joanie's room" although it is now occupied by a stepbrother. Mary moves into her new husband's house and fights to use her broken-down bathroom scales instead of his new ones because "everything in the house is his—there's not even room in the kitchen drawers for any of my utensils." John moves into his bride's home and can't shake off feelings of sadness because his collection of books remains stored in the garage: "There's no room to build extra bookcases anywhere."

Even when former homes have been completely remodeled and all the outside landscaping changed, ghosts of the former spouse remain, and the newcomers are the outsiders. We are impressed by the number of couples who try to begin their lives together in the former home of one of them, but eventually decide to acquire a place of their own because the hoped-for ease and sense of belonging have not materialized. In many instances, when couples move to a place of their own they are astonished at the positive effects of the move on the happiness of the family.

Adults do not always recognize the dilemma of children who spend only part of the time in the household. It is difficult for the children to feel as though they belong to the household or to the neighborhood. Therapists can be of assistance in such situations by helping the adults to find ways of making a more comfortable place for the children—a spot of their own, even if only a private drawer. Some families help their children to make friends in the area by including neighborhood children in appropriate activities. They also help by acknowledging, accepting, and talking about feelings of strangeness. One 12-year-old commented on these feelings of not belonging when he said, "Instead of saying I sleep in the study when I'm there, I wish they'd say it's my room that they use for a study when I'm not there."

B. Living with Strangers

As a rule, people feel more attached to those who are more familiar to them or more similar to themselves. Parents are able to pick out their baby's clothes from among those of a number of babies because they recognize their own child's scent. Thus, it is understandable when a stepmother says, "My stepchildren don't smell right." Another woman comments, "My stepson's skin texture is so different from my own son's—it feels foreign to me." Many stepfamily individuals come together as virtual strangers and do not allow themselves the necessary space and time to become familiar with one another.

Even after eight years living full-time with a stepfather, one teenage boy commented that he still couldn't interpret some of the remarks and actions of his stepfather: "The first eight years of my life I didn't live with him and I don't think I'll ever be able to make that up." Obviously the bonds between those who enter the stepfamily already knowing one another are stronger than the bonds between those who have not been together or lived together previously. On the other hand, older children who have been good friends before their parents married one another sometimes become distant after the remarriage because sharing a bedroom, a bathroom, or a parent is often uncomfortable.

At times of family tension, new stepfamily households will often divide along biological lines. Shifts in these former alignments need to occur if a satisfactory integration of the family unit is to take place. At times, the task of the therapist is to help adults, in particular, accept the fact that steprelatives who come together under one roof as strangers need time to develop their relationships. They may even find that they have insufficient common interests or personal similarities to create more than a bond of tolerance between them; accepting even this relationship creates a connectedness.

C. Impact of Family of Origin

We find that the adults' sibling relationships and earlier feelings of exclusion and rejection can have a profound influence on the sense of alienation experienced by members of stepfamilies. For example, important earlier "exclusion" situations that existed in the family of origin may intensify the common "left out" emotions of stepparents in newly formed stepfamilies. These feelings of alienation may continue to be so strong, even in the face of major attempts on the part of other family members to include the new person, that the couple relationship is threatened. Of course, any member of the household may have unrealistic fears of exclusion from the new unit because of personal sensitivities built up earlier because of rejection by family, friends, or peers at work or school. The need to belong has become magnified by significant experiences of exclusion in the past. This is illustrated in the case of Dee and Hal who came to therapy at the point when they were considering a divorce from one another because of their constant fighting.

Although Dee and Hal entered therapy at the beginning of their second year of marriage, they had made little progress towards stepfamily integration. Dee had two children—a daughter in college and a son who lived primarily with his father. Hal had two girls who spent approximately equal time with their mother and stepfather and with Dee and Hal. Drawing their family genogram (Genogram 6) was initially only an exercise to them because their anger at one another was so deep that

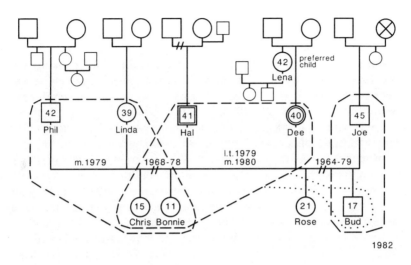

Genogram 6

they could do nothing but attack each other. Later, important historical elements became clear to them.

When asked about earlier relationships, Dee spoke with strong feelings about seeing her older sister Lena being "doted on" by her parents while she had been criticized by them all her life, betrayed at times by her father, and made fun of by her mother. Hal added that Dee's parents were still rejecting her. Dee and Lena, her sister, had only recently become good friends after many years of bitter rivalry.

Hal, on the other hand, had lived with his father after his parent's divorce when he was five. He loved his father and felt he had tried very hard to please him but had never been successful. Dee agreed that Hal's father was very critical of Hal.

Further discussion of these important dynamic factors, however, did not occur until several months after the initial appointments. In the meantime, Dee and Hal met separately with the therapist because both were so angry that nothing positive took place during their joint sessions. Both desperately needed emotional support, which the therapist was able to give during their individual appointments. Slowly, their self-esteem increased until they could benefit from joint sessions alternating with individual appointments. The therapist finally was able to help them make important connections between their past experiences and their present difficulties.

Since coming into therapy, Hal had made many positive changes in structuring the household, the most important ones being that he was paying attention to Dee's needs even while his daughters were in the household, and he was gradually limiting his almost-daily telephone contacts with his former wife, Linda. For her part, Dee was controlling her fault finding of her husband by dealing with her anger at the moment —through doing something she liked, talking to friends, or writing down her complaints to discuss in her next individual therapy session.

While these changes were helpful, the couple's lack of empathy for each other continued to precipitate violent scenes between them. Major sensitivities which Dee and Hal had brought with them into their marriage—sensitivities particularly susceptible to activation in a remarriage situation—were creating a vicious cycle. With the therapist leading the way, the cycle was discussed, explored and written down so that the couple could clarify for themselves what was going on between them when their relationship began to deteriorate. The important elements were conceptualized in the following manner:

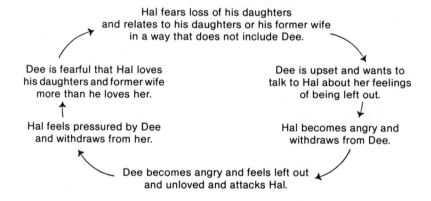

As the tension mounted, the cycle often escalated into physical violence between them. The therapist tried to help Hal and Dee find ways to deal less destructively with their anger at the same time that they sought to understand their difficulties.

Another dynamic cycle relating the past to the present proved to be a breakthrough that resulted in their accepting themselves and each other as they had not been able to do previously:

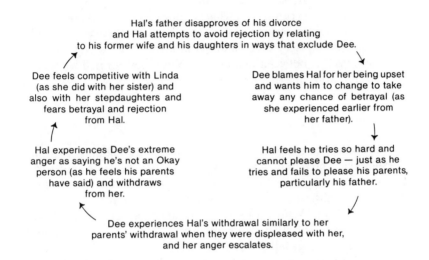

Hal's father disapproves of his divorce
and Hal attempts to avoid rejection by relating
to his former wife and his daughters in ways that exclude Dee.

Dee feels competitive with Linda
(as she did with her sister) and
also with her stepdaughters and
fears betrayal and rejection
from Hal.

Dee blames Hal for her being upset
and wants him to change to take
away any chance of betrayal (as
she experienced earlier from
her father).

Hal experiences Dee's extreme
anger as saying he's not an Okay
person (as he feels his parents
have said) and withdraws
from her.

Hal feels he tries so hard and
cannot please Dee — just as he
tries and fails to please his parents,
particularly his father.

Dee experiences Hal's withdrawal similarly to her
parents' withdrawal when they were displeased with her,
and her anger escalates.

When Dee and Hal could see their interaction as circular, they each were able to take more responsibility for their own feelings and actions and stopped attacking one another. The antecedents of their behavior became understandable to them. It became easy for them to see how their remarriage had magnified their existing emotions: Hal's divorce and remarriage was frowned on by his parents and he feared their rejection as well as rejection from his daughters and former wife, Linda; Dee was in a position in which Linda was a female who had come into Hal's life earlier than she (symbolic older sister); in the household, Dee had female "rivals." Dee's anger triggered Hal's feelings of low self-esteem, while Hal's withdrawal produced similar feelings in Dee. Both then needed support from the other and were unable to give it, and the vicious cycle continued to escalate. In recognizing that the strength of their reactions was rooted in their pasts, they were able to be more supportive of one another and no longer expected that the other person could always act in ways to prevent their sense of being isolated from one another.

BUILDING RELATIONSHIP BONDS

An asset in living in a stepfamily household can be an awareness of the process of bonding and the necessity for nurturing interpersonal relationships. As one father/stepfather said, "In a stepfamily nothing is taken for granted. You become very aware of what is going on and you see what it takes to make and keep relationships. You don't take people for granted." Many times, however, therapists see stepfamily adults who have lost sight of the fact that all relationships between people take conscious effort. Following are some of the relationships that need to be nurtured.

A. Couple Relationship

In a stepfamily the couple subgroup is newer and frequently feels much more fragile than the parent/children subgroup. It needs time and attention for the relationship to grow. Often the adults become so involved in attempting to meet all the children's needs that they give no thought to deepening the bond between them. We are not saying that the needs of the couple count more than the needs of other family members. Rather we have found that many stepfamily couples fail to consider their need to take time to have fun together and to have a separate relationship. This benefits the children as well as the adults because time together enhances the couple relationship while also allowing freedom for the children to have a separate relationship. It also supplies a model for the children when they have families of their own.

Of course, there are individual differences in the types of activities and the amount of time together desired by couples, and it is likely that in many instances balancing the needs of all the household individuals will not allow for complete satisfaction of each person's wishes and needs—not an unusual situation in life. However, it is certainly not productive for adults to deprive themselves of pleasure simply because of not being able to fulfill all their needs. The adults must have adequate reserves in their internal emotional reservoirs if they are to be able to be caring to others. Therapists are often in a position to point out this connection.

One powerful emotion that can prevent adequate bonding within the new couple relationship is the guilt that parents who remarry often feel if they form a strong bond with their partner. Remarried parents frequently have feelings that developing a primary relationship with their new partner is a betrayal of the relationship they have had with their children ever since their births. In a biological family, this conflict does not arise because the couple relationship came first. While having children tends to hold biological families together, this is not true for stepfamilies (White & Booth, 1985). In most instances, there needs to be a development of a solid couple bond for a couple in a stepfamily to stay together. Since divorce entails considerable dislocation and upset for children (Wallerstein & Kelly, 1980), the needs of the children seem better served if the couple is able to form a bond so that satisfactory stepfamily integration may be achieved. From the adult's point of view, the couple relationship needs to be of primary concern. Then, if all goes well, the couple remains together as one household unit when the children become independent and leave home. The following couple illustrate the danger of not making time for their relationship to grow:

Because they were increasingly angry with one another and felt discouraged and depressed, Ethan and Rebecca came to a stepfamily retreat weekend which included discussions led by a clinical social worker. They had been married for five years. Rebecca had no children and Ethan had three children, aged 12, 11, and 8, who saw their mother infrequently.

Ethan worked days and Rebecca worked the night shift. Money was a problem and they shared equally in caring for the children without any outside help. Except for their wedding weekend, they had never been away from the children overnight for the five years of their marriage until the weekend retreat. During the few hours they were together during the week and on weekends, they devoted themselves to being "good parents," helping with homework, teaching the children to fly kites, going on picnics. As they talked about their lives at the retreat, the other participants formed an opinion summarized by one man who said, "No wonder you're feeling discouraged and mad at each other. You don't have anything going for yourselves."

This discussion produced a profound impact on this couple. Rebecca began to voice her need to be with her husband alone at times and to do fun things together with him, and Ethan saw clearly that his children needed to see him enjoying himself with Rebecca. (They had been burned out as parent and stepparent and actually were becoming inconsistent in their treatment of the children and lashing out at each other in their frustration.)

Ethan talked about some of his guilt at forming a relationship with Rebecca and about his realization that the children seemed to be reacting negatively to the mounting tension in the household. He saw that his depression and unhappiness did indeed affect his children's sense of stability and well-being. A positive shift in their relationship became apparent to the group, and following the weekend retreat Ethan

and Rebecca instigated a child-care arrangement with two other couples so that they were able to look forward to and enjoy a weekend
together every few months. They also decided to take one or two hours
each week to go out for coffee after dinner while the children stayed
home and did their homework on their own.

As we mentioned in Chapter 3, remarried parents may have great difficulty
forming a solid couple relationship with their new spouse at least partially
because in their own family of origin they experienced their parents' couple
relationship as distant or poor and the parent(s)/child relationship as the
primary and important one. For these adults, the structuring of stepfamilies
(with the parent/child relationship preceding that of the new couple) represents a return to their earlier growing up experience. These remarried
parents lack experiential models of a good couple relationship or of simul-
taneously satisfying adult/adult and parent/child relationships.

Awareness of each other's earlier bonding experiences can often change
the partner's perception of present bonding difficulties and bring an understanding that the difficulties are situationally determined: "I guess it's not
because you don't love me; it's more that you never did see your mother and
father together very much and your model was your close relationship with
your mother." This is illustrated in the following case.

Daniel had one daughter who lived with him because his former wife
was confined to an institution. After three years, he married Tara, a
woman who had not previously been married. After two years of marriage,
Tara insisted that they seek therapeutic help because she continued to
feel outside the family unit and had grown to dislike her 13-year-old
stepdaughter, Marlene.

Daniel and Tara were seen individually, and together, on an alternating basis. Tara had not been openly hostile to Marlene and the girl had
friends, was doing well in school, and was not seen in therapy during this
period. Several important insights during their first four months of
therapy paved the way for Tara to begin working her way into the family
system through a solidification of the couple subsystem. Initially Tara
was vociferous about her anger at Marlene, while Daniel sat back and
claimed to be unperturbed by what was going on. Slowly Tara recognized
that her basic anger was at her husband for his passivity and failure to
support her.

At this point, Daniel became increasingly aware of his anger at his
wife and of his belief that his daughter was a sweet, charming girl who

was ill-treated by her stepmother. For a time the relationship between Tara and Daniel grew more and more stormy and they had proportionately more individual therapy sessions than before (early mobilization stage—Chapter 4). Each needed these less emotional individual sessions to keep the tensions between them at a manageable level. Then, in an emotional conjoint session, they saw an important dynamic interactional pattern that fed on itself and escalated quickly.

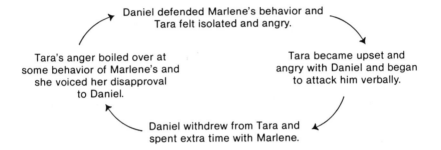

It became clear that Daniel was having difficulty responding to his wife's needs and that Tara, in turn, was very demanding in her wish to "banish Marlene."

Therapist: Daniel, I'm wondering how things were when you were growing up. Did your parents work well together?

Daniel: No, they certainly didn't. I don't think they had much of a relationship.

Therapist: What about your relationship with them?

Daniel: Oh, it was great! I was comfortable with Mother but I was not as close to her as I was to my Dad. He and I went fishing together a lot. He supported anything I wanted to do.

Therapist: So what you experienced was a family in which you felt a close relationship with your parents, but you didn't notice much going on between them.

Daniel: That's right.

Therapist: What about you, Tara?

Tara: I guess mine was totally different. I was an only child and I did get along well with my parents, but they were always very loving to each other. (tears) That's what I keep wanting from Daniel.

During the next few sessions, Daniel realized the roots of his strong need to defend (support) his daughter, and Tara realized her wish to duplicate the closeness she had experienced between her parents. The differences in their early models became clear to them and this removed to some extent the "personal sting" from their behavior towards one another. Very slowly, with this new understanding, they were able to alter their interactional patterns so that Tara gradually became part of the household. During these months, 13-year-old Marlene came to therapy with her father and stepmother from time to time to work out the changes in the relationships between all three of them as they moved together towards greater cohesiveness and family integration.

B. Stepparent/Stepchild Relationships

Stepparent/stepchild relationships are receiving considerable research attention at the present time (Clingempeel, Brand & Segal, 1987; Crosbie-Burnett, 1984; Hetherington, 1987) which is yielding many important results with implications for therapy. A basic finding is that the character of this relationship is the best predictor of the happiness of the stepfamily (Crosbie-Burnett, 1984). Other research information indicates that marital satisfaction is not the same as stepfamily satisfaction (Clingempeel, Ievoli & Brand, 1984; White & Booth, 1985) as it is possible to have high ratings of couple satisfaction together with low ratings of family satisfaction.

These research data are giving the same message from two different points of view—that satisfactory stepparent/stepchildren relationships do not necessarily follow from a good couple relationship. Clinical information confirms these findings: stepfamily couples often report experiencing closeness and happiness as long as the children are not with them. Indeed, existence of difficulties in connection with the children is the top stressor cited by stepfamily couples (Messinger, 1976). Our expectation is that families with good stepparent/stepchildren relationships will probably have a good relationship between the couples. Since the converse is not necessarily the case, the stepparent/stepchildren relationship becomes a better predictor of family satisfaction than is the couple relationship.

As we see it, there is a message for us as therapists. Stepparent/stepchildren relationships are independent relationships and may need therapeutic intervention per se even though a good couple relationship exists. However, if these stepparent/stepchild relationships are the focus of therapy prior to adequate bonding between the couple, the stepfamily system can disintegrate because the biological parent feels as though he/she is losing the child and is becoming the outsider in the family. With a couple having a satisfactory relationship, it may occasionally be important to work with the stepparent/ stepchildren subgroup together without the bioparent in order to improve these steprelationships. Whatever the contact, common interventions that are helpful include:

- Encouraging stepparents to have one-on-one fun time together with their stepchildren since bonding takes place more readily when they are relating dyadically. One young stepson remembers the beginning of his affection for his stepfather as the day his stepdad took him to the water slides near their home and they went down the slides together.
- Helping stepparents and stepchildren share with one another their likes and dislikes and their past experiences.
- Exploring what the children would like to call their stepparent. Following the children's lead in this important area can be important to the relationship. (See pages 223-225 for a more complete discussion.)
- Educating the adult, especially, about the time it takes to form relationships and the need to enter in neutral rather than in high gear in regards to *enforcing* the house rules. The stepparent does need to be part of the *determination* of rules, however (Visher & Visher, 1979).
- Pointing out that there needs to be fairness in the relationship and that this can be present from the first contacts, although caring takes longer to develop.
- Clarifying that love is not limited in amount.
- Giving assurance that the stepparent is not trying to replace the biological parent of the same sex (even when that parent has disappeared or is deceased).

As stepparent/stepchildren relationships develop, it may be important to help the remarried parent (alone or with the partner) pull back and allow space for the new relationships to form. During these changes within the household, the remarried parent may need additional support and attention from his/her spouse.

There is considerable evidence from both clinical observation and empirical research that a good stepparent/stepchild relationship is often damaged by an attempt to be a parent substitute (Anderson & White, 1986; Mills, 1984). Children are sensitive to what they see as any attempt to replace their other parent who is elsewhere in actuality or in memory, and they may resist letting their stepparent into their lives. Preschool children are usually different from older children in this respect since they have fewer memories of a former family and their ideas of "family" are not as rigidly fixed. If the adults in their lives permit it, young children can often enjoy having additional "parents."

There are many satisfactory roles available for stepparents (Mills, 1984). Therapists can be helpful by working with stepfamily couples to determine suitable roles for their particular family, and by helping the adults relinquish their expectations that the stepparent become a parent.

It has been said that one advantage of an ambiguous role is that it allows more freedom and a multiplicity of choices. This certainly seems true for stepparents. The important element is finding a role that is satisfying to both stepparent and stepchild (Crosbie-Burnett, 1984; Mills, 1984). Even within one household, several different roles may be indicated. One 20-year-old girl who had been in a stepfamily for over five years said that she particularly appreciated her stepfather's love and caring in giving her and her younger brother and sister what each needed—parenting of the youngest, help and encouragement to the next oldest, and comradeship and support to her.

Hetherington, Cox & Cox (1985) have found that stepparents are best accepted if they enter by walking the middle ground, being neither withdrawn from the family nor too actively involved. Roles tend to change over time. However, if the goal of the remarried parent, or of the stepparent, or of both, is for the stepparent to become a parent, the adults usually find themselves frustrated and angry.

As a rule, forming a satisfying stepparent/stepchild relationship is an essential ingredient for good integration and identity. Perkins & Kahan (1979) note:

If a family member places himself or is placed in the position of being inside the family perimeter but outside the interpersonal subsystem, he will have a different experiential domain from the other family members, and will feel dislocated and cut off from the family. This is exactly the experience of many stepparents; they are caught in the intraspace, inside the family perimeter, but outside one interpersonal subsystem, that of the children. Likewise, stepchildren are often caught in the intraspace without access to the marital subsystem. (p. 177)

Many times, therapeutic intervention is necessary to help move the stepfamily in a forward integrative direction.

C. Parent/Child Relationships

A remarried mother illustrates a part of the children's loss of access referred to by Perkins and Kahan (1979) when she says:

My daughter and I lived together in a single-parent household following my divorce. During that time, when I came home at the end of the day I wanted to talk to someone about what had happened, so I talked to my daughter. Now I'm married and when I come home I talk to my husband. I've just realized how many things have changed for her since my remarriage.

Therapists frequently need to sensitize the adults to how many changes a remarriage can bring for children, not the least of which is a feeling of being cut off from the parent who has remarried. The feelings of the children are not just fantasies. Their contacts with their parent are diluted and fewer in number since they are now sharing time and space with one or more other persons. If no one-to-one time between parent and child or children remains, there is a tendency for children to feel that they no longer have a direct contact with their parent and their sense of isolation and loss is increased. In their attempts to work as a couple and to integrate the new unit, many parents and stepparents do not plan to make time for the parent and child to have time to talk alone together or to do something together that they both enjoy.

Children may often wish for much more personal time than is possible or productive for the household. Acknowledging that there may be a wish for more time while meeting, as much as advisable, a child's need for a special connection can be helpful in enhancing all the relationships in the household. In certain situations where there are disturbed relationships between a child and a parent in the stepfamily household, it may be helpful to see the child and the parent together in therapy. In our opinion, this is rarely a productive subgroup, however, since therapy then reinforces a preexisting subgroup at a time when old relationships need to change and new relationships are being formed. Parent/child relationships need to be maintained *within the total stepfamily context* or the household may remain divided along biological lines.

D. Other Steprelations

We know of few guidelines for therapists regarding stepsibling relationships. Stepsiblings can be important to one another as companions, role models, or supporting figures when children feel cut off from their parents. Many teenagers talk of steprelationships in very positive terms if the adults have given the children the feeling that all of them are treated fairly within the household. In our experience, if there are difficulties between stepsiblings that are more than would be expected or have continued to be problematic, they may signal that there are difficulties with equal treatment involving the couple, so the whole family unit (rather than just the stepsiblings) needs to be included in therapy as soon as it is productive to see all of them together.

As yet, little research has been directed toward stepsibling relationships or the effect of separating siblings after a divorce. Clinically, we know of a number of situations in which siblings did not live together after a remarriage. It appears that the separation has worked well for these children, provided they do have regular times to be together and see their other parent.

Stepgrandparents can be important relatives for stepfamilies. Children are often more willing to accept a new set of grandparents than to accept a stepparent. Thus, if grandparents are willing to build bridges rather than walls, they can become constructive influences in the integrative process of the stepfamily (Furstenberg, 1981).

FAMILY IDENTITY

Keshet (1980) clearly illustrates the changes that need to take place as stepfamilies develop into functional units, stressing that:

> The transition within the stepfamily from an affiliation of divided subsystems to a more unified whole is a complex and gradual process. The stepfamily will always have strongly bounded subsystems to which members remain loyal. . . . The individual members and subunits of a stepfamily can, however, learn to join together to reach common goals and to enjoy common satisfactions. (pp. 530-531)

In this connection, Anderson & White (1986) state that "a stepfamily can have moderate levels of biological parent/child coalitions and perhaps still function effectively as a family unit (p. 418)." However, they note that if these coalitions remain strong, the stepfamily may become dysfunctional. We believe that therapists can be helpful with this necessary integration process in many ways described in this volume.

CONCLUSION

Frequently, the development of new alliances is fraught with difficulty because stepfamily individuals have membership in more than one subsystem and this can create conflicts as individuals are pulled by competing loyalties. A particularly deep conflict is that of remarried parents who have loyalty to their children and also to their new spouse. Resolving these loyalty issues can be important tasks in therapy and will be addressed at some length in Chapter 9.

As stepfamilies reorganize their relationships and structure their families, they gain a feeling of belonging and identity as a unit, which Wald (1981) refers to as "blending and becoming." Even though the family boundaries are "permeable" (Messinger, 1976; Messinger, et al., 1978) and there may be less cohesion than in biological families, there are many deeply satisfying rewards in belonging to a stepfamily, the members of which hold themselves in high esteem and value the bonds they have worked hard to create.

CHAPTER 8

Life Cycle Discrepancies

My husband has two children in their 20s and I have a 15-year-old daughter and a 6-year-old son who live with us. The problem is that my husband doesn't want to be a parent to them. We're at such different places.

—Remarried mother of two

There are interacting individual, marital, and family life cycles. In biological families these cycles usually are congruent. In stepfamilies, they often are not. Indeed, McGoldrick & Carter (1980) consider a wide discrepancy in life cycle stages as a predictor of remarriage difficulty. These discrepancies can be apparent to those thinking in such terms, but remain beyond the awareness of many remarried couples who are caught in their life cycle discrepancies.

For example, Velma and Terry, married for the first time, typify a couple with congruent life cycles. They both started their jobs the summer after graduation. They honeymooned for two weeks and then set up housekeeping in an apartment equidistant from their jobs. They enjoyed furnishing their home and developing friends and activities together. At the end of three years of marriage, their daughter Tina was born. They were proud parents and took great pleasure in watching their daughter grow and develop.

In contrast, Bill and Betsey had also been married for three years. However, Bill was 45 and had been married before; his 15-year-old daughter and 12-year-old son lived with him and Betsey most of the time. Betsey was 30 years old and had not been married before. After a three-day honeymoon, Bill and Betsey moved their furniture, the children, Betsey's two cats, and Bill's dog into a three-bedroom apartment. Bill's daughter spent the major portion of her time with her friends while her younger brother stayed with his mother as much as he could. Both children "played up" to their father when they were with him, and excluded their stepmother.

Betsey had always dreamed of having children and longed for a child of her own, while for Bill, having a wife and two children was all the family responsibility that he wanted.

For biological families there is an orderly progression from the marriage and honeymoon period, to the birth and development of children, career advancement, the gradual separation and departure of children, and the dealing with loss as grandparents and parents die.

In stepfamilies the couple may be at very different individual stages. There is no marital stage without children since children are there from the first, often moving towards independence and individuation rather than wanting family closeness. The specter of potentially significant losses also is present from the very beginning. Indeed, the remarriage itself becomes an additional phase in the life cycle of the individuals (McGoldrick & Carter, 1980), an added and important transition requiring many personal adjustments. Stanton (1981) has said that "dysfunctional families develop problems because they are not able to adjust to transitions which occur within the family life cycle" (p. 365). In our view, stepfamily members come together and are facing major transitions prior to any development of smooth family functioning. No wonder many stepfamilies experience significant stress and seek outside assistance early in their existence.

Sager et al. (1983) consider that these developmental discrepancies produce various and at times incompatible "tracks." They note: "The task for the clinician is to be aware of the many simultaneous tracks on which the systems and their members are likely to be operating and to ascertain if needs are being met well enough in the different systems" (p. 39).

There are many different types of stepfamilies: stepfamilies formed following the death of a spouse; those formed after a divorce; those in which the children reside in the household; those where both adults have children; and those in which only one of the couple has children from a previous relationship. These different patterns produce different dynamic configurations and different life cycle discrepancies.

There are several major areas that cause confusion for stepfamilies because of their life cycle discrepancies, and we find that stepfamily members frequently need help in recognizing that their sense of confusion may be related to life cycle differences that have produced competing and incompatible needs. Recognition and acceptance of these differences as "givens" in remarriage situations can create a climate in which understanding and negotiation lead to a satisfactory resolution.

STEPPARENTS WITH NO CHILDREN OF THEIR OWN

In stepfamilies in which only one of the adults has had a child, the discrepancies in the couple's life experiences are great. Thus, their individual, marital, and family life cycles are not congruent.

In the example cited above, when Bill married Betsey he had lived 45 years, had been married previously, had been a parent for 15 years, and had climbed the corporate ladder to the top. Betsey, on the other hand, was 30 years old, had not experienced a committed couple relationship, and had never been a parent. She enjoyed her work in the loan department of a local bank and hoped to move into the public relations department. There were many discrepancies in their life cycles, but it was their conflict over having a child that brought them into therapy.

Before their marriage, Betsey and Bill had agreed that they did not wish to have children. Three years after their marriage, this premarital understanding had disintegrated and the tensions between them were mounting. Betsey had expected that her two stepchildren would satisfy her need for a family, but this had not occurred. She liked them well enough, but as her biological clock ticked on she grew increasingly preoccupied with thoughts of becoming pregnant and having a child of her own.

Bill felt betrayed by this shift in his wife's attitudes. Since he had no desire to return to diapers and the P.T.A., he withdrew from all conversations having to do with increasing the size of the family. Anger grew between them until they exploded at one another. Betsey called for a therapy appointment for both of them to try to resolve the issue of having a child.

In a number of areas Bill and Betsey had worked out satisfactory solutions, and the relationships between Betsey and her stepchildren was growing stronger. Even so, in their anger at one another the adults were withdrawing so that their lives touched less and less frequently. The therapist pointed out how far apart Betsey and Bill had grown and suggested that they would probably need to concentrate on less conflictual situations before they could talk productively regarding the question of having a child together. The couple accepted this opinion and began to share other less significant and more immediate hurts. It took six to seven months to work out power and intimacy issues so that they were finally able to work together as a couple. For the first time in their marriage they could speak of "we" rather than "I" without threatening their basic sense of self.

Finally Betsey and Bill began to talk to one another about having a child. Because they found it impossible to deal constructively at home with this topic, they accepted the therapist's suggestion that for the time being they confine their problem-related communications to their therapy appointments. Betsey had decided she wanted to have a child and Bill continued to be adamantly opposed to this. He felt burdened with family issues already and saw no way they could add a child without reducing their (to him) precarious standard of living and creating added household pressures.

As they talked, they became aware of the power struggle that was escalating between them. Each felt unsupported by the other, often covering the pain this caused by being angry with each other. Eventually Bill was able to let down his guard and share his feeling that he was inadequate and selfish because, as he put it, "Who could be against motherhood?" The therapist pointed out that, given Bill's life cycle stage, it was certainly understandable that he felt as he did. He had fathered two children who were now in their teens, and he had attained a rewarding though demanding position at work.

Betsey, in turn, said she did not want to be a parent without Bill's wholehearted help. She expressed her distress that she had such a deep need for something about which her husband was less than enthusiastic. Again the therapist clarified the basis for the incompatibility of their needs—Betsey had never been a mother, and having teenage stepchildren did not satisfy this need for her. These interventions made it possible for Bill and Betsey to recognize their impasse in other than personal terms, and they were able then to empathize with each other's position, both at home and in the therapist's office. Some months later they reached a mutual understanding to have a child, and both were pleased when Betsey became pregnant.

Sager et al. (1983) report on a similar situation in which the couple eventually decided to divorce. In this latter instance, therapeutic sessions had produced understanding of the life cycle discrepancies between them and the realization that these differences created a situation in which "their needs [were] no longer being met *enough* to continue their relationship" (p. 287).

While in our experience more stepmothers than stepfathers with no children of their own want to have a child, the wish to experience biological parenthood is by no means restricted to women. A reverse situation can exist when a parent who has remarried wishes to have a child of the present marriage, while the new spouse is refusing to become a parent because of an unsatisfactory experience as a stepparent. When the stepparent also remembers his or her own parent as being an ambivalent or unhappy parent, the need to remain childless can be especially strong.

Melinda, the stepmother of 10-year-old Doug, outlined her dilemma to her therapist when she said, "I have no experience to go on. My mother hated being a mother and I got married and have a less than satisfactory on-again, off-again relationship with my stepson. I'm scared I couldn't be a good parent, and I'm not really wanting to try."

In this stepfamily, Melinda's husband, Neal, enjoyed being a father and he interpreted Melinda's reluctance to consider having a child to mean that she did not truly love him. By the time the couple came to see the therapist, their relationship had deteriorated to the point where they were considering a divorce.

In therapy, Neal slowly realized that his wife's reluctance to have a child was not a reflection of her commitment to him, and Melinda began to recognize that parenting and stepparenting were not necessarily the same experience. As Melinda and Neal's relationship improved, so did her acceptance of Doug. Now stepmother and stepson began to enjoy one another, but even so, Melinda's wish not to become a mother remained very strong.

At this point their therapist suggested that since Melinda had spoken often about a poor relationship between herself and her own mother she might find it beneficial to have a few individual therapy sessions. Melinda accepted the suggestion and decided to see a therapist whom she had seen before her marriage to Neal.

As Melinda explored her relationship with her mother, she discovered the strength of her negative feelings towards her mother. Her individual therapy continued for 9-10 months. Melinda's mother had died a few years before she and Neal were married and Melinda had not recognized previously the impact of her relationship with her mother on her own marriage.

Melinda and Neal did not continue with their joint therapy until after Melinda had completed her individual sessions. They then returned together to once again discuss the question of having a child. A decision was reached relatively quickly as Melinda realized that she was expecting her husband to make up for the rejection she had felt from her mother. She had also fantasied that he would look after her as her mother never had. Instead he had wanted to become a parent and look after a child.

Melinda had not been able to share these insights from her individual therapy with Neal until they met together with their therapist. Once she opened herself to Neal, he responded so positively that Melinda felt nurtured by him, albeit not in the parental way she had fantasied. They moved emotionally closer to one another and Melinda tentatively began to raise the possibility of parenthood. Soon they were making plans to have a child. During her periods of continuing ambivalence about becoming a mother, Neal responded with understanding rather than anger. Melinda's ambivalence decreased and she did become pregnant.

Much to her surprise, Melinda thoroughly enjoyed being a mother and considered that she was really quite competent at it. This sense of adequacy as a parent had a very positive effect on Melinda's relationship to her stepson. She saw herself for the first time in an effective parenting role with Doug, to which he responded positively. Indeed, all the household relationships became relaxed and full of warmth.

In other situations, men and women who have never had children want the freedom to play together as a couple without the necessity of arranging for baby-sitters for young children or some type of supervision for older children. They do not easily understand the sense of commitment that the remarried parent has to his or her children. Thus, the differences between husband and wife are often seen as a reflection of personal commitment, or lack of it, to the marriage, rather than as incompatible needs arising because of discrepant family life cycles.

TEENAGERS IN NEW STEPFAMILIES

Teenagers do not usually welcome the birth of a stepfamily. They have lived for some time in at least two other households and their ideas of "family" are more formed than they are for younger children. They also are reaching, or have reached in later adolescence, the stage in their individual development in which they are searching for "who they are" and are becoming more autonomous. They are moving away from the family unit in the direction of peers and an eventual emancipation from the family.

Into this gradual developmental progression may come disruption in the form of a parental death or divorce, a time of living in a single-parent household in which they often take on the role of companion or spouse-surrogate to their parent, and then a remarriage of that parent. Suddenly, with their parent's remarriage, they are asked to enter into the building of a new family unit. All this is occurring while they are working on their developmental task of individuation from their family. No wonder one 16-year-old lamented, "Two parents are two too many—who wants any more?"

Frequently teenagers in stepfamilies, in their search for their own identity, wish to live with the biological parent with whom they have not been living, and this wish comes into conflict with the residential adults' need to form or consolidate their stepfamily unit. When the stepfamily is in the first several years of its existence, it is common for the new stepparent to feel that teenagers' interest in their friends is related to a lack of acceptance of new steprelations. As a result, the new couple often tries to force the adolescents into family interactions and activities, with dire consequences in the form of acting out and family stress.

> Beth was 14 years old when her father, Louis, remarried. She and her younger brothers had spent about equal time in their mother's home and with their father. The boys continued to be with their father as much as before, and they got along well in the household, but Beth began to give reasons why she could not be with Louis and his wife, Elsa.
>
> When Beth did stay in her father's household, she did not enter into the household activities; instead, she listened to her Walkman radio and, according to her stepmother, "sulked around."
>
> Louis and Elsa were distraught and sought therapeutic help. They met with the therapist and reviewed the many ways they had attempted to engage Beth and include her in their household. The new couple, Beth, and her siblings and stepsiblings were seen together for four appointments, approximately two weeks apart. Alternating with those sessions, Louis and Elsa were seen together to give them needed support and validation and to help them understand the group sessions and to move forward.
>
> Major dynamics emerging in the family appointments that involved Beth included:
>
> 1. Beth had felt that her father had been lonely prior to his remarriage and that he had needed her, but that this was no longer true.
> 2. Beth resented having to share her father with Elsa and her children.
> 3. Beth's school friends were in her mother and stepfather's neighborhood and she wanted to be a part of their afterschool and weekend activities, and not with her father as much as previously.
> 4. Beth's stepsiblings (who were slightly older than she) were angry that she had rejected all their efforts to get to know her better and to include her in the household.

Beth's loss of direct contact with her father once he had remarried received initial attention in therapy, and ways in which the two of them could share special times together were worked out. After this connection had been reestablished, the primary concern for Beth centered around her wish to reduce time in her father's household and increase her contact with her friends. Beth's stepsiblings were helpful to her in articulating Beth's needs to the adults, since they understood very well her need to be with her peers. This identification and support from her stepsiblings began a bonding process between them and Beth, with positive repercussions in the household.

In their appointments as a couple, Elsa and Louis dealt with their sadness at relinquishing their expectations of "one big, cohesive group," but gradually accepted Beth's withdrawal as representing a way in which she had attempted to gain the space required for her to meet her developing need for peer relationships.

Adolescents in stepfamilies move out to a place of their own at an earlier age than do teenagers in nuclear families (White & Booth, 1985). It is our impression that sometimes this is in response to exclusion by the adults who are attempting to protect their own relationship from unresolved and severe conflicts between themselves and the adolescents. At other times, moving out is one way in which young adults in stepfamilies handle both internal and external conflicts that arise because their developmental need for increased autonomy is clashing with the needs of the new couple who are in the "nesting stage."

Unfortunately, the clash is frequently viewed by the adults as a threat to the very existence of the new family unit. Information and therapeutic understanding of the inevitability of life cycle incompatibilities in a remarriage family can provide the necessary validation that allows family members to accept the evolution of the family unit over a longer than anticipated time span.

FAMILY LIFE CYCLES

Even when both adults have been married previously, their family life cycles can be very different.

The two adults in one stepfamily had wide discrepancies in the length of their previous marriages, the ages and sex of their children, and the length of time in a single-parent household, to name a few important differences. Elmer had been married twice previously and had a 15-year-old boy from the first marriage and a 9-year-old boy from the second, while Myra had one previous marriage that lasted only eight months and resulted in the birth of twin girls who were now three years old. Myra had had little marriage experience and knew nothing about raising boys aged 9 and 15, while Elmer had forgotten what it was like to have three-year-olds in the house and had had no experience with little girls. We recommended that the couple take a parenting course and child development class together to help them deal more easily and realistically with the many new experiences that each might encounter.

In another situation, a man who had been divorced after 21 years of marriage married a woman with a 10-year-old son, David. Tom's children were grown and on their own and Marie's son lived in Marie and Tom's house most of the time. David's biological parents, however, did talk together infrequently about their son. The stepfather's expectations of David were based on what he thought he remembered about his own two children when they had been 10, a matter of 20 years earlier. Tom was appalled at the noise and mess that followed his stepson around, and Marie was hurt and angry at his critical remarks about the child she had been raising "virtually alone" for five years.

Tom had grown up in an extremely authoritarian household, while his wife's family of origin had been lax and her parents had shown little concern about the behavior of their children. Both adults wished to alter these earlier childraising patterns, but they had become polarized in their behavior and were finding themselves reacting to David as they remembered the way their own parents behaved.

At their therapist's suggestion, Marie and Tom attended a child development course and joined a group of parents who met together twice a month. This educational experience helped both of them to develop more appropriate expectations of a 10-year-old boy, while their therapy sessions enabled them to learn to work together to solve the many stepfamily challenges they faced, due in part to the different places they had reached in their individual, marital, and family cycles. As the new couple were able to develop a closer marital relationship, Marie's contact with her former husband regarding David no longer caused the difficulty in the household that it had previously.

GENERATIONAL DISRUPTION

Disruptions in family life cycles can also intimately involve the grandparent generation. The expected progression is interrupted and the character of the family tree changes.

Six years ago Halene had been married at the age of 40 to a man with children in their 30s. Halene's mother had wanted her daughter to marry, but she was upset when Halene married Leon because he had been married before. Halene felt that her father withdrew from her to please her mother. Halene sought counseling because of her tenseness and upset whenever she had contact with her mother.

During the course of therapy, Halene accepted the fact that she might never be able to gain her mother's approval in the way she wished and that her younger brother might always be her parents' "favored child." Her own self-esteem no longer was dependent on her parent's approval. During a week's visit with her parents, she found that she was able to relax and enjoy her brother and his family, and she found herself even "kidding around" at times with her parents. Leon joined the family group for three days and by the end of the visit Halene felt her husband had been received more warmly by her parents than ever before.

Shortly after Halene's return home from her visit, her mother's sister died and left Halene a beautiful antique rocking chair. Halene's mother took the chair to her home and promised to send it to Halene. Several months later the following interchange took place in therapy:

Halene: I'm getting really angry with my mother. She's never sent the lovely rocking chair Aunt Cynthia left me. She was my favorite aunt and it means a lot to me that she wanted me to have the chair.

Therapist: Does your mother know how much it means to you to have the rocking chair?

Halene: I'm sure I told her but now she's up to her old trick of making me feel guilty. She says the chair matches so much of her furniture and fits a bare spot in the living room. It's clear she doesn't want to let me have it. I'm going to see if my brother will go in and just take it and send it to me. She'll just have to get another rocker. This one's mine, it's not hers.

Therapist: What reaction do you think your mother would have if your brother did that?

Halene: She'd be mad at me, not him, but I'd have the chair, and I don't care. I've written her and talked to her on the phone several times about it. We've gotten into a real struggle over it.

Therapist: Is it a new chair, or has it been in the family?

Halene: Oh, it's been in the family for a long time. That's one reason it means so much to me. I remember it from when I was just a little girl. I used to sit and rock in it when I visited my aunt.

Therapist: Do you think your mother is worried about what will eventually happen to the chair?

Halene: I don't know. I never asked her. I told my niece she'd have it some day.

Therapist: Does your mother know that?

Halene: I guess not. *(Pause)* Say, maybe she thinks it will go to my husband's family. Hey, I better tell her what my plans are. You know it might make a difference.

Therapist: Um hum.

Following this session, Halene wrote to her mother and told her how much the rocking chair meant to her, her remembrances from her childhood, and her inclusion of the chair in her will for her niece. Halene also offered to buy her mother a new rocker for the living room to replace the old one. A few weeks later, the chair arrived. Halene's mother also wrote a note saying she found she didn't need another chair after all.

AGE DIFFERENCES

A common discrepancy in stepfamilies occurs when a parent marries a person whose age is close to that of the stepchildren. Generally, it is the wife who is considerably younger than her husband, though at times it is the reverse. When a man with children marries a woman 15-20 years younger than himself, it can mean that the new wife and her stepchildren are similar in age. The generations exist in function, but there is not the usual age differential between the couple subsystem and the children's generation. Frequently, remarried parents in this position feel that they have simply added one more child to their family unit. When this happens, the stepfamily tends to remain in an unstable position. For solid integration to occur, there generally needs to be a strengthening of the hierarchical boundaries despite the similarity of ages, with the couple carrying out the usual administrative functions of the family.

By seeing these couples together without the children, therapists are immediately acknowledging the existence of the couple as a separate entity. Not only do these two adults need to fulfill a certain function in the household, they also need to work out an intimacy between them that is satisfactory to each. If this does not happen, there is a likelihood that the stepparent and stepchild may draw together in a nonproductive bonding because of similarities in the level of their life experience. The fact that a young stepmother, for instance, can understand and empathize with the rebelliousness of a stepson eight years her junior can be helpful to a therapist working with a family with an acting-out teenager. If, however, the adults have not developed a good couple relationship, it can be easy for the difference in family function between stepmother and stepson to become blurred, and their relationship can take on intimate sexual elements. Simply stated, in these situations in which the usual age separation between generations does not exist, generational differences apply despite the similarity in age. The therapist's conceptual clarity on this point can result in reducing the confusion in a stepfamily where this clarity has been absent.

One unrealistic expectation we have noted in the stepfamily pattern we have been discussing is the anticipation that the children will view the new young stepparent as a parent figure. Indeed, the children's stepgrandparents may be closer in age to their parent than is the stepparent, and these adults may become more "parental" to their stepgrandchildren than the stepparent. These stepgrandparent/stepgrandchild relationships can be particularly important in stepfamilies formed following the death of a parent. The therapeutic tasks, then, are to help the family strengthen the generational boundaries and find suitable and satisfying interpersonal roles and relationships, given a deviation from the usual age differences in families.

CAREER DISPARITIES

Another source of remarried confusion is a wide discrepancy in career phases. If the adults consider their work to be simply a source of income and not a "career" with built-in goals to which they aspire, there may be little tension in this area, even when one has been working for 10 to 15 years and the other has only recently entered the work force. Frequently, however, one spouse, usually the man, has worked up the employment ladder over a period of time, while the other is still in some type of career training or has been gainfully employed for a much shorter period. It is our experience that couples where this disparity occurs have very often not conceptualized the source of resulting tensions and tend to take their conflicts as personal failure and as indicating that they are deficient in some respect.

Claire and Sydney had been married for four years. Sydney had two adult children aged 25 and 27 who had never lived with the couple, while Claire had a daughter who was 18 and in college. Sydney was a computer expert who had risen from working in the field as a technician to heading the marketing department for a large and successful electronics firm. He now had a month's vacation each year and looked forward to retirement in 10 years. Sydney wished to purchase a vacation home on a lake as he had spent a number of years "dreaming about retiring there and fishing to his heart's content."

Claire, on the other hand, had gone to work at the telephone company to support herself and her daughter after her divorce. Now that she and Sydney were married, she had been able to return to school and study to be a nurse. She was employed at a local hospital, loved her work, and hoped to become a supervisor before long. She worked various shifts and had little time off. Claire's favorite way to relax was to read or knit, but while she enjoyed quiet weekend days at home, she often liked to go dancing or to the movies in the evenings.

Claire and Sydney worked out many of the stresses of their relationship arising from the joining of their two family groups, but they began to argue over weekend plans and future arrangements. Eventually, they sought professional assistance as these arguments began to erode other aspects of their relationship.

Each entered therapy feeling discouraged and disappointed in one another and in themselves. They felt "selfish and self-centered" and feared that they could not stay together. After drawing out their individual hopes for the future, the therapist called to their attention the many differences between them that were occurring because they were at different phases in their careers. Recognition of the inevitability of these disparities helped them let go of their self-blame and freed them to work out a future that met enough of the needs of each.

They began looking for a cottage near a lake that was close enough to Claire's work so that she could join Sydney there on weekends when her schedule permitted and she wished to do so. At other times, Sydney would drive home so that they could be together there and participate in more active evening entertainment than reading in front of a fire at a vacation cottage. Sydney was able to identify with Claire's career aspirations and she accepted that he would want to retire after working for 40 years. They decided to delay further long-range planning for a few years.

Claire and Sydney's emotional responses to one another shifted so that their arguments over finances subsided and they again found sexual and emotional pleasure in being together.

SUMMARY

The specific incongruities we have discussed are imbedded in a larger cultural context that often contributes to the difficulty stepfamilies experience in attaining a necessary family solidarity. Society continues to think in terms of a life cycle which progresses from birth, through adolescence, to marriage, birth of children, individuation of the children from the unit, and integration of loss in later years. With the divorce and remarriage explosion of the 1970s and 1980s, this model is hardly suitable and helps to create lowered self-esteem for the millions of individuals travelling this path. As was stated in Chapter 1, an important element in effective therapy with stepfamilies is the therapist's acceptance of the life cycle complexities inherent in remarriage families.

CHAPTER 9

Loyalty Conflicts

I told myself I loved my child and his child exactly the same. Then I noticed that when my child leaves her milk, I pour it back into the bottle. When his child leaves her milk, I give it to the cat.
            —Mother/stepmother to therapist

Boszormenyi-Nagy & Spark (1973) have pointed out that "Loyalty commitments are like invisible but strong fibers which hold together complex pieces of relationship 'behavior' in families as well as in larger society" (p. 39). They further note that in nuclear families "the most fundamental loyalty commitment pertains to maintenance of the group itself" (p. 39). However, stepfamily members come together with a complex mixture of loyalties from the past and often, for the children at least, very little loyalty to the stepfamily group. Forging a trust in the new group and developing an identity as a unit and a loyalty to the group are complicated processes.

As a result of their previous alliances, stepfamily members bring with them bonding patterns that often lead to triangulations. In our experience, the triangulations illustrated in Figure 6 are common in stepfamilies.

As we have diagrammed them, the individual at the apex of the triangle feels caught in the middle between the other two, sometimes joining with one and at other times with the other; the remaining two persons vie with one another for the commitment of the person at the apex. While there are alliances and loyalty conflicts in nuclear families, the resulting triangulations tend to be less "set in concrete." In a biological family, a father and daughter may form an alliance to keep the family room tidy, or a mother and daughter may join together in opposition to the father in connection with TV viewing, but there is often a fluidity to the alliances depending on the issue and also on the maturation of the child. A child may prefer the company of the father at

164

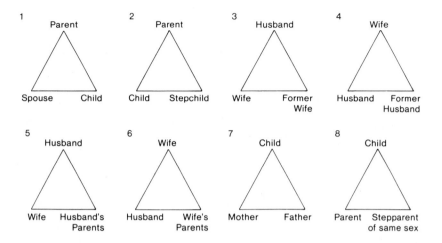

Figure 6. Common Triangulations in Stepfamilies

one age and of the mother at another. In stepfamilies, because of the prior bonding patterns, triangulation derives from the external structure of step-families rather than arising from intrapsychic processes. The alliances usual-ly are more visible than in biological families and engender strong emotional responses.

Loyalty requires trust, and stepfamily members come together with little trust in the steprelationships or in the family as a unit. A major therapeutic task is to help with the development of trusting relationships through emo-tional sharing of pain and fear and caring. Through these relationships, a loyalty to the group can develop. The individual "in the middle," as a rule, is the person with allegiance to each of the other two; a remarried father, for example, is a part of the parent/child subgroup and also of the new couple subgroup. As a general principle, when individuals from two different gener-ations are involved, the family relationships are likely to be disturbed if the primary coalition is between the two generations.

If a remarried father, for example, remains more closely allied to his child than to his wife, there will probably be a disturbed relationship between him and his wife and between his wife and his child. Similarly, if a past relation-ship and a present one are involved, as in triangulation with a former spouse and a present spouse, and if the present relationship is not the primary coalition, it is unlikely that the couple or the present and the former spouse will be able to relate well. When children are the ones being pulled in dif-

ferent directions, it is usually the adults who need to work out their conflictual relationship, thus freeing the child to relate to both adults.

With so many important connections between households existing in the
suprafamily system of stepfamilies, the resolution of competing loyalties is
an extremely complicated undertaking. Sometimes, instead of assisting individuals in relating to each other, the therapeutic task becomes one of helping
individuals deal with the pain of cut-off relationships with individuals who
are important to them.

ADULT LOYALTY CONFLICTS

A. The Remarried Parent

There are two major loyalty conflicts for remarried parents: 1) feeling
caught between the new spouse and the children, and 2) feeling pulled by
children and stepchildren. Sager et al. (1983) consider that a major source of
tension in stepfamilies is the internal conflict of parents over love for their
children and love for their new spouse. In functioning nuclear families, the
couple relationship is usually solid before a child is added to the family
constellation. In stepfamilies, the bonds between parent and child predate
the couple relationship. Frequently, these remarried parents experience
strong feelings of guilt, as though they are betraying their relationship with
their children if they develop an intimate couple relationship.

Lewis et al. (1976) and Framo (1981) speak about the importance to
nuclear families of a primary couple relationship. Clinicians working with
stepfamilies are finding that lack of commitment between stepfamily couples leads to vertical splitting of the unit along biological lines (see Chapter
2), which delays or prevents the development of family integration. The
integrity and viability of the stepfamily is in jeopardy if the remarried parent
does not allow him/herself to bond adequately with the spouse: "The
difficulty in keeping the adult-pairing love separate from parent-child love
reappears as a common problem of Rem [remarriage] families" (Sager et al.,
1981, p. 9).

The bonds between children and parents frequently become extremely
close during the single-parent household phase. When the parent remarries,
tension between the children and the new spouse may develop as each side
vies for the affection of the remarried parent.

In their fear of abandonment, children as well as adults test the loyalty of
the remarried parent:

Steve, age 10, had been living with his father, Frank, 50% of the time since his parents' divorce when he was seven years old. When his father, a social worker, became seriously involved with Mary, Steve was upset.

One weekend, shortly before Frank and Mary were to be married, all three went to a movie together. Mary and Steve went inside to find seats, while Frank remained in a long line to buy popcorn for all of them. After a few minutes, Mary reappeared and with considerable emotion told Frank she needed his help. Steve would not sit with her, insisted on sitting way up in front, and was saying, "When Dad comes in, he'll sit beside you. He won't sit with me."

Frank and Mary went into the theater and Frank put his psychological background and understanding to good use when he went to his son and said, "Up here is too close to the screen for us. Please come back and sit with Mary and me. I want to sit beside both of you. I don't want to have to sit there without you. I love you both and I want to be with both of you."

Steve walked up the theater aisle with his Dad, and Frank sat with Mary on one side and Steve on the other. Remarried parents are well advised to not make "choices" when there is no need to do so and to be careful not to "set themselves up" by creating confrontational situations.

Loyalty conflicts and boundary ambiguities are intimately entwined, as loyalty pulls prevent the formation of clear interpersonal boundaries. In a certain sense, therapists can educate remarried parents and give them "permission" to form a new adult/adult relationship. Exploration of the remarried parents' own childhood experiences can also be important as they may be recreating the pattern in their family of origin in which they perceived the primary relationship to be the parent/child relationship. (See Chapter 3.)

When remarried parents have stepchildren as well as children of their own, this can cause another deeply disturbing dilemma. Once again, guilt is a prominent emotion. Many stepparents feel guilty if they *don't* love their stepchildren as much as they love their own children; they also feel guilty if they *do* love their stepchildren as much as they love their own children. If they are nonresidential parents and residential stepparents, a common reaction is to feel guilty and resentful about giving of themselves to their stepchildren when they feel deprived of the same opportunity to give to their own children.

Frequently we see unconscious loyalty issues at the root of conscious confusion over stepparenting roles:

Debbie and Peter had been seen by a therapist for about 10 months. During this period they had progressed from being barely able to listen to one another (Mobilization Stage) to working reasonably well as a couple (Action Stage). Recently they had been discussing Debbie's confusion about what Peter expected of her in her role with his 12-year-old daughter, Celia. A repetitive interchange emerged:

Debbie: I don't know what your expectations are of me.
Peter: I appreciate whatever you do for Celia. What you're doing now is just fine.
Debbie: I really need to have you set some definite, some very specific rules about when I'm to be responsible for Celia.

During one session, Debbie was angry because she would need to look after Celia the Saturday before Thanksgiving, this day being the only time she would be able to be alone with her sister who lived out of town and would be visiting. Peter was going to visit with his ill father that day and said he would take Celia with him. Thus, Debbie could be alone with her sister. At this point Debbie insisted Peter should visit his father alone.

No matter how much they discussed this matter, nothing was settled. The therapist, recognizing the likelihood of an important internal conflict, suggested that Debbie might wish to come for an individual appointment so that she would have the opportunity to explore her feelings about her role as a stepparent to Celia in more depth without needing to be concerned about Peter's reactions.

The individual session was productive and brought into Debbie's awareness deep emotional concerns that had been hidden beneath her confusion over what her husband expected of her. These were the feelings Debbie talked about, in the order in which she recognized them:

• Guilt that she didn't feel the same about her stepdaughter as she felt about her own son.
• Her strong desire to have her son know that no other child would threaten her relationship with him.
• Resentment of some of the "mothering" she had felt called upon to give her son because of the model of "overmothering" she had observed in her own family of origin.

Then a crucial interchange occurred:

Debbie: Not knowing what my role with my stepdaughter is gets worse the more I like her.
Therapist: Are you scared you may grow to love Celia?
Debbie: (tearfully) Yes, I guess so.
Therapist: Are you scared you might love her as much as you love your son?
Debbie: (sobbing) Yes, that really scares me.
Therapist: As I remember it, when you were growing up, you saw your parents loving your sister more than they loved you.
Debbie: Yes, they still do.
Therapist: So you didn't have the experience of seeing parents loving more than one child.
Debbie: No, I didn't.
Therapist: So maybe you got the idea that a parent can only love one child . . . that if you love Celia you can't also really love your son.

Debbie had thought that she was responding to her husband's pressure, but as many emotions from the past and from the present welled up in her, she knew that the pressure was from inside herself. She continued to cry, then slowly began to talk of sharing her insights with Peter. She felt she wanted the next appointment to be a joint session with her husband.

Debbie did talk to Peter and in the future the question of her role as a stepmother was not a topic of discussion.

For remarried nonresidential fathers, also, the conflict can be acute as their many memories shared with residential stepchildren forge new and strong bonds at the same time that lack of contact dilutes their relationship with their own nonresidential children. Understanding their feelings in this way reduces their loyalty conflicts and allows remarried fathers to accept the shifts in their emotions. They also can look forward to the possibility of more contact when their children may alter their residential pattern or become young adults with the freedom to form relationships with whomever they wish.

B. Conflicts with Former Spouses

At least one of the adults in a stepfamily has had a previous intimate relationship. At times after a remarriage, husband and wife join together against the former partner. Frequently, the motivation seems to be an effort to bond together as a couple and create a tight stepfamily unit. At other times it may serve as a way of avoiding intimacy, since concentration on a third person can prevent closeness between the couple. In the latter instance, if the conflict becomes resolved (i.e., a court battle ends), then the couple may begin experiencing difficulty as marital issues surface because the spouses now are faced with developing their own emotional connectedness.

A common source of tension for remarried husbands and wives is feeling caught between their new partner and their former spouse. If a wife, say, has not finished the process of separating from a former husband, she may find herself pulled in two directions as she spends considerable time on the telephone talking to her ex-husband about matters not concerned with the children, and then attempts to give special time to her irate husband who is feeling left out.

Gwen found herself in such a position. Her conflict continued until she was able to relinquish her need for approval from her former husband (which was not forthcoming) and move away from him in a psychological sense. When this happened, her phone calls became focused on issues involving the children. At times, Gwen's husband communicated with her ex-husband instead of Gwen and tensions between the couple in connection with Gwen's relationship with her former spouse slowly subsided.

For Fred the conflict took a slightly different direction:

Fred had been remarried for three years. He had two children, Hannah, 8, and Martin, 6, who spent alternate weekends with him and his wife, Florence. A crisis arose when Fred and Florence had planned a weekend away and Fred's former wife, Julia, decided to take a class and asked Fred to take the children three weekends in a row. Fred wanted to see his children and also feared anger and harassment from Julia if he refused. He thought that Julia might not let the children spend their regular weekends in his household if he said no. So Fred and Florence canceled their weekend reservations.

Florence was angry, first at Julia, and then at Fred. The weekends with the children became very tense. Florence called Julia and they had a heated argument on the telephone, while Fred alternated between "placating" Julia and "placating" Florence. In couple therapy, Fred's passive responses to his fear of loss of a relationship with his children and Florence's need to control could be explored only after the therapist pursued *their* feelings whenever either of them began to dwell on the character and emotional reactions of Julia.

Slowly, Fred and Florence inched their way out of this volatile triangle; they began to be more tolerant of each other and then of Julia. Fred became much freer in his interactions with his former wife and no longer felt that every one of her requests automatically required his acquiescence. Changes also occurred between Florence and Julia, although Julia was not included in the therapy sessions. Florence initiated several telephone calls to Julia and interacted in a detached but civil manner. After this, all three adults were more relaxed in their dealings with one another.

Unfortunately, many volatile situations may not work out as smoothly as this one did.

Such was the case for Lance, his wife, Angela, and his former wife Paulette. Lance and Angela never achieved enough self-esteem to accept their own or each other's needs, despite seeing several different therapists. Paulette also continued to remain engaged in unhappy interactions with them. Lance and Angela left therapy, still stuck, and wishing that their various therapists had magic wands—a wish also shared by the therapists!

C. Conflicts Involving In-Laws

Ambivalent relationships with in-laws are the theme of numerous cartoons and jokes. In stepfamilies, these relationships often are burdened with an even greater intensity of negative emotion and ambivalence, especially when children are involved. Grandparents can have a difficult time accepting a new "in-law" who becomes a stepparent to their grandchildren.

The importance of working with the adult "in the middle" is illustrated by the difference in outcome in two therapy examples involving grandparents. In both stepfamilies a longstanding and unproductive triangulation existed with the husband, who was an only child, caught between his parents and his new wife. In both situations the couple was seen in therapy.

In the first instance, the therapist attempted to "de-triangulate" by urging Ida to talk to her mother-in-law, despite the fact that her husband, Leonard, felt his primary loyalty was to his parents. This approach did not work out, and the couple dropped out of therapy. As we see it, Leonard's primary loyalty to his parents stood in the way of a satisfactory relationship between them and Ida. The mother-in-law felt no need to accept Ida since she was the recipient of the primary loyalty of her son.

In the second stepfamily, during the initial therapy session Jerry stated that he visited his parents with his son and that since his parents and wife, Karen, did not get along, "these visits do necessarily exclude Karen." The therapist worked with the couple to strengthen their commitment to each other, and then worked with Jerry to help him make a separation from his parents. As he accomplished this, he let his parents know that on most occasions he would not want to visit them without Karen. Miraculously, so it seemed to the couple, Jerry's parents approached Karen and a relationship began to develop.

As a general rule, the pivotal person feels helpless and pulled in two directions. In actuality, that person is a member of both subgroups and thus is the most powerful person in the triangle. Reframing the dilemma in terms of power can be one step in enabling the individual to use this power to make an important primary commitment to his/her own generation when different generations are involved. This can pave the way for the other members to change what they need to change in their relationships with one another.

D. Loyalty Conflicts for Grandparents and Other Kin

Grandparents, aunts and uncles have many of the same types of loyalty conflicts. We believe that these loyalty conflicts are exacerbated in our culture because we have grown away from an extended family network with active parenting of the children by numerous relatives. It is important to point out that new relationships do not detract from important positive existing relationships.

Helen's sister, Cecile, and her husband had been divorced. Helen sought counseling when her former brother-in-law, Ivan, began living with a woman he intended to marry. During the single-parent household phase, Ivan had had primary care of his and Cecile's son Jonathan, with Jonathan seeing his mother once or twice a month. Genogram 7 illustrates those involved.

Helen had three sessions with a counselor. During the first hour the precipitating event was discussed:

Helen: Since the divorce, we've seen Jonathan and Ivan a lot. Jonathan and my daughter are about the same age and really like to play together, and we all like Ivan, and Jonathan's with him. His family isn't close, so he's always been close to us. We haven't heard from my sister much at all. She's moved farther away and doesn't call or come over.

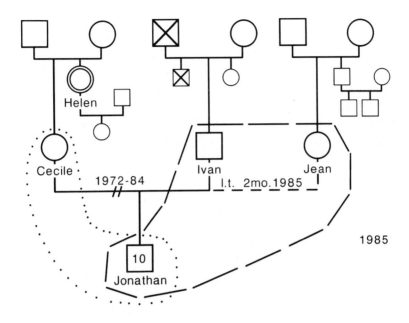

Genogram 7

But I don't know what to do. What if I like Ivan's new girlfriend? I've met her and she seems nice.

Therapist: Can you tell me a little more about what you're afraid of?

Helen: Am I being disloyal to my sister if I like Jean?

Therapist: Do you feel differently about your sister now than you did before the divorce?

Helen: No. I don't see her much, but we have fun when we're together, the way we used to.

Therapist: Do you think that if you have a good relationship with Jean it will make a difference to your relationship with Cecile?

Helen: No, I guess not. I'd never thought about all this before.

Therapist: Are you concerned about how your sister will feel if you see Ivan and Jean?

Helen: Yes, that does bother me. I wouldn't want her to think I don't still love her.

Therapist: Can you talk with your sister? (Helen nods in the affirmative.) Do you think you could talk to her about your feelings and have her understand?

Helen: Yes, I think so. That's a good idea. I'll think about it.

During the next several weeks Helen explored other reactions she was having to the situation and was waiting for an appropriate time to talk with her sister, Cecile.

One important dilemma for grandparents arises when they already have grandchildren and acquire stepgrandchildren. Just as stepparents with no biological children tend to have fewer loyalty conflicts, so stepgrandparents with no biological grandchildren find it simpler to accept stepgrandchildren. If they acquire stepgrandchildren after having had relationships with grandchildren (not necessarily in the same unit as the new stepgrandchildren), then the grandparents often worry about the reaction of their grandchildren if they show caring behavior towards the new stepgrandchildren. Not only are they concerned about their grandchildren's responses, they are also worried about the feelings of their son or daughter (the stepparent) if they *do not* show caring behavior towards their stepgrandchildren (Furstenburg, 1987).

Recently we have encountered a number of grandparents/stepgrandparents whose deep emotions about family have surfaced when "family pictures" have been taken. Once again the question is raised about who is in the family. Grandparents/stepgrandparents may act in ways that reveal their feelings that stepchildren (and perhaps their parent) have no right to be in this picture.

Helping stepfamilies develop a solid sense of family selfhood is an important therapeutic task given the many internal and external ambiguities that arise.

CHILDREN'S LOYALTY CONFLICTS

A. Conflicts Between Parents

After a divorce, virtually all children experience loyalty conflicts, their severity depending for the most part on the postdivorce relationship between the two parents: the more amicable the parents' contacts, the less severe the loyalty conflicts for the children. After a remarriage, there usually is an exacerbation of loyalty issues for the children as a stepparent enters the suprafamily system. Once again the children may find themselves caught in the middle between threatened and hostile bioparents. Even young children often are able to express their feelings with clarity and poignancy, though not usually to their parents—"It's like a game of ball and I'm the ball"; "my parents are shooting arrows at each other and the arrows go right through me." We find the children reacting predominantly with anger and depression as they wrestle with strong feelings of helplessness.

Because of their lack of maturity and their dependence on their parents, young children in particular need their parents' help to reduce their loyalty binds. Later, as children mature, they are more able, with understanding and outside support, to remove themselves from their central position, leaving their two parents to handle their own issues with one another. In conflicts with parents and stepparents, the children may have no one in their generation with whom to align. It becomes the responsibility of the adults to work out a relationship that frees the child to relate to each adult and not be caught between warring or subtly hostile adults.

Heather consulted the therapist she and her former husband, Lloyd, had seen prior to their divorce because her four-year-old son, Brian, had suddenly become anxious and upset and cried whenever he was to go with his father for the weekend. Because the divorce agreement ordered it, Heather was required to let her son be with his father, but his screaming before the visit was very painful for her.

The therapist met with Heather and empathized with her pain and her concern about Brian's distress. Heather gave the therapist permission to call Lloyd and make an appointment to talk with him about his experience with Brian.

Because of her previous contacts, the therapist had an existing relationship with both of Brian's parents and this undoubtedly simplified and shortened the therapeutic process in this situation.

During two meetings with Lloyd, the therapist explored his relationship with Brian, even considering the possibility of child abuse which had been raised by Heather. Her assessment was that nothing detrimental for Brian was taking place when he and his father were together. Lloyd had not remarried and no one else was living in the household.

As the therapist explored the situation with Heather, she began to gain an awareness of subtle ways in which Heather was sending negative messages to her son about his father. In pinpointing the events taking place at the time Brian became anxious and upset, Heather recalled that she had installed an answering machine so that she could screen her incoming telephone calls and in this way refuse calls from Brian's father. Brian was often present when his mother refused calls from his father, although she accepted calls from others. Brian also had heard Heather talking to her present husband and her friends in a negative manner about her former husband.

The therapist helped Heather to gradually become aware of the negative messages she was giving Brian about his father. Heather saw that she was attempting to pull Brian towards herself and her present husband, and she could begin to see the root of her son's anxiety and distress. Since Brian's symptoms were extremely upsetting for his mother, she took steps to reduce the loyalty conflicts she had been producing.

Heather once again talked to Brian's father on the telephone and she was careful not to make negative remarks about Lloyd in Brian's presence. The boy's behavior changed quickly and once again he enjoyed being with his father as well as with his mother and stepfather.

Parents are frequently unaware of the ways in which they are putting their children in the middle between them. Once they see the connection between their actions and their children's upsetting behavior, they often can be quite cooperative in changing their unproductive behavior. Parents as well as the children benefit from changes since the adults have also been upset by the distress or acting out of their children. In the case just discussed, it had been an action of Brian's mother (the purchase and type of use made of the telephone answering machine) that had upset her son and precipitated the crisis. Consequently, Heather herself was able to quickly alter the situation. However, it should be noted that even though unilateral changes can produce shifts throughout the suprafamily system, as happened in this case, when more complex interactional patterns are causing the problems it can be much more effective to see all the involved adults, sometimes conjointly. (See Chapter 4.)

When children are older, their parents and stepparents may not be as aware of their upset. Indeed, as children often express their emotions in disruptive, withdrawn, or depressive behavior rather than by open emotional expression, the adults are likely to be angry with the behavior and make no attempt to understand what feelings lie beneath the actions. An important intervention in therapy is to help the children share their feelings with their parents and stepparent. Often, the adults, for the first time, recognize and understand the effects of their own behavior on their children. This can become a powerful motivating force for the adults to learn new ways of interacting.

In a therapy session with Stan, 18, Cris, 16, and the four adults in their two households, the adults saw them both cry and heard Stan say, "When your parents get divorced, all you want to do is crawl into a hole and come out when it's all over," and Cris say, "You don't want to hurt either one of your parents and there's nothing you can do." These two sons had felt caught in the middle between their two parents. After experiencing her sons in this way in therapy, the boys' mother said with feeling, "I'm going to try to never put you boys in the middle again. I see how much it hurts you." Following this appointment, adult cooperation replaced competition and Stan and Cris's depression lifted.

B. Conflicts Between Parent and Same-Sexed Stepparent

Isaacs (1982) states that when stepfamilies get stuck they do so because of three major situations, one of which is that "an adversarial relationship between the new partner and the child's other parent is established" (p. 125).

In these situations the child gets caught in the crossfire between the stepparent and the parent of the same sex. Even when animosity between the two adults is at a minimum, children can suffer from guilt because they fear that liking their new stepparent is being disloyal to their other parent. Younger children may not yet have absorbed the message that "each American child learns, early and in terror, that his whole security depends on that single set of parents" (Mead, 1970), so they may accept stepparents easily. However, if they have older siblings, even young children may learn that it is not acceptable to relate warmly to a stepparent because this may jeopardize their relationship with their other parent. As an example, when a five-year-old on a week's vacation with his father and stepmother called his stepmother "Mom," his 12-year-old brother said to him sharply, "Don't you ever let me hear you call her that again."

The message that children need to hear is that it is acceptable to love more than two parents. When animosity exists between the two adults, or when children feel that stepparents are attempting to replace their other parent, children usually retreat or withdraw to the security of the earlier biological relationship. At times, however, children may be in a position to receive more from a stepparent than their bioparent is able to give them. Unfortunately, in many of these situations the children are not able to accept what the stepparent has to offer because of their guilty feelings.

Fathers are still expected to be more peripheral than mothers in the raising of the children and in the responsibility for the emotional climate and the running of the household. It is logical, then, that children might feel even stronger loyalty pulls between their mothers and stepmothers than between their fathers and stepfathers.

Therapeutically, to reduce the loyalty bind for a child, the parent and stepparent need to relate civilly to one another if at all possible and be willing to let the child relate to each of them. Frequently, a first therapeutic step is to help the parent recognize that he/she is very important to the children, since parents need to feel secure as a parent to be able to accept their children's relationship with a new person. Eventually, the adults in the children's two households may need to be seen together.

Lena Baldwin was 12 years old when her father, Edward, remarried. Lena and her five-year-old sister, Victoria, lived with their mother, Kelly, and stepfather, Morton, and spent weekends with their father and Enid, their new stepmother. Lena, however, was refusing to come to be with Enid and her father and was surly and withdrawn the few times she did visit. Edward was upset and made an appointment with a therapist.

During the appointment the therapist drew Genogram 8 and learned the following important information:

- Enid and Edward had lived together for a year before getting married. During this time, Lena had seemed to enjoy being with them, but after the marriage she changed rather abruptly.
- Lena's mother, Kelly, would not talk to Enid, even on the telephone.
- If Edward was to be away on business for any part of the weekend, Kelly would not let Lena and Victoria come that weekend.
- Enid and Edward were working together well, but were baffled and upset by Lena's behavior and didn't know what to do.

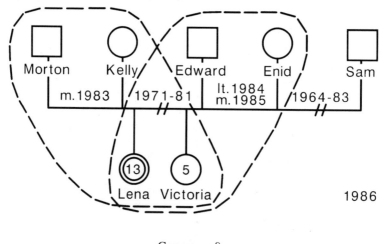

Genogram 8

With Edward and Enid's permission, the therapist telephoned Kelly, told her that she had met once with Lena's father and stepmother, and asked if she and her husband would come for an appointment.

Kelly: Why do you want to see us?

Therapist: I understand Lena has some wishes not to visit as before with her father and stepmother.

Kelly: That's true. I can understand that. There's a new person in that house and Victoria's comfortable but Lena isn't.

Therapist: Are you saying that you do not mind having Lena stay on the weekends with you instead of being with her father?

Kelly: (pause) No, I'm not saying that. I think she needs to see her father, but I'm not sure how much she really is with him when she's there.

Therapist: So you would like Lena to see her father but you think things need to be worked out differently.

Kelly: Yes, that's it.

Therapist: There may need to be some changes, and you and your husband's input could be very valuable. It would be helpful to have the opportunity to talk with the two of you.

Kelly: Who would be paying for the appointment?

Therapist: This would be your appointment. My fee is _____ for one and one half hours. Do you have insurance?

Kelly: Yes we do, but I would have to talk to my husband about this.

Therapist: Please do. If he would like to talk to me, please have him call. If you have more questions, please call me again. Would you like me to call you back in a few days or would you prefer to call me to let me know your decision?

Kelly: I'll call you.

Kelly and Morton did make an appointment without any further conversations. During this session, the therapist had her initial impressions of the tensions between Kelly and Enid confirmed. Kelly was having great difficulty letting Lena relate to her stepmother now that she felt this to be a long-term relationship. The therapist supported Kelly's desire to be a good mother, pointing out the many ways she was providing what her daughter needed. As Kelly began relating ways in which she felt she was a good mother to Lena, she relaxed and agreed that changes were needed. Kelly and Morton reluctantly accepted the suggestion that the four adults and Lena meet together to see what might work better.

During their initial meeting, Lena was particularly tense and moved her chair close to her mother. The therapist attempted to ease the adults' tension by having them complete the genogram. As they began to talk together, Lena relaxed. Lena did not say much, but was tearful when her mother suggested that perhaps it would be better if she didn't visit with her father and stepmother. At this point, Kelly recognized her daughter's distress and began to shift to a more conciliatory approach.

The next session included only the four adults. When Morton did not come at the appointed time, the therapist asked Kelly if she would call and see if he were coming because she felt it was important for them all to be there. The session did not begin until Morton arrived.

During this appointment, the adults were more free in their expression of anger at each other over what they saw as impediments to Lena's being with Enid and Edward. When their anger enlarged to other issues, the therapist intervened to return them to this topic. Slowly the therapist shifted their anger to their fears; Lena's mother was able to say she feared that her daughter would be confused by having a mother and a stepmother, and Enid was afraid she could never develop any relationship with Lena. Towards the end of the appointment, Enid commented that she thought Kelly was a good mother to Lena and Victoria, and Kelly, shortly thereafter, acknowledged that she considered Enid, as a stepmother, to have the hardest role of them all. The session ended on this positive note.

The third appointment included Lena. The adults even joked a little together, and Lena watched closely as her mother and stepmother talked together. During the week, the two women had also talked on the phone in Lena's presence to arrange a new appointment time. The group talked together, making changes in the weekend arrangements to accommodate Lena and the adults. Lena endorsed the idea of counting on being with her father and stepmother regularly every other weekend, whether or not her father would be there all the time. Another appointment was made for six weeks in the future, but this meeting did not take place as both households felt that the situation was working comfortably.

Kelly was still not cognizant of the depth of her insecurity, but even so she was feeling comfortable enough to relate minimally to Enid. From the therapist's point of view, Lena's enjoyment of each household had much less to do with the specific arrangements that were made than it did with Lena's perceptions that her mother and stepmother were able to talk together without arguments. The two women had been able to empathize with the fears each had expressed and this had opened communication channels. This was enough to dissolve Lena's conflict and allow her to relate to her stepmother without fearing the anger of her mother.

Of course, there are stepfamilies in which the adults are not able to disengage themselves sufficiently from their own interdependencies and personal emotions to respond positively to the needs of their children. In these situations, if therapists have an opportunity to see the children they may be able to offer needed support. Young children can find a stable relationship with a therapist, and older children can be helped to see the adults in a different way, looking at them more objectively and seeing what they are really like. As children are able to accept the human qualities of their parents and stepparents, both the positive and the negative, they are better able to be more detached and not feel to blame for the actions of the adults.

The dilemma for therapists in these situations is to be there for the child, at the same time not encouraging loyalty from the child at the expense of loyalty to the parents and stepparents. If children withdraw rather than experience a helpful detachment from their parents, they may feel caught in a conflict of loyalties between parents and therapist. In these situations, children frequently begin to resist therapy as a way of solving their conflict.

Unless an alliance is maintained with the adults, the therapist may be scapegoated by parents/stepparents when they are threatened by the children's behavior, or seen by the children as producing another conflict of loyalties—a triangulation with the child, his/her adults, and the therapist. As we view it, the task for the therapist is to maintain contact (without breaching confidentiality) with the important adults if they are not being seen as a family unit, so that the adults do not feel that their authority in the family is being undermined. The child needs to experience the support of the therapist, but without sensing a therapist/child alliance that promotes hostility between parents/stepparents and therapist. The therapist becomes an important person to model the value of objectivity in order that children be able to see parents and stepparents as neither saints nor ogres, but as worthwhile human beings with the ability to make decisions and act in ways, within the limitations of their situation, to make their lives more satisfactory.

One young man who earlier had seen a therapist to help him adjust to his stepfamily counseled a teenage friend about to experience the remarriage of her mother by saying, "The adults in a stepfamily try really hard. They make a lot of mistakes but they're really trying. It can work out if you just give it a chance." In this case, the young man was able to transmit to his friend what he had learned in therapy. This perception became an important factor in the friend's eventual positive stepfamily experience.

SUMMARY

The structure of stepfamilies is one in which it is virtually impossible to avoid at least twinges of guilt, jealousy, anger, and depression as interpersonal loyalties come into conflict. With knowledge and empathy, therapists can provide a vital service to stepfamily members, since acceptance and understanding of these human reactions are first steps in building adequate self-esteem. This, then, can lead to the exploration of ways to cope productively with the myriad of situations arising from the swirl of emotions which accompany the many complex relationships of remarriage.

CHAPTER 10

Boundary Problems

The kids think our bedroom is theirs too. Their mother says they're used to watching TV with her there. I say we need some privacy.
— Stepfather of two

In an article entitled, "Family Boundary Ambiguity: A New Variable in Family Stress Theory," Boss & Greenberg (1984) define boundary ambiguity as "the family not knowing who is in and who is out of the system" (p. 535). They continue by stating that "it is the ambiguity rather than the event itself that predicts the family level of stress" (p. 535).

Although Boss and Greenberg do not include stepfamilies in their discussion, we consider that this paper gives a valuable description of a fundamental source of stress on stepfamilies. Frequently, there is lack of agreement between stepfamily members as to who is in the family (Pasley, 1987); add to this the loyalty conflicts discussed in the previous chapter and it becomes clear why there is high stress in stepfamilies due to the ambiguous boundaries of the family. In our experience, the boundary ambiguity of stepfamilies produces stress that can impact the stepfamily suprasystem on a number of levels and in many important ways.

BOUNDARIES BETWEEN HOUSEHOLDS

A. Custody and Visitation

After a divorce, two basic determinants of the boundaries between the households of the children are the custody and visitation arrangements that are worked out between the divorced parents. At the present time, there is a movement in favor of joint custody as a means of encouraging both parents' involvement with the children, and therapists are consulted frequently regarding questions concerning visitation, access, and custody issues. Although more research is of vital importance, empirical studies of custody and visitation patterns are yielding helpful information in this important area (Greif, 1979, 1982; Steinman, 1981; Steinman et al., 1985; Derdeyn & Scott, 1984). While there can be special circumstances in individual situations, we find that the guidelines emerging from the research support clinical impressions, and give a rudimentary framework for helping families in this crucial area.

First of all, a clarification of terms is in order because often there is confusion about the term "joint custody." It can mean "joint *legal* custody" or "joint *physical* custody," the former assuming the two parents have legal rights to make decisions affecting their children following a divorce, while the latter refers to equal rights for the two divorced parents to have their children reside with them. Joint physical custody does not assume equal time in each household, but when the parents have joint physical custody the time spent by the children in each of their two households tends to be more equal than when one parent has sole physical custody.

In research reports, "joint custody" frequently refers to both joint legal and joint physical custody (Ahrons, 1981; Bowman & Ahrons, 1985). In addition, we make a distinction between contact and custody, since we find that confusion arises when this differentiation is not made; custody is a legal arrangement, while contact refers basically to the visitation of parents and children.

There is now considerable evidence that it is important, in most situations, for children to maintain contact with both parents after a divorce (Hetherington, Cox & Cox, 1976; Hetherington, 1979; Hess & Camara, 1979; Wallerstein & Kelly, 1980). When there is contact, children report less divorce trauma (Rosen, 1979) and good overall adjustments and self-esteem are promoted. The adjustment of fathers following a divorce also responds positively to contact with their children (Greif, 1982; Jacobs, 1982).

Isaacs (1986) reported that the first year following a divorce is the most critical period for future child adjustment. Another finding was that contact between nonresidential parents and their children is important, but the regularity rather than the frequency and length of contacts was the most important feature. Isaacs found that quality contact during this period can lead to good child adjustment even when the quality of future contacts is minimal. Conversely, poor quality postdivorce contacts during the first year have lasting deleterious effects on the children, even when there are improved parental contacts later. There are some indications that during the single-parent household phase, children may do better if they reside with the parent of the same sex (Santrock, Warshak & Elliott, 1982).

Since contact with both parents following divorce has been found beneficial and 75% of children have had no contact for over a year with their fathers two to five years after the divorce (Furstenberg et al., 1983), investigators of various custody arrangements have examined the question of a relationship between custody and contact. Joint custody, implying both legal and physical custody, has been found to keep fathers more involved with their children (Ahrons, 1981; Steinman, 1981), and for this reason joint custody has often been considered as the decision-making/living-arrangement of choice following divorce (Greif, 1979).

After a *remarriage,* the question of contact and custody becomes less clear. Adolescents have reported stress at being cut off from a parent (Lutz, 1983). Even after a remarriage, joint custody continues to keep fathers more involved in parenting their children (Bowman & Ahrons, 1985). However, adolescents in stepfamilies, although they may desire contact with both parents, often do not like joint custody arrangements (Crosbie-Burnett, 1985). It may be that teenagers in both single-parent and stepparent households have reached a point in their development where they are moving away from family and towards their peers, so that they wish to have a primary residence near the majority of their friends. Indeed, it is during these years that teenagers are wrestling with questions of identity and they often choose to live with their other parent, which would usually be the father. Such changes frequently take place (even without a legal change of custody) and often are beneficial, particularly for boys (Giles-Sims, 1984). Similar changes for girls can be more problematic (Ihinger-Tallman, 1985). Helping residential parents accept these changes in household composition and boundaries often is of major importance.

It has been our own clinical impression as well as the impression of other therapists with whom we have talked that children who are cut off from a parent have poorer overall adjustment and have greater difficulty forming relationships with their stepparents. This impression is supported by research on stepfather families (Furstenberg & Nord, 1985). However, the situation in stepmother families is less clear. The contact between nonresidential mothers and their daughters appears to delay for a time, though not prevent, the formation of a good relationship between stepmothers and stepdaughters who are living with their fathers and stepmothers (Furstenberg & Nord, 1985; Clingempeel & Segal, 1986). Why this is so needs further study. One question we have is whether or not an important causal factor may be tensions between mothers and stepmothers and the daughters' identification with their mothers, so that the daughters' loyalty conflicts are exacerbated. In addition, we feel that it would be easy for girls who live with their fathers after a divorce rather than with their mothers to perceive this arrangement as severe rejection by the mothers and be conflicted in their relationship with their mothers. For boys in the same situation, it can make logical sense to them that they live with their same-sexed parent. Hopefully, clinical observation and empirical research will continue to investigate these questions.

As far as we know, there are no studies that have looked at cut-off relationships with parents after a remarriage. In fact, it is our impression that research projects on stepfamily relationships sometimes suffer from tendencies to eliminate families from studies in which the nonresidential parent lives at a distance, where parent/child contact is limited, or where there is no contact between nonresidential parent and child. Clinically, we find that many children who are cut off from a parent build idealized images of that parent and have no way to check the reality of their fantasies.

When residential parents recognize the tendency of their children to idealize absent parents in this way, they are often more willing to work out ways for children to get to know that other parent. When the other parent is highly unreliable in some way—for example, having a problem with alcohol—then it may be necessary for the contacts between parent and child to take place in a supervised environment, and perhaps for only short time periods.

Even though stepparents do report having an especially difficult task if they are competing with a "perfect" idealized absent parent, the residential adults in stepfamilies often deal with the ambiguity of household boundaries by promoting cut-off relationships between the children and their parent who is elsewhere. Having the children remain full time in one household certainly does reduce the stress of transitions and interactions with another parental household; however, these children are often the ones who become depressed, upset and lacking in self-esteem. They wonder if there is something wrong with them that makes them unlovable—otherwise why would their parent have no contact with them?

The task for a therapist treating a cut-off child is one of helping the child recognize and accept that the decision to cut off contact was connected to something going on with the adult and not connected to who the child was or is. Indeed, it is unfortunate that many cut-off relationships occur not because the parent *does not* care for the child, but because the parent *does* care a great deal and finds disappearing from the relationship a way to cope with the pain of separation. In our experience, education regarding the needs of children following divorce and remarriage sometimes helps nonresidential parents maintain contact through the painful times until a time when the pain is much less acute.

Many different dual-residential arrangements are being tried successfully, from a year in each household to alternate days and weekends. The age of the child (very young children appear to need one primary caretaker) and the ability of the child to handle transitions (Huntington, 1986) are two important factors to be considered in working out residential arrangements. Assessing realistically the needs of the particular child can give important information about advantageous scheduling.

One mother described the pattern that had existed for her preschool-age son for two years as follows: "Timmy was only four when he started spending one month with me and my husband and alternate months with his father and stepmother. We had said there would be no contact between him and his other household during the month, but Timmy taught us right away this wouldn't work. It was too long away. So he has telephone contact during the month and goes to the other household for dinner about once a week. He seems to like this arrangement a lot."

We believe that when it is the children who reduce or cut off contact with one of their parents when they become teenagers, they do not experience the same loss of self-esteem that accompanies a parental cut-off. The therapeutic task in these situations is to help the adults shift visiting times, if possible, to meet the changing needs of children of that age, and to maintain some type of contact (e.g., telephone, written) so that greater contact can more easily take place in the future. When younger children choose to reduce or stop seeing a parent, it typically signals problems between the adults in the child's two households. At times, of course, a child's reluctance to be with one parent may need to be investigated to assure the well-being of the child when in that household.

In summary, the issue of beneficial custody arrangements following remarriage needs clarification. Much of the research on custody issues has made no distinction between single-parent households and stepfamily households following divorce. We believe this is a major error. There are structural and emotional differences between these two types of households and it may be that the most beneficial custody arrangements in single-parent households are different from the most beneficial arrangements after a remarriage.

As far as contact or access is concerned, it is our belief that present evidence indicates that in the long term the majority of children do better and the stepparent/stepchild relationship may actually be improved if the children have at least minimal contact with both of their biological parents, even though it may create greater boundary ambiguity between households. Unfortunately, the stress caused by the increased boundary ambiguity between the households when children move back and forth leads many adults to attempt to "close ranks" and exclude the other biological parent. The following sections suggest ways in which boundaries can be strengthened within the structure of the stepfamily suprasystem.

B. Permeable Household Boundaries

Because of the need for children to move between households, Messinger, Walker & Freeman (1978) consider that stepfamily households need to have "permeable" boundaries to allow the children to have the freedom to go back and forth easily and gain from the diversity of experiences offered by their different households.

In America the "expected" time of emancipation from home comes, as a rule, when children graduate from high school and go to college or move away from their family of origin. For single-parent households and stepfamilies it is different. As one mother of a young son said tearfully, "I knew he'd leave home at 18, but not at 4." Sharing children between households can be deeply wrenching, and it seems to us that the animosity that builds up between the two households often has as much to do with the fear of more loss of relationship with the children because they may prefer the other household, as it has with leftover bitterness and anger from the time of the divorce.

We have found that it can be helpful to talk with parents and stepparents about these fears (see Chapter 5). At times, such a discussion allows these formerly unconscious or preconscious feelings to emerge and be acknowledged. Often, the reality of the fears can be assessed, and where it seems necessary the adults in the two households will, hopefully, be willing to reassure one another that they will work together on any changes.

Even though the boundaries between stepfamily households are not as clear as between other households not joined together by shared children, we feel that it is important for there to be definite boundaries. Children may have membership in two households, but each household needs to feel that there is a clear psychological and, for many adults, a clear physical boundary around each of the two households. Often, the children would like their two biological parents to remain in frequent contact, to celebrate holidays together, and to feel free to enter the living space of the other. We certainly know stepfamilies in which there is a strong and clear psychological boundary around the household, and where the adults feel a deep security in their couple relationship and in their relationship to the children, and therefore are comfortable with frequent contacts of a social nature between the two households. In most households, however, if a former spouse feels free to enter the house when not specifically invited, the adults in the household feel that their household boundary has been pierced and they have been invaded. When the couple agrees on the boundary limitations, such breaches tend to be resolved, but all too frequently the stepparent senses a lack of an adequate boundary when the remarried parent has not yet made a psychological separation from his or her former spouse and this failure is reflected in the boundary ambiguity.

Betty and Ralph entered the therapist's office for the first appointment and immediately signaled boundary difficulty when Ralph said: "Do I have to phone my ex-wife each week to tell her what I'm doing with the kids?"

Ralph's former wife had disappeared for three years and his children had remained with him after the divorce. Now she had returned to the area and wanted to be a parent to her children, and Ralph and Betty were unsure how to handle the situation. In this case, the therapist helped them to see that it was important for them to feel that they had a separate and private life with the children and that the children and their mother also needed their own psychological and physical space. This did not mean, however, that the two households could exist comfortably without communication in connection with the plans for the children that affected both of the households directly—for example, arrangements for the children to go back and forth between the households, holiday plans, and special events that could alter the visiting pattern.

This family was one that found that they needed the reduction in ambiguity that comes from maintaining a strict visitation schedule, using sitters for times they would not be home over a weekend in which the children were scheduled to be with them. The regularity of the schedule became a "constant" that helped the children and the adults in the two households to reduce tense contacts and feel more security in planning ahead.

Giving children time to adjust when they shift from one household to another can reduce a great deal of friction, and filling in important information gaps for the children creates a sense of belonging. We are impressed by a 10-year-old girl who wrote about her experience and suggestions to stepfamily adults:

I'm 10 years old, and I live in a stepfamily. My mother got divorced from my father when I was two years old. Now I live in two houses. I change to a different house every week. I have been doing that for two years now. It works very well for me. The one thing that is nice is both of my parents live in the same town. That way I can go to the same school. Also, I have the same friends. It was my idea to go to each house every week. At first my parents disagreed about this, but they tried it. After awhile they liked doing it that way. I like it very much also.

Everything is not perfect. One problem is that every time I go to a different house, I feel like a stranger. The reason why it feels like being a stranger is because, after you get back from a different house, the rest of the family might be talking about something that happened while you were gone, and you don't know anything about it.

If you are in a stepfamily and just got back from the other house, I think it would help if your Mom or Dad told you about what happened that week when you were gone. After they tell me that, I feel that I'm a part of the family again. When they tell me that they missed me, I feel better, too. Another thing that helps me is that I can call the other house on the phone any time. I also come home in the middle of the week to eat dinner and visit the other family. It isn't easy all the time, but I know they all love me, and after I've been home a couple of days, I don't feel like a stranger anymore. (Fesler, 1985, p. 6)

Stepfamilies frequently need a great deal of therapeutic help in working out this type of arrangement and in reducing household boundary ambiguity, while at the same time maintaining enough permeability of boundaries so that the children can move back and forth comfortably between their two households.

C. Relationships Between Former Spouses

Despite the good news that researchers give us regarding the neutral or even positive relationships that many former spouses are able to maintain following a divorce (Ahrons & Perlmutter, 1982; Furstenberg & Nord, 1985), clinicians bring the bad news that many divorced couples are not able to build a constructive boundary between them. Instead, many former spouses are not psychologically separated from one another, some being bound together by a need to receive positive affirmation from the other, some locked together by bitterness and hostility.

The absence of an adequate psychological separation between former spouses can have many negative repercussions in a new marriage. It can create a barrier to the formation of a solid relationship with the new spouse and cause confusion and acting out by the children of the former couple.

The lack of commitment Tess felt from Mort was rooted in his inability to separate from his first wife. Mort would not allow Tess to accompany him when he picked up or delivered his children from their mother's home, and he refused her pleas that she be included in the weekend outings he planned. Eventually, Mort was able to recognize that his wish for approval from his former wife was preventing him from shifting his allegiance to Tess and developing a solid couple relationship.

Peter and Yvonne illustrate another dynamic which on the surface appears to create a strong new couple but can instead mask a fear of intimacy and lack of true closeness. This is an unrelenting barrage of anger against a former spouse which binds the couple together through court battles, endless heated discussions, and the draining of immense amounts of money and emotional energy. For Peter and Yvonne the battle against her former husband continued for three years. At the end of that time, the court awarded Yvonne the retirement benefits for which she had been fighting, and the glue in her and Peter's relationship disappeared. They entered therapy shortly thereafter, because now they were faced with the task of attempting to build an intimate marital relationship to replace the fighting and anger against Yvonne's ex-husband which had held the couple together.

When there is a lack of commitment between the new couple, the children may quickly perceive this and behave in ways to divide the couple even farther. A common fantasy for children is of their bioparents getting together again, and older children sometimes report conscious plans they engineer in an attempt to bring this about. At other times, children are unaware of why they are behaving badly, but looking at the consequences of their behavior can provide a clue to at least some of its motivation.

Fourteen-year-old Melissa left school at noon and hitchhiked downtown with another student in her grade to walk the streets and smoke pot. When Melissa was late coming home, her mother, Trudy, called the school and learned that she had been absent during the afternoon. Trudy had been divorced two years before and had married Jack four months previously.
Trudy was very upset, but decided it would not be right to burden

Jack with this problem and so she called Melissa's father, Britt, who had not remarried. The two had not seen each other for over six months, but Britt came right over to Trudy's house and they sat down to decide what to do. While they were still talking, Melissa came home and received a big hug from her mother and a scolding from her father. Melissa's truancy became worse rather than better. Trudy and Britt tried punishing Melissa, bribing her, and talking to her. It did no good; the behavior continued.

After several months, Trudy sought help for her daughter. After listening to Trudy's description of what was going on, the social worker began to suspect that Melissa had unwittingly found a way to bring her bioparents together. Melissa's personally destructive behavior was perhaps being rewarded by the fact that it succeeded in reuniting her parents for a little while. The therapist made an appointment for Trudy and her husband Jack and outlined the issue as she saw it. She further suggested that if Jack and Trudy worked together with Melissa when she acted in ways that upset Trudy and contacted Melissa's father only in connection with positive rather than negative behaviors, Melissa's truancy might be reversed.

Britt was upset at the turn of events and did not cooperate with the new plans when Trudy and Jack explained the situation to him as they now saw it. Jack, however, appreciated the opportunity to help his wife rather than having her turn to her former husband, and Trudy began to limit her contacts with Britt to neutral or positive matters concerning Melissa. Melissa's behavior improved and her truancy ended.

This situation intimately involved Melissa, her parents, and her stepfather, Jack. While the therapist chose to work only with Trudy and Jack, there were, no doubt, other productive combinations once the bond between the new couple had been strengthened. Indeed, Britt might have been more cooperative had he been included in the sessions when that became appropriate, even if a different therapist had been necessary because of the alliance between Trudy and Jack and the psychologist they were seeing.

Had the couple relationship between Trudy and Jack been adequate, their including Britt and Melissa from the first might have been the most productive approach. However, we believe the new couple needs to be validated first so that it is clear that the therapist sees this union as the primary one. If this is not done, it is easy for the remarried couple to feel that the therapist believes the former couple to be the "true couple." In our experience, the new couple will be able to work with the adult or adults in the children's other household only after their own couple relationship and psychological boundary have been established.

Warm relationships between former spouses can certainly lead to positive outcomes for all concerned, provided there is security in the new couple relationship. Sometimes, however, frequent contact between former spouses "to work together for the children" may obscure the fact that one or both of these parents has not yet truly separated. In these cases, the new spouse may feel isolated and guilty at wanting less contact between the former spouses . . . "after all, he's such a good and concerned father to his children." We are suggesting not that psychological separation is synonymous with lack of contact, but simply that the boundary around the new couple must contain within it intimacy and loyalty that satisfy both partners and distinguish this relationship from a much less intense relationship between former spouses.

Hostile relationships with ex-spouses frequently come up for discussion in support groups or therapy groups for stepfamily adults. These leftover feelings from the past cripple present relationships and can be difficult to resolve because ordinarily they cannot now be worked out with the former spouse if that has not been done before. They may need to be worked out unilaterally. The sharing and support that can take place in a group setting, between individuals who may be at very different places in their separation from former spouses can provide a valuable and helpful perspective for those still struggling with these issues. Until this separation is made, it is difficult for the parents and stepparents in the children's lives to form any type of parenting coalition.

We have used a simple visual illustration with couples that has been extremely illuminating and helpful to many of them. In describing some of the major family roles for individuals as they progress through life we have stated and drawn it this way:

First you are an individual, then you marry and become part of a couple; then, when you have children, you become a parent.

1.

When there is a divorce or death of a spouse, the couple drops out and the individual and parent roles remain.

2.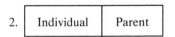

3.	Individual	Parent	Couple

Frequently, when a remarriage takes place, the parent role does not shift and the "couple" role gets added on to the end, rather than being between the individual and the parent role as in a first marriage. This usually results in stepfamily difficulties.

4.	Individual	Couple	Parent

The task is for the parent who has remarried to once again return to a situation similar in position to that in first marriages. The adults need this security, and the children need the example of a committed couple as they mature, leave home, and form their own adult relationships.

Seeing this diagram has clarified for numerous couples the uneasiness and stresses that previously they have not been able to conceptualize adequately. Being able to visualize their situation in this manner has enabled them to work on productive solutions.

D. Parenting Coalition

It seems clear that children function better and are much happier when their parents and stepparents have a civil relationship with one another. While this can benefit the children directly, it can also benefit the adults indirectly in that the children are happier and respond to the adults in a more positive manner. In addition, the adults themselves have a greater opportunity to escape the anger and helplessness that can arise when they are joined together by negative emotional ties rather than by a working arrangement.

"Parenting" can be used to indicate a wide variety of caretaking activities, from that of a parent role to being an adult friend, or a support for the parent. Rather than having two parents who are setting important parameters for the family system, there are three or four adults, the *parenting coalition,* who are setting important parameters for the stepfamily suprasystem. The need for joint action gradually disappears except for nodal family events (e.g., graduations, weddings, births, deaths) as the children mature and move into independent living.

The Bennett family is an example that illustrates the profound difference a parenting coalition can make. Genogram 9 shows two generations of

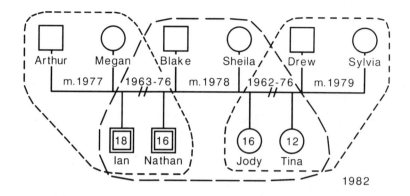

Genogram 9

the family. (The name Bennett is used to represent the suprasystem. Actually, there are three different surnames.)

After Blake and Megan's divorce, the boys, Ian and Nathan remained with their father. After Sheila was divorced from Drew, the girls, Jody and Tina, remained with her. When Sheila and Blake were married, all four children lived primarily in their home.

Sheila and Drew had worked hard to coparent their girls after their divorce. Then, after both were remarried, the four adults, Sheila, Drew, Blake and Sylvia, formed an effective parenting coalition. In fact, during the sessions with the counselor Sheila remarked, "Drew is an ideal ex-spouse. He sees the girls regularly and has a good relationship with them, and he doesn't interfere with our household." The two households cooperated well together, with Sylvia taking the role of "being a friend to the girls" and Blake slowly taking on a parental role with them.

In contrast, the bitterness and anger between Blake and Megan had continued for the six years since their divorce and the four adults, Sheila and Blake, and Megan and her husband, Arthur, had not spoken together for one-and-a-half years before arranging to all come together to talk with a counselor.

Some of the adults were reluctant to meet together, but all did make the commitment. The counselor met with the young people first, then with the adults, and finally with the entire group. The sessions were intense—filled with anger and with poignancy and sadness. The counselor kept the sessions focused on the present, pointing out how the anger between the boys' parents and stepparents was affecting both Ian and Nathan. The girls and their father and stepmother said relatively little since the connections between the girls' two households were satisfactory to all of them.

An important turning point came in a session when the adults were being seen together. After considerable anger had been expressed, Sheila was able to tell Megan that she considered her to be a good mother to the boys. Soon after that, Megan began to cry as she thought about not being with her sons more, and the counselor supported her feelings of sadness. Rapport began to develop between Sheila and Megan and the cloud of anger began to dissipate. Later on, Ian and Nathan were able to express deep feelings of being caught in the middle between their parents. Megan saw their upset, perhaps for the first time, and voiced a resolve to stop fighting and "putting them in the middle."

Many important developments followed from these sessions. The ability to empathize with the vulnerable feelings of other members of the stepfamily suprasystem defused the anger and bitterness and permitted the boys' parents and stepparents to begin working together in connection with Nathan and Ian. In the sessions, there had been a noticeable positive correlation between the emotional well-being of the boys and of the girls and the ability of their parents and stepparents to form a parenting coalition. Nathan and Ian had had many upsetting times and were very tense, while Tina and Jody had settled down relatively quietly after their mother and father remarried. It is likely that the manner in which Tina and Jody's parents and stepparents cooperated became a model that helped Blake and Megan to resolve to change their negative behavior.

The four adults became highly motivated to shift the destructive relationships between Ian and Nathan's two households and this did indeed happen. Now both sets of young people had parenting adults who worked together in constructive and nonhostile ways and the boys' anger and upset gradually disappeared. In appreciation, Ian said, "Instead of trying to make life difficult for each other, they're trying to help one another now."

Of course, there are many stepfamilies who are not able to work out a parenting coalition. At times, the contact between the two households is made through the stepparents, or by the stepparent and parent of the same sex. The most important element in most of these situations, however, is that adults deal directly with one another and not through the children, unless the children are adolescent and can make the arrangements without feeling "in the middle." It is when children are in the middle, perhaps being used by angry and hostile parents as pawns or messengers, that they become (or remain) disturbed.

E. Control Over the Household

Commonly there is less control in stepfamilies than in nuclear families because of the presence in memory or in actuality of influential individuals in other households. When a former spouse has died, the continued presence of that person can exert a powerful influence on the stepfamily household. One widower talked of the difference between a remarriage following death rather than divorce: "After a divorce you want things to be different; after a death you want to replicate the past. A remarriage reactivates your grief and so many situations that arise in the household pour salt in the wounds. The former relationship becomes idealized and you try to make the new person fit the old patterns."

Whether the wish is for a change or for a repetition, the household will be similar in some ways, yet different in other ways, to whatever has gone before. Positive memories from the past can be enhancing; intrusions from the past can be demoralizing.

It is evident that when the ex-spouse is in the area and there are continuous contacts of one kind or another, you have a family suprasystem where not all of the variables are under the control of the members of the stepfamily; this often leads to feelings of helplessness and loss of control.

In their effort to combat feelings of helplessness, some individuals attempt to control everything—the children's every move, the actions of the former spouses, and the behavior of the present spouse. One stepmother painted a clear picture when she said, "Since I couldn't control the big things I wanted to control (her husband's ex-wife, the existence of two stepchildren who moved in unexpectedly), I became a 'brush your teeth, wash your hands, clean your room' person to the children because those things I could control." Other individuals react by withdrawing, becoming depressed, and giving up all control. Helping adults and children accept their limitations *and* their control is important to the well-being of stepfamilies.

Warner's two children, aged 11 and 13, lived most of the time with him and his second wife, Anita, in the new home the couple had recently purchased. When the children's mother came to take them somewhere on weekends, she frequently would walk into the house while she was waiting for them, help herself to a cold drink out of the refrigerator, use the bathroom, or make a telephone call. Warner and Anita were feeling violated and they both had become depressed and ineffectual in their dealings with the children and their mother.

The adults were quick to respond positively to therapy. The therapist helped them realize there were limitations in the situation that angered them, and their anger and feelings of helplessness led them to abdicate the control that they did have. While they could not control the behavior of the children's mother, they could control what went on in their own household. After brainstorming various solutions, they decided to see that the children had possessions they wanted to take with them ready and by the door, so that when their mother arrived they could run out to greet her immediately. The extra time and physical energy it took to oversee these preparations and to alert the children when their mother drove up were much less draining than the emotional energy they had expended earlier. As a result, the boundary around the household was clarified.

F. Household Regulations

Therapists often need to work with stepfamily adults to accept the parameters of their own boundaries. There are no identical or mirror image households. In each household, the ambience is distinctive, and the ways of acting and interacting are unique. Tolerance for these differences between households is important for stepfamilies. Of course, there are behaviors that may occur in a few households that are detrimental to children and require strong action by the parent in the children's other household, but in general children are able to adjust to a variety of environments when they have the impression from their parents and stepparents that they have permission to find satisfactions in each of their households. If, in contrast, the message is that one household is right and the other is wrong rather than simply different, the children often have difficulty moving back and forth. As a rule, the advantages for children of having more models from which to choose outweigh the disadvantages of "culture shock."

Adequate self-esteem as a parent or stepparent is usually the primary factor that creates the personal security to allow this tolerance for and acceptance of the different households. Frequently, the therapeutic task becomes one of helping the adults' self-concept improve so that the other household is not a threat.

Unfortunately, a common situation is one in which adults in one household are talking negatively about the adults in the other household and there seems no way to have these parents and stepparents all sit down together in an attempt to alter this destructive pattern. In such situations working with one parent or couple may enable that person or couple to create a satisfactory solution for the children. The comment made to her children by a mother who was caught in such a situation was very effective in defusing the children's conflict. When the mother learned that her former husband and his new wife were making negative and damaging remarks about her and her present husband, she said to her children, "I'm sorry they feel that way about us, but they aren't in this household so it's not possible for them to know what it's really like here." This comment did not criticize the other household, yet it allowed the children to make their own assessment of their two different environments. Other parents and stepparents have been able to adopt a similar stance when offered this model for handling a comparable situation.

Another difficulty for some adults is their wish to cross household boundaries and have the children experience in household B the consequences of behavior that occurred in household A. Unless the adults in both households are working together more closely than is usual, ignoring household boundaries in this way can lead to frustration and anger. Ordinarily, consequences need to stay within the household. For example, a mother might say to her daughter, Mary: "If you aren't home by 12 o'clock, you'll be grounded for three days." In this case, she expects her ex-husband to ground Mary for the third day because Mary will be in his household at that time. However, Mary's mother cannot control what happens in her ex-husband's household, and acting out, frustration, and anger can result if she tries. Instead, Mary needs to finish the stated consequence (the third day of being grounded), in the "involved" house when she returns.

A variation on this theme is when a father says, for example, "If you don't get your homework finished you can't go to your mother's tomorrow." Denying contact with the other household is usually an unsuitable consequence and can produce turmoil between the households. This father needs help accepting the limits of his control and finding more appropriate behavioral consequences.

BOUNDARIES WITHIN THE HOUSEHOLD

Boundaries within stepfamily households also can be ambiguous. One day two individuals are in the household, the next day there are 10; during the school year three children are present, during holidays these children are gone, but two others have taken their place. The boundaries stretch and shrink like a rubber band, producing stress; as soon as there is comfort with the territory, the band is snapped again to take a different shape. It is not surprising that stepfamily members frequently need help in coping with this fluidity.

A. Intergenerational Boundaries

During the single-parent household phase of the process from divorce or death to a remarriage, parents and children tend to form a tight unit, with children frequently becoming parentified children. They feel responsible for their parent (usually the one they perceive to be the "weaker" or less powerful parent) and become psychologically the parent of their parent. Often, children have become confidantes and surrogate spouses to a parent during this time when there is no adult partner in the household. The generational boundaries become blurred and when a remarriage takes place, restoring the intergenerational boundaries can be very difficult; children feel displaced and angry and parents feel guilty and torn. Satisfactory family functioning, however, does appear to depend on adequate boundaries between generations (Minuchin, 1984) and changes may need to take place. In our opinion, family communication and gradual shifting of subgroup patterns can be much more productive than sudden shifts with little verbalization.

> Sarah, a young woman of 25 with no children, married Edward, a widower of 41 with a 17-year-old daughter, Claire, and two younger sons. Claire had taken over the management of the house since her mother's death, doing the shopping and cooking and becoming a confidante to her father.
>
> Sarah moved into Edward's home and immediately set about "to make the kitchen hers." Without discussing the matter with Claire, Sarah totally remodeled the kitchen and then set about establishing herself as the woman of the house. Major tensions arose, which eventually took four months of therapy to reduce to a manageable level. Emotional communication and extensive negotiation were the key elements of the therapy.

Strengthening intergenerational boundaries also can be an extremely important therapeutic task when the stepparent's age is close to that of a stepchild (see Chapter 8).

B. *Couple Boundary*

Forming a solid couple bond can be difficult in stepfamilies. So much is going on all at once—adjusting to the couple relationship, working out relationships with stepchildren, dealing with former spouses in connection with the children, and attempting to keep the household running smoothly. Nourishing the couple relationship too often gets lost in the midst of competing needs. Yet an adequate couple relationship seems crucial to the success of the stepfamily.

We see two major stumbling blocks to forming an adequate boundary around the couple: the remarried parent's guilt and fear of loss of relationship with their children. In Chapter 3 we discussed some of the influences of the family of origin on the formation of this relationship. Parents are concerned that by developing an intimate and emotionally close relationship with their new partner they are betraying their children and destroying the relationship they have had with them during the single-parent household phase. Yet, if the couple does not make a commitment to each other, the whole unit may be in jeopardy and the children will once again experience the trauma of a divorce.

The precipitating event that brought Terry and Louise into therapy was the trip that Terry took to Hawaii with his two children, leaving Louise and her son at home. The vacation had been planned by Terry without consulting his wife, and when Louise learned of the plans she was hurt and angry. When she attempted to have her husband alter them he refused, saying that this would disappoint his children, and that Louise was being very selfish.

Terry and Louise were seen alone and conjointly in therapy for nearly a year before a satisfactory couple bond was created so that the children could be included. During this initial period, Terry's deep attachment to his son and daughter and his lack of commitment to his wife became clear. A conflict between Terry and his stepson had also emerged. A major turning point in therapy came during an individual session in which Terry broke through his usual emotional reserve and in tears said, "I begin to see I don't have to give up my relationship with my children if I have one with my wife."

Louise became more understanding of her husband's fear of losing his children and the couple began to work together in a tentative fashion. Slowly their bonds were strengthened and no longer did they threaten each other with divorce. Not surprisingly, many tensions in the household subsided as Terry and Louise began to work together as a couple.

When there is a functioning adult couple, it makes possible to include in therapy other important subsystems within the household, such as that of siblings or a generational group composed of all the children in the household.

C. Personal Boundaries

There are wide variations in the amount of personal space and privacy needed by individuals. The amount of "alone time" also varies greatly from person to person. In stepfamilies with the typical increase in the number of people and decrease in the amount of space, stepfamily members often feel deprived of enough time or space or privacy. Added to this deprivation are feelings of anger at themselves because they find their needs unacceptable.

As we see it, these personal needs are important ones and if they are accepted as important, there are solutions that can be worked out in all but extreme cases.

Jessica, 14, felt "inundated" by her two stepsisters, a half brother, her mother and her stepfather. She had been an only child until she was 11 and then suddenly she was sharing a room with a stepsister. As for the rest of the house, she found someone in every room, including the bathroom, and what she called "the incessant babble of voices" was ever present. She kept wondering what was wrong with her because all this activity did not seem to bother anyone else.

In this case, it was a school counselor who worked with the family and helped family members become more tolerant of individual differences in their need for personal privacy and to work out ways to better meet their needs. Jessica discovered that her stepfather had feelings similar to her own and a rapport developed between them.

This particular stepfamily had the financial ability to create a study and play space for Jessica in a section of their garage. Meanwhile, her stepfather worked out an arrangement for having time alone to read in a small study.

In a similar situation in another stepfamily with less financial capability, time *alone* in a shared bedroom was arranged.

It generally takes discussion and conscious planning to create personal space in stepfamilies. A woman who has lived alone for 10 years becomes a stepmother to two children; a man who has never been married before becomes a stepfather to three children who have had the run of the house, including the bedroom, when they were living with their mother before her remarriage; two adults, one with four children and the other with three, marry and move into a four-bedroom home. Paradoxically, carving out necessary personal time and space can be an important ingredient for stepfamily integration.

SUMMARY

The complexity of the stepfamily suprasystem allows for significant disagreement about who is inside and who is outside of the household, about the various subgroups, or about the family unit itself. As a result, there is boundary ambiguity in many parts of the stepfamily—between households and between parenting adults, as well as within households where intergenerational boundaries may be problematic and personal space a complicated matter.

Since satisfactory family functioning depends upon the existence of nonambiguous household intergenerational and subsystem boundaries (Boss & Greenberg, 1984), a basic therapeutic task with stepfamilies is the development of suitable and adequate boundaries. Without them, the family "cannot reorganize, the process of morphogenic restructuring in the system is blocked, and the system is held in limbo" (Boss & Greenberg, 1984, p. 535).

However, when children are moving between households, there is a need for "looser" (more permeable) household boundaries than in biological families. For many stepfamilies, a pattern emerges over time so that boundary changes no longer create instability. Change becomes "a given," and acceptance of less cohesion becomes a facet of satisfactory stepfamily identity.

CHAPTER 11

Power Issues

I sometimes wish I didn't exist. Then my Mom and Dad could have got a divorce and gone their separate ways instead of fighting about me.
— Adolescent stepchild

A sense of personal power contributes to the development of self-confidence. Conversely, feelings of helplessness undermine self-esteem and characteristically lead to unproductive emotions and behaviors. Structural family therapists have been concerned with power issues in families since the 1960s (Minuchin et al., 1967) and consideration of power structures in stepfamilies has recently begun to receive attention (Crosbie-Burnett, 1984; Furstenburg, & Spanier, 1984; Giles-Sims, 1987; Sager et al., 1983; Visher & Visher, 1979).

Power has been defined as "the relative influence of each [family] member on the outcome of an activity" (Aponte, 1976, p. 434) and is the motivating force that "activates the system and carries it through an action" (Aponte & Van Deusen, 1981, p. 313).

DETERMINANTS OF POWER

To date, most studies of family power have looked at the balance of power between couples in nuclear families (Crosbie-Burnett, Giles-Sims, & Plummer, 1986; Giles-Sims, 1987). In stepfamilies there are many more factors to be taken into consideration, yet some general considerations apply to any marriage. As Giles-Sims (1987) states it, "Marriage relationships virtually require some degree of mutual dependence, making it more or less imperative that each partner be able to influence the other's actions to some degree. . . . Imbalanced relationships tend to be unstable, because partners each experience distress. Those receiving less than fair rewards tend to feel angry and resentful and those receiving more than fair rewards feel guilty" (pp. 152-153).

In stepfamilies we find that structural factors such as the number of children each partner has and the custody and visitation agreements become important. Other factors influencing power relationships include: age, sex, educational background, financial assets, financial support of the children/ stepchildren, and alliances within the household. Clinical observation is supported by research in this area showing that more power is associated with: having custody of the children; being older; being male; being better educated; having a higher income; providing more financial support of children/stepchildren; and having interpersonal alliances (Crosbie-Burnett, et al., 1986; Giles-Sims, 1987).

Some of these attributes apply to all types of families, but in stepfamilies there tends to be less homogeneity of age and income, and the presence of stepchildren makes for very different power dynamics. While the relationship between the marriage partners in a remarriage has been found to be more egalitarian than in first marriages (Giles-Sims, 1987), other factors can create important imbalances that require therapists to help the couple find ways to work out a more equitable balance between them. For example:

> Timothy was 10 years older than June and had custody of his two sons. June had not been married before. Although both Timothy and June had high-paying jobs and financial equality, Timothy had considerably more power in the household than did June because of his age, sex, and alliance with his sons. As a result of therapy, Timothy and June initiated changes that increased June's power and enhanced their relationship. Timothy stepped back and June spent time alone with her stepsons and took over some of the responsibilities in connection with their sports activities. In addition, June included herself in the financial decisions connected with the family.

The power structures in stepfamilies can differ from those in nuclear families in a significant fashion because of the fact that the children have parents living in two different households. In our experience where there are two or more households involved, the common legal and institutional arrangements lead to the following adult hierarchy:

1. Residential parent*
2. Spouse of residential parent

---

*In some instances, residence is changed without a legal custody change. In most cases, the residential parent is the custodial parent.

3. Nonresidential parent
4. Spouse of nonresidential parent

In general, the adult with the greatest suprafamily system power is the residential parent; the adult with the least power is the spouse of the nonresidential parent.

The relative positions of the nonresidential parent (no. 3) and the spouse of the residential parent (no. 2) in the hierarchy can vary depending on the issue. In mediation, for instance, courts tend to consider the nonresidential parent ahead of the spouse of the residential parent, and at other times the courts enter suits against the residential adults, not including the nonresidential parent and/or spouse. Legally, both of the child's bioparents have access to school records, but in practice the residential parent and spouse are the ones to receive school mailings. One advantage of joint custody is that it avoids a custody hierarchy and leaves the adults in a more equal power position.

While there may not be legal or institutional consistency in the status of the nonresidential parent and the spouse of the residential parent, the order given reflects the psychological hierarchy as experienced by many stepfamily adults vis-à-vis the children. Psychologically, children in stepfamilies are in a position to exert more power than in nuclear families where both parents are in one household. As a result they often acquire a standing in the hierarchy that is greater than that of at least one (or more) of the adults. When this happens, one or both households can get fixated in an early stage of stepfamily development.

At times, stepfamily adults seek therapy with the hope (not necessarily conscious) that support from the therapist will alter the balance of power — there will now be an influential person on "our side." We believe it is important for therapists to be able to conceptualize these external attributes of power when working with a stepfamily, because there may be many important dynamics that have unconscious roots in this power/lack of power schema. When one therapist pointed out the relative power positions of adults in stepfamilies, the mother/stepmother in the couple suddenly recognized one source of her anxiety and said, "No wonder I'm feeling upset and out of control; I went from being a custodial single mother to being married to a noncustodial father."

There is a lack of control in stepfamilies that stirs deep feelings of helplessness: "Helping stepfamily members cope with the lack of control in many areas is not an easy task, but understanding and acknowledging the difficulties and delineating the areas of control can be very helpful" (Visher & Visher, 1978, p. 255).

REACTIONS TO HELPLESSNESS

A. *Remarried Parents*

Individual experiences in the area of dependency in the family of origin may be powerful determinants of how a person will react to a future sense of helplessness. For adults who have had poor dependency relationships in childhood, the lack of control and ambiguity in stepfamily life can be extremely difficult. In addition, if one adult has felt unfairly treated by a former spouse or by the court in divorce proceedings, the need for control can be even greater. If a hostile relationship between divorced parents is added to this personal vulnerability, an all-too-common situation occurs wherein parents seek the power of the law to enhance their position. Often it is the nonresidential parent who goes to court to try to gain greater access to the children or to change the custody or living arrangements. This often happens at the time of the remarriage of this nonresidential parent (Ahrons & Perlmutter, 1982). It is our impression that this happens primarily when the other parent—the residential parent—has not yet remarried. Perhaps this is because the nonresidential parent now considers that the court will lend its power to form an alliance with the new couple. As a rule, as we see it, this recourse to the authority of the court enhances the power of the person(s) seeking this support and reduces the power position of the parent who has not remarried, who is then moved to fight against any changes.

When Stacey remarried, he and his new wife, Natalia, decided they would like to have Stacey's two children with them more than the twice-a-month they had previously been with their father. Stacey and his former wife had had a bitter divorce and he had felt totally helpless in his dealings in connection with his children. Feeling unable to talk with the children's mother, Stacey spent thousands of dollars on attorney's fees each year for three years in an attempt to have his children with him and Natalia more of the time. The children's mother felt angry and threatened and fought to retain the control she had; one court battle after another took place. Instead of bettering his situation, these battles resulted in Stacey seeing his children less and less frequently even though he was legally entitled to continue his previous visitation pattern.

Eventually, the depressed and frustrated nonresidential father turned to a counselor for help. In addition, he and his wife became members of a group of stepfamily adults, a few of whom had been waging similar battles. Gradually, Stacey was able to give up the struggle with his ex-wife and accept and enjoy the few times he did see his children. Much to Stacey's surprise, his children began to telephone him between visits and they began to visit with him and his wife more often.

This is not an unusual outcome. By accepting that family control is less after a divorce or remarriage, Stacey no longer was dealing with his strong sense of helplessness by fighting for more power. Instead, he channeled the control he did have into productive actions—planning pleasant outings when his children were visiting, responding in a relaxed way to telephone conversations with the children, and using the money that became available, now that he was no longer paying attorney's fees, for initiating special times for all of them, and making expenditures that enhanced his and his wife's happiness. Now that Stacey was no longer waging a battle, his former wife was in a position to consider changes without feeling she was "losing."

Another source of difficulty for a remarried parent is the need to share power with his or her new spouse, particularly where the children are concerned. When, over time, there is no balancing of power in the household, tensions tend to arise between the couple.

Glen and Brenda (Genogram 10) were such a couple. During two initial therapy appointments, they gave the following information:

Glen's two children, who lived with their mother in another state, were with him and Brenda for three weeks in the summer and one week near Christmas. Brenda's older daughter lived primarily with her father, while 11-year-old Cleo lived with her mother and stepfather. Brenda sought help because of the violent arguments she and Glen were constantly having over Cleo, who Brenda maintained was a darling well-behaved child who was treated very badly by her stepfather, Glen. Brenda also considered that Glen's children were absolute hellions who ran through the house with muddy shoes, didn't flush the toilet, and smeared peanut butter and jelly all over the walls with their dirty hands. According to Brenda, Glen was angry at Cleo all the time and tried to set very strict rules for her, but set no rules for his children when they were there.

Glen talked of his and Brenda's premarital agreement that *he* would look after her and *she* would look after her daughter. This was not working out at all because this gave him no say in the house and his stepdaughter treated him badly. He would try to hold back and talk to

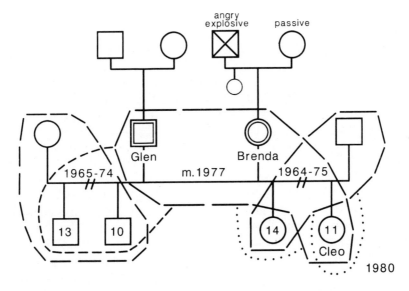

Genogram 10

Brenda about it, but she would argue with him until finally he blew up at her and also at Cleo.

During their first two appointments, the couple agreed on nothing except that the therapist was correct when she said that both seemed very angry and resentful, and both appeared to feel helpless and unappreciated. They also agreed that they did want to work together as a team and were having great difficulty doing that. When given the task of deciding what area they wished to discuss first, Brenda and Glen quickly lapsed into their former hostile interactional pattern and could not agree on what to discuss. Neither one was able to share power with the other, even in this basic task.

Eventually, the source of Brenda's fear became clear when she reported that she had grown up in a family in which she and her sister were "pinned against the wall" by their father who often became angry and was given to explosive behavior. Brenda's mother was passive and did nothing to protect the girls from their father.

The premarital rule had been formulated because Brenda feared that Glen's treatment of her daughter would be similar to the "lickings" Brenda remembered from her childhood. Because the agreement created a continuing situation in which Glen had little power in the household, he flexed his parental muscles when his own children were there, and he exploded at Cleo and Brenda from time to time. A vicious cycle was dragging them down:

Glen was to look after Brenda and
not have any authority over Cleo.

Brenda feared Glen's treatment of
Cleo and in her effort not to be
passive like her mother, set strict
rules for Glen's interaction with Cleo.

Cleo was unpleasant to Glen and
he grew increasingly angry,
eventually exploding.

As for Glen's childhood, he had been given very little personal power when he was growing up, and so he feared and was angry at the authority of his wife just as he had been angry and fearful of his mother's overcontrol. By exploring these issues in therapy, the couple began to recognize the validity of their reactions *in the past* and the ways in which these feelings and expectations were not necessarily valid *in the present*. They became aware that the residues of their past were creating major problems for them and actually producing the situations they feared. Very slowly and tentatively they began to build some trust between them and work together as a couple.

In another situation, a woman who sought therapy when she began having arguments with a new partner with whom she was living wrote in the course of her therapy the following analysis of a fundamental cause of her second divorce and her present difficulties:

I married Fred after four years of dating and living together. It was the second marriage for both of us. I brought to this marriage my nine-year-old daughter, Judy, from my first marriage. During my courtship with Fred, I wanted Judy and Fred to like each other so that there would be no conflict. However, I always felt that Judy was mine. I had raised her and taken care of her successfully by myself after the divorce.

That was the first time in my life that I had lived on my own. I had been an only child; my mother had been overprotective and always told me what to do and how to feel because she wanted "only the best" for me. She was the good, loving parent, in her eyes, and my father was the "bad guy" who was called upon by her to do the punishing. She said she regretted having to report my misdeeds to my father because of his severe punishment, but she let me know she had no choice. Some of my parents' most bitter arguments started because my father felt my mother sided with me against him. He was right! At any rate, I don't ever remember them *sharing* parental control and responsibility.

I got married the first time never having lived independently. My husband had all the control in the marriage. I did what he told me to for five years. During the sixth year, I rebelled against his authority and finally separated from him. I was very scared to be on my own for the first time, and with the additional responsibility of a five-year-old child. I had tremendous anxiety regarding my ability to cope on my own. But I did it—I managed very well. I was proud, very proud. And Judy was living proof that I had succeeded without anyone telling me what to do.

So when Fred entered the picture, I was not going to allow him to have anything to say about raising Judy. I had to be the only one she looked to for guidance, discipline—everything. Fred tried to participate at times in Judy's raising, but I always intervened. I wouldn't allow it. I wanted Judy and Fred to live in my household side-by-side without conflict, but also without relating to each other closely. I wanted Judy to be loyal to me, and I wanted Fred to be committed to me. I was to be *the* important person they each looked to for direction and to satisfy their needs.

I wanted each of them to love or need only me, not each other. I was so afraid that if I gave up any of my authority or importance to anyone else that I'd lose all and be under their control.

Fred seemed to resign himself to that kind of arrangement—I took care of him, and I also took care of Judy. Things went along like that relatively smoothly until Fred and I had a son, Greg, together a year after we were married. I wanted Judy and Greg to be close to each other and to me. I still wanted to be the one center of each child's life and of Fred's life. I wanted to be the "director" for both children, but where Greg was concerned, Fred had legitimate parental rights.

It seemed to me at the time that the escalating arguments between Fred and me were caused by different ideas on how children should be raised. In retrospect, I can see clearly that arguments increased because Fred appropriately wanted to have some say-so regarding his son's raising, but I wasn't willing to relinquish any of my parental control. I was so sure that if I let him have *anything* to say about Greg he'd take over completely and run the whole family, including me. I was fighting in any way I could because I was so afraid that if I gave in to his way I'd lose my position of power and importance—and to me, that meant that I'd lose myself.

I knew nothing of sharing and compromise. I knew only that if I didn't control each person in the family and keep the members kind of separate from each other I'd be overrun or smothered. I really felt that I'd be at their mercy or be nothing.

The marriage deteriorated, and I deteriorated because I felt pulled in too many different directions in trying to maintain a relationship with the *kids* excluding *Fred;* a relationship with *Fred* excluding the *kids;* a relationship with *Fred and Greg* excluding *Judy;* a relationship with *Judy* excluding *Greg and Fred. I got tired—* couldn't do it any more. So I opted to take both children and leave Fred (feeling perfectly justified in doing so, incidentally). That way I escaped from the threat of losing— losing especially, I thought, the position of being the only person the children had. I was their only giver, their only source of support and guidance—I was everything to them and they needed me. My position alone with the children gave me a tremendous feeling of power—and no one was going to take any of that power away from me. I earned it—I deserved it. I was not able to see that that kind of power was also a terrible, lonely burden.

A number of women discover during the time of heading a single-parent household that they are capable and manage well on their own. Their self-esteem may have risen but, as was the case with this mother, when they remarry they resist returning to what they fear will be the reduced status of their first marriage. Men who have been passive in their former marriage may also have the same fears. For many, the sharing of power stirs deep fears. Learning what these fears are, where they may have originated, and the necessity and value of sharing power can be extremely important therapeutic tasks.

B. Stepparents

In new stepfamilies, stepparents have considerably less authority in connection with their stepchildren than do the children's parent. In stepfamilies of certain types, this inequality can exist without causing difficulties: in stepfamilies formed when the children are teenagers on their way out of the household, or in stepfamilies in which the adults wish their roles to be less balanced, the couple can work together to see that the needs of the stepparent are not overlooked in this arrangement. For the most part, however, if there is not a gradual shift in the direction of more equal co-management, the stepparent remains as an outsider and feels alienated and alone. Where both adults have children and both, therefore, are stepparents as well as parents (the so-called "complex" stepfamily of White & Booth, 1985), two separate groups can exist under one roof; however, there is a danger of a split occurring so that two single-parent units exist again, either figuratively, or literally through a divorce.

Co-management is frequently an ideal in a stepfamily, but it does not necessarily mean taking on a parent role. It does mean sharing in the decision-making for the family. In fact, in the specific area of discipline, empirical and clinical evidence shows clearly that stepparents who attempt to take on a disciplinary role too quickly impede rather than enhance stepfamily integration (Brown, 1986; Hetherington et al., 1985; Stern, 1978; Visher & Visher, 1982).

We have yet to address a group of stepfamily adults that does not list "discipline" as a major source of tension, and in most instances the same is true for stepfamily couples who seek therapy. Since productive handling of disciplinary issues is different in stepfamilies than in nuclear families, therapeutic intervention in this area can be immensely helpful.

Frequently, remarried parents expect their new spouse to be a parent to their children, not recognizing that this role is ordinarily doomed to failure because the stepparent is not viewed by stepchildren as having the authority to be an enforcer of limits. We often say that discipline cannot be enforced without the consent of the disciplinee. Therefore, prior to the development of a friendly relationship, stepparents usually cannot wield much power except through force—which is, of course, destructive psychologically if not physically.

Stepparent and parent need to work together from the first on what they wish the house rules to be, and then the stepparent needs to be supportive of the parent when he or she enforces the rules. When children can be included in the decisions about rules, they usually respond positively and are therefore more willing to meet the standards. It is our impression that the adults are often surprised at the strictness of the limits and the magnitude of the consequences for noncompliance suggested by the children.

In stepfamilies, there are many actions and ways of doing things that are different from what the members have experienced before; this is true for every stepfamily member. As a result, the adults commonly have a strong desire to have an endless list of "do's and don'ts." We suggest that the family concentrate on only a few areas that seem to be the most important, and let the myriad of other things go. If this doesn't happen, everyone feels under attack and tenseness destroys the opportunity to relate comfortably with one another. Mills (1984) points out the value of stepparents and their partners being flexible about which roles and rules are most comfortable.

A common complaint of stepparents, especially stepmothers, is "But I'm alone with the children a lot, what do I do then?" In our experience, "what happens then" basically depends on the relationship between the couple. Parents need to call the family together and say to their children that their stepparent is in charge when the parent is not present. If the parent and stepparent are supportive of one another and are working well together, the empowering of the stepparent by the parent in this way can lead to a workable arrangement. However, when the couple is fragmented, this approach will not work well because the children ordinarily recognize that the step- parent does not actually have any power because of lack of support of their parent. One parent illustrated this when he responded to suggestions similar to these by saying poignantly and with sudden awareness of some of the difficulties in the family, "I can see the problem — my wife doesn't give me as much authority with the kids as she gives the babysitter." This couple had some power issues to settle before the stepfather would be respected by his stepchildren.

We are not suggesting that interpersonal issues between stepparent and stepchildren include the children's parent. It is not a house rule that Jimmie ask before borrowing his stepfather's tools or that Jane return her stepmoth- er's coat in the same condition in which she borrowed it. These are interper- sonal problems that need to be negotiated between the two people involved. In fact, in the productive handling of such situations lies one important route to learning about one another and thus building a relationship.

In response to lack of power, stepparents frequently *appear* to be the ones in charge. They are what we call high profile stepparents, verbal and involved, shouting at the children and in one way or another "throwing their weight around." Further scrutiny, however, often reveals that the alliance between parent and children is actually very strong so that the stepparent, in reality, has very little power in the household and is attempting unsuccessfully and in a nonproductive way to exert some control.

Benson and Henrietta were seeing a therapist because their stepfamily household was chaotic. Benson had a son, 16-year-old Michael, who lived with them. Occasionally, Michael saw his mother who lived in another state. The therapist saw the three together and noted that Henrietta controlled the session by talking a great deal and complaining at length about Michael's lack of responsibility at home and his seeming unwillingness to do his share of the household chores even when he said he would cooperate. Michael and his father said little during the one-and-a-half hours.

In a session with the couple only, Benson was more verbal and said several times that he felt that his wife's demands were reasonable and that he supported her authority in running the household. Henrietta continued to be emotionally agitated and talked of the ways in which she had attempted unsuccessfully to get Michael to cooperate. The therapist agreed that it sounded like a frustrating situation and made another appointment to see the three of them together.

Henrietta did not appear for this appointment and the therapist met with Benson and his son. Benson talked of "staying out of it" and letting his wife run the household. When asked by the therapist whom each of them saw as having the power at home, both stated that Henrietta was in control. During this appointment, both Benson and his son were verbal and the therapist began to see the strength of their alliance. Emotionally, Benson was supporting his son's noncompliance; in fact, the therapist suspected that Michael was acting out his father's anger at Henrietta. Instead of Henrietta actually being in charge at home, the therapist now saw the control exerted by Benson and Michael.

Henrietta kept saying that she would come for another appointment with her husband, but each time Benson or Benson and Michael came alone, bringing with them Henrietta's apologies and the reasons she could not be present.

We concur with their therapist that Henrietta did not have power in the household and responded by unsuccessful attempts to feel some control through having Michael clear the dinner table, keep his room clean, and put his soiled clothes in the laundry hamper. As this did not happen, her voice became more strident and her complaints to her husband more frequent. Benson listened to his wife and said that 16-year-old boys are very inconsiderate.

Henrietta as the stepparent was not in a powerful positon vis-à-vis Michael, and her husband was remaining passively in the background and consciously expecting her to be in a position of authority with her stepson. In her helplessness, Henrietta was aggravating the situation. It is likely that she had hoped to gain an ally in the therapist and had felt disappointed and more alone, so that she did not continue in treatment.

In our opinion, if other stepfamily members are to be seen with the couple for an initial appointment, the first session needs to be clearly understood to be for evaluation of the situation only. If the couple has a solid relationship (see "Action" stage in Chapter 4), then it may be productive to include others in the therapy. In the above family situation, an alliance between the couple needed to be developed before Michael was included, although he might have been seen separately if this seemed advisable. We might also have seen Henrietta and Benson individually in an attempt to strengthen each one's sense of adequacy. Educational comments and material might have been a first step to helping Benson take an active role with his son and enabling Henrietta to step back from the unsuitable stepfamily position she was attempting to occupy.

We have previously noted that an important therapeutic consideration is the recognition that in most cases stepparents are not initially the ones with the power to control the running of the household unless the stepchildren are young. Unfortunately, their attempts to deal with their helplessness often increase rather than decrease the household tensions and at times they are seen incorrectly as wielding the power.

C. Children

We think of the issues for children in stepfamilies as being in three general categories, or the three L's—Loss, Loyalty, and Lack of control. Just as with the adults, children can have strong reactions to feeling helpless and having no control over their lives. One task in therapy is that of helping the children gain mastery over their own lives in areas that will be of benefit to them.

Many times, following a death or divorce, children are given control beyond their years or responsibility. For example, they may be asked whether or not a parent should marry a particular person. Such responsibilities and choices are adult concerns and can put an unfair burden on children, even though they may like the power that it gives them. In fact, when children have been given too much responsibility during the single-parent household phase, they can be more than usually upset when their parent remarries, because of the sudden and dramatic shift in their position. In therapy, such a displaced child will probably need to find areas of responsibility and control to replace those that were abruptly terminated without the consent of the young person, even though the child resented them during the single-parent phase.

In nuclear families, children find ways to "play one parent off against the other" when the parents are not working well together. With their biological parents in two different households, children in stepfamilies often gain an inordinate amount of power by playing one household off against the other.

The children's power becomes greater than that of the stepparent or of one or more of the other adults. For the children this is an ambivalent spot to be in; on the one hand it is helpful to feel a sense of control, yet on the other hand there is an insecurity in not having strong adults to count on to be protective and truly nurturing. The needs of the children are important, and their input is valuable, but the adults are the persons with the ultimate authority for their households. Ideally, they need to work together to promote the best interests of the stepfamily suprasystem.

If the adults are not cooperative and the children are allowed to manipulate the situation, either between households or between parent and stepparent, children will find themselves in the conflictual middle position. Helping children gain "productive mastery" can be a therapeutic goal.

One 13-year-old boy found ways to see a good friend with whom he had lost contact when his mother remarried. He also learned productive ways to talk with his mother and stepfather to persuade them to arrange for him to take a woodworking class that was of great interest to him. As he found that he had the power to effect these desired changes in his life, he slowly dropped the disruptive behavior that had been the method he had employed previously in his attempt to gain mastery over his life. Within certain parameters which he could not change—his mother and father's divorce; where he now lived; the amount of money to be spent by the adults for his activities—he had found that he was not helpless in controlling many elements in his life that were important to him.

In another instance, seven-year-old Jeremy was being seen by a therapist. He refused to get ready for school in the morning, and could never find his soccer shoes when it was time for his mother or stepfather to take him to soccer practice. Many times Jeremy had left the shoes at his father and stepmother's apartment. Working with the youngster and at times with the adults, the therapist helped Jeremy to gain more control over his life. When the adults began letting the consequences of lost shoes fall on Jeremy, he soon got the message that there were many things in his life that he could control. In addition, in the morning Jeremy was now allowed to wear to school what he chose, he could choose one of four different breakfasts, and he had the choice of a special treat to take to school for after lunch. (There were limitations of course, since he was dependent on available clothes and food.)

When he couldn't find his soccer shoes, Jeremy's mother and stepfather no longer became angry or called his father or helped him search—

it was up to Jeremy to let them know when he had his shoes and wanted to go to soccer practice. Soon Jeremy realized that it was up to him to control whether or not he attended soccer practice. Now he was in charge of parts of his own life that were important to him rather than attempting to gain a sense of mastery through unproductive behavior.

Often children feel guilty and responsible for the death of a parent or for the divorce: "If only I had not slammed the door in Mom's face, if I had just done what my father told me to do, then my parents wouldn't have split up or my father wouldn't have died of a heart attack." These are the thoughts that can run through children's minds. While these thoughts can cause children considerable unhappiness, they do bring with them one positive aspect: giving the child a feeling of control.

Helping children gain mastery over aspects of their lives before attempting to remove their feelings of guilt and responsibility can work well. If they come to feel, before experiencing areas of control and mastery, that there was nothing they could have done to prevent the death or divorce, children can become increasingly depressed by their feelings of helplessness. If, on the other hand, they have experienced mastery of their environment, they do not need the earlier unrealistic sense of control to feel the sense of personal power that we all need to have in our lives.

POWER STRUGGLES BETWEEN HOUSEHOLDS

When parents in nuclear families do not trust one another, there can be frequent power struggles between them. When parent and stepparent in one household do not trust the parent and stepparent in the children's other household, a similar pattern often emerges. When this happens, the needs of the children can get lost in the ensuing struggle. In some situations, the confrontation is clearly recognizable; in other households it is more subtle. A pediatric allergist, in reflecting on his caseload, realized that 90% of his emergency nighttime calls were for children who were in a single-parent household or a stepfamily. He commented that in most instances he had detected underlying hostility between the children's two households so that as children changed households medicine had been forgotten, directions for giving the medicine were not included, or the other household had not been informed of a current allergic difficulty. Even in these subtle ways one household was in control and putting the other at a disadvantage; at times, this battle over medicines and health escalated between the households.

Most conflicts are more open. When it is not possible to see all of the involved adults together, we have had satisfactory outcomes by working with the adults in only one of the households. Since it takes two to fight, the power struggle cannot continue if one household will decide to back off from the conflict. This suggestion needs to be reframed for adults who may think of backing off as a "chicken thing to do" rather than an *active* decision to make a strategic withdrawal. When the adults in both households are willing to come together to see a therapist, the opportunity for future, as well as present, cooperation is enhanced because understanding rather than distrust can develop between the two households.

In the following example the two households were those of the children's father and stepmother and their maternal grandparents:

After Claude and Maggie had been married for 10 years and had two sons, Eric and Warren, Claude became severely alcoholic. When the boys were 9 and 7, Claude and Maggie were divorced. The boys remained with their mother and Claude moved away. He continued to see his sons a few times during the year and they had good times when they were together. Claude continued to drink heavily for a year. When he lost a third job because of his drinking, he entered a rehabilitation program; this time he was successful in his attempt to stop drinking. Soon after this, Claude and Josie met and six months later they were married.

Following the divorce, Maggie had been depressed and spent seven months in and out of psychiatric hospitals. When she was in the hospital, Eric and Warren stayed with Maggie's parents. Soon after Claude's remarriage, Maggie was killed in an automobile accident and the two boys went to live with their maternal grandparents (see Genogram 11).

A power struggle developed between Eric and Warren's two households—the father's and the grandparents'—over where the boys were to live. At one point, Claude kidnapped the boys after school and drove them to his home. The grandparents retaliated by stealing them back. There were heated arguments over the telephone and more snatchings after school. The boys' school work began to suffer and the situation came to the attention of the school authorities. Eventually Claude and Josie and the grandparents were required by the court to meet with a counselor.

The counselor met with the four adults together and pointed out to them that their behavior was hurting the boys and that was the reason the school had needed to act to protect Eric and Warren. The adults glared at one another and said very little.

During the next appointment, the mood was different. The adults

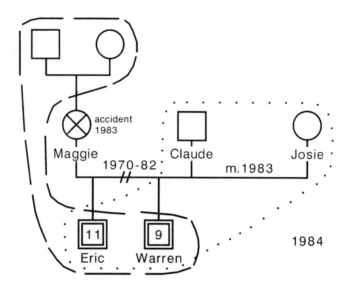

Genogram 11

were more thoughtful, and during this meeting the critical moment came when Claude said to Maggie's parents with tears in his eyes, "I don't know what the boys would have done without you." Shortly after that, the boys' grandmother said, sadly, "I always really knew that the boys would want to be with you sometime. I think it's really best for them because they'll see that everyone loves them. But I thought it would be further off, not so soon."

For the first time, the two households became allies rather than enemies. Living arrangements were changed gradually. Now that Claude and Josie and the grandparents had formed a "parenting coalition," the power struggles and tensions swirling around the boys dropped away and slowly Eric and Warren began to function adequately again.

SUMMARY OF THERAPEUTIC INTERVENTIONS

No matter whether it is an individual or a household that is feeling powerless, the following can be helpful therapeutic interventions:

• Acting as a support to create a more equal power structure;
• Helping individuals to shift towards more equal distribution of power;

- Outlining clearly what the situation is and the advantages of sharing power;
- Exploring the antecedents of individual reactions to helplessness;
- Working to help stepfamily members control what *they* can control and let the rest go;
- Assisting with the recognition of limitations and the personal control within these parameters.

CHAPTER 12

Closeness and Distance

Really my fear about my sexual feelings about my stepmother kept me from expressing some of my positive emotions towards her.
— Retrospective report of teenager in a stepfamily
(Visher & Visher, 1979, p. 177)

The relationships between people in a new stepfamily household frequently are awkward and self-conscious. Often, a lack of closeness is an important agenda item for stepfamilies coming for therapy. Adults and children usually have an acute awareness of the many interpersonal encounters that take place. Couples may feel uneasy in exposing their closeness to the watchful scrutiny of their children and stepchildren, and ties between the other individuals have not had time to form.

As for the children, even those from different families who have known and liked each other previously face different relationship parameters when their parents marry one another. Relating under one roof and sharing not only your parent, but the bedroom and bathroom, to say nothing of your TV, telephone, space at the dinner table, or your new hair dryer, can instantly produce relationship tensions not experienced earlier on the school playground. The "presence" of those with whom you have not lived can crowd out the familiar interactional flow so that you feel "observed and not alone," even when new household members are in their rooms at the far end of the house from you.

The more that stepfamily individuals are together, the more opportunity they have to experience one another in a less self-conscious manner. Just as it can be more difficult to relate easily to a friend you have not seen for some time than to one with whom you have recently shared time, the relationships between residential stepparents and stepchildren and between stepsiblings

222

who live together a great deal of the time can become consolidated more quickly than when there is less contact. Even parents and children who are nonresidential lose emotional contact with each other as they mature and change apart from one another.

While this "awareness" of interpersonal interactions can result in feelings of discomfort at times, these experiences also teach stepfamily members what is involved in developing and maintaining all types of human relationships. Understanding of others comes more easily with practice, and interpersonal relationships are not as easily taken for granted. As one 18-year-old girl in a stepfamily said, "I'm more understanding of other people's problems now, and I think I'm a better friend."

HOW STEPCHILDREN REFER TO THEIR STEPPARENTS

A 34-year-old man reflecting on growing up in a stepfamily remarked that for three to four years he and his stepmother had a comfortable relationship "until the day she asked me to call her mother. From then on there was a tension between us." We believe this comment clearly illustrates what can be an important issue for therapy: What do children call their stepparents? As we see it, if the adults follow the children's lead in these matters, satisfactory stepfamily relationships are more likely to occur than if children are asked to satisfy the wishes of their adults.

Once again it appears that in their desire to emulate the idealized nuclear family, adults frequently request, or even require, that stepchildren call their stepparent by relationship terms such as Mother or Father, or Mom and Pop. The adults, in contrast, nearly always call their stepchildren by their given names, free from any relationship connotation. In our experience, no matter what the adults may say about not wishing to replace or substitute for a child's other parent in another household, the child hears the message that saying "Mother" or "Father" to a stepparent is a rejection of their bioparent in favor of the stepparent.

Conversely, though much less frequently, a child may ask to call a stepparent by a relationship term, and feel rejected by that person when the answer is "no." Even when the relationship term is rejected by the adult in an attempt to demonstrate to the child that the stepparent is not attempting to alter the child's relationship with the parent of the same sex, to children a stepparent's refusal is seen as a rejection of their efforts to establish a closer relationship.

Over time, depending on their individual needs, what children choose to call their stepparent may change. However, the use of a relationship term does not necessarily measure the closeness or quality of the stepparent/stepchild relationship. At first, as one stepmother of preteenage stepchildren said, "You're lucky if they call you anything," to which another woman replied, "In our household my stepdaughter would approach my husband and me and say rather vaguely, 'Dad and whomever.' Obviously I was 'whomever'!" The usual pattern is for the child to use the stepparent's first name, and frequently this is where the matter rests, particularly if the children are latency age or older.

Unfortunately, society is of no help to stepfamilies in this regard. In some instances, remarried parents and stepparents worry about how friends and neighbors will judge the relationships between the stepchildren and their stepparent when they hear the children calling the stepparent by his or her first name rather than using a relationship term. Clara offers a good illustration of this. Clara, who had no children of her own and who acquired two young stepchildren, was talking with a good friend about her stepchildren. Clara's friend interrupted her to ask, "Are you saying that your stepchildren call you by your first name?" When Clara's answer was "Yes" her friend said with some feeling, "Oh, that seems so cold to me."

This is an area where it is important for the therapist to use accurate language. During an initial session with a large stepfamily with children "from both sides," the therapist asked the children, "What do you call your stepparents?" Several of the children responded animatedly with important psychological comments as to the reasons for their choices. With one question the therapist began to form a positive alliance with the family as he demonstrated his understanding of stepfamily structure and his expectation that they might use nonrelationship terms.

In a different family the guilt carried at times by the children was well illustrated—and resolved—during their second appointment as a family:

Susan (stepmother): I've tried so hard to be a parent to you, but I'm not your mother. I like you three children a lot, but I don't love you the way a mother would. (Later, Susan commented that she had waited for the sky to collapse at this confession. Instead . . .)

Charles (age 13): I've always wondered how you felt about me calling you by your first name while the others call you Mom.

Susan: Oh, that's only natural. The other two are a lot younger than you are. You've known your mother for a lot longer than they have.

At this point the five of them, husband, wife, and his three children, began to talk together about things they wanted to do as a unit. Prior to this time, Susan had been somewhat removed from the children, with

Charles and Susan making assumptions about the feelings of the other and experiencing guilt about their own feelings. Sharing and clarifying their disturbing assumptions enabled the family to draw closer together in an appropriate and productive manner.

DISCOMFORT WITH DISTANCE

In our experience, generally it is the adults in stepfamilies rather than the children who are upset by the lack of strong emotional ties between stepparents and stepchildren. Even though caring and warm feelings exist, the ideal of (perceived) nuclear family closeness casts its shadow over the stepchild/stepparent relationships and makes them seem pale and colorless by comparison. The adults become dissatisfied, worry about the quality of their nonbiologic ties, and may attempt to elicit the same concern in a therapist.

Eighteen-year-old Steve told a group of family therapists about being sent to a psychiatrist at age nine because he did not converse easily at the dinner table. His recollection was that his mother and stepfather, with whom he lived most of the time, interpreted his lack of verbal animation as being due to Steve's lack of acceptance of his stepfather and anger over his parent's divorce and his mother's five-year-old remarriage. As Steve said, "I felt fine about having a stepfather, and I wasn't mad about being in a stepfamily. I got mad at them, though, for sending me to see a psychiatrist. It's embarrassing when you're nine to be sent to see someone like that. Your friends think you're pretty queer. So I wasn't mad at first, but then I did get mad about that and so they all felt they were right from the very first. But they really weren't. I was comfortable just not talking any more than I did."

Steve continued by saying that he cared a great deal for his stepfather, who was his role model. Perhaps by now Steve's mother and stepfather are satisfied with the warmth of the stepfather/stepson relationship, but apparently their earlier perceptions and concerns did not match Steve's own experience.

Frequently, when adults and children meet separately in therapy, children are privately expressing love and affection for their stepparents at the same time that their stepparents are discussing their reactions to what they perceive as a lack of caring by their stepchildren. The adult concern is often manifested as an inability to translate positive actions of the children into "caring" because the actions do not match the expectations and dreams of the adults.

Stepparents often rush in too quickly to try to forge closer stepparent/stepchild relationships without allowing time for a more gradual and steady progression from strangeness to familiarity and trust. With the stepfamilies pressure for closeness, it can be difficult, but necessary, for therapists to resist rushing in prematurely to promote closeness. In fact, looseness and freedom in the relationships may be essential to development of warm and caring steprelationships.

In a case reported in *Family Kaleidoscope* (1984), Minuchin helps a family in which the stepmother/stepson relationship has deteriorated following a sudden close bonding at the beginning of the formation of the stepfamily. Distrust and loyalty conflicts had surfaced for the stepson when his stepmother psychologically moved in too rapidly and prematurely short-circuited the task of slowly overcoming an initial distance in their relationship. In therapy, a warm and trusting relationship between the stepson and stepmother was gradually reestablished.

All too often, stepgrandparents, stepparents, and stepchildren assume they "ought" to feel closer to one another than they do. The resulting guilt feelings prevent them from developing as close a relationship as they might have if they had felt free to establish bonding patterns between them in a more gradual manner. Many times there also is external pressure from the parent of the children for steprelations to burst into full bloom without a period of germination and growth. This fantasied closeness is ordinarily seen erroneously by the remarried parent as the way to insure happiness for the children who have gone through a period of unhappiness following the death of a parent or a parental divorce.

In such families, there are several therapeutic needs: 1) for validation that a family unit indeed exists with bonding patterns that do not mirror those of functioning nuclear families; 2) for education to arrive at more realistic relationship expectations, even to accepting that the steprelationships might not ever be described as close; 3) for help in filling in past histories and sharing fears and concerns as well as positive feelings; and 4) for the reframing of stepfamily goals so that the family can view the need to self-consciously develop bonds as a positive characteristic. When bonds do form, they are often "bonds that are incredibly rich and strong because they had to be created on purpose" (Papernow, 1986, p. 15).

DISCOMFORT WITH CLOSENESS

Often there seems to be no acceptable interpersonal distance in stepfamilies! Just as a lack of the familiar idealized nuclear family closeness is cause for alarm, so is its opposite: warmth and closeness between stepgrandparents, stepparent and stepchildren, or between stepsiblings. One reason for this discomfort is that children having an emotionally close relationship with a stepgrandparent, or especially with a stepparent, can produce guilt because "children are reared to love and trust only their natural parents" (Thies, 1977, p. 59).

For stepparents with biological children living primarily, or even part time, in other households, guilt is also a common response to a growing closeness with stepchidren. One man expressed it eloquently when he said, "For a long time I considered that love was finite, and that if I had one bucket full and gave it to my stepchildren, I was depleting my supply and therefore had less to give to my own children." Adults and children may need to be made aware that love is infinite and increases the more it is shared.

Since positive shared experiences lead to increasing closeness in a relationship, it is to be expected that steparents who have little meaningful contact with their biological children and have many important connections with their stepchildren will form a strong psychological bond with their stepchildren, and will tend to feel less psychologically connected to their biological children. Even then a deep and special love can remain between them. Steve, who talked of his excellent relationship with his stepfather, illustrated this point when he said, "My Dad is irresponsible and sort of a flake, but I love him. I'm not sure why. I guess it's just because he's my Dad." As in all families, over the years contact between the adults and children shifts and changes and forms many different shapes and patterns; each variation may produce alterations in the bonding between the individuals concerned.

The self-conscious nature of steprelationships frequently leads to an over-interpretation of situations. The following interchange illustrates the way in which "normal" child's play can cause discomfort and concern in a stepfamily:

> *Grace:* I've been remarried for two years and have a four-year-old daughter and a three-year-old stepson. I'm upset about the way they play together. I don't know if I need to be, but I am.
> *Therapist:* Can you tell me more about what you mean?
> *Grace:* Uh, it has to do with sex.
> *Therapist:* Are they playing "doctor" together? Is that it?
> *Grace:* No, it's not that. They're playing house. She's the wife and he's the husband, and they talk about being married. They play this a lot.
> *Therapist:* Is there something sexual they talk about or pretend while they're playing?
> *Grace:* No, it's not that. It's just that they're not really brother and sister and maybe they could get the idea of getting married when they get older.

Therapist: I see. You're wondering if letting them play house could lead to sexual activity or to the idea of a real marriage later on.

Grace: Yes, that's it. What do you think?

Therapist: Am I correct in thinking that you would not be worried about this if they were biological brother and sister instead of stepbrother and stepsister?

Grace: Yes, that's right.

Therapist: You are saying that you realize young children *do* play house together and pretend that they are married. (Grace nods in agreement.) So you might say they just enjoy playing house together the way children of that age do. Maybe they will continue to play together a lot, but more likely they will each relate more to friends they make at school.

It is true that once in awhile stepbrothers and stepsisters do marry one another, but that usually happens if a remarriage has brought them together as older teenagers or young adults. Your two have been together since they were very young.

Grace: So I'm looking at it differently than the children are?

Therapist: I think so.

Grace: I guess they just like playing house together the way young kids do and it'll drop out later like in any family.

Therapist: Does your husband feel the same way about it?

Grace: No, he says they're just little kids. I think I'm going to think about this some more 'cause I probably don't need to worry about it.

In this stepfamily, Grace was concerned with the closeness of the children as manifested in a type of play typical at this age. More frequently, it is the children who react to warm stepparent overtures by drawing back and resisting overt gestures of affection if stepparents approach too quickly. Preschool children may soon accept a display of warmth from stepparent or stepsiblings provided they do not sense this is upsetting to their parent in the other household, but older children require a much longer time to feel comfortable with closeness. Teenagers may even be on their own before they relate warmly to stepsiblings and the parenting adults in their lives.

An amusing as well as illuminating example of a 10-year-old's reaction to closeness occurred in the initial therapy session with David and his large stepfamily. His stepmother and an older stepsister had both expressed the feeling that they often would like to give David a hug but they weren't sure how he would feel about it. The therapist then turned to David and asked him if he could tell them how he would feel if they hugged him. At this point

David literally fell off of his chair. After all of them, including David, laughed, the therapist helped David right his chair and encouraged him to put his feelings into words. David said it would feel "very strange."

While concern over closeness and distance between family members does occur in all types of family structures, in stepfamilies the individual's antennae are attuned to catch and perhaps intercept interactions that would be accepted and often go unnoticed in nuclear or single-parent households.

SEXUAL ATTRACTION IN STEPFAMILIES

Sexuality ordinarily is a prominent and visible ingredient of new stepfamilies because the couple are living through the honeymoon period in the presence of the children, and there may be stepsiblings of different sexes who are dealing with the sexual issues of puberty and adolescence. Sometimes, mothers and daughters become competitive with one another for the affection of the new husband (Schulman, 1972) and sons may be attracted to their father's new wife.

In recent years there has been considerable research in the area of sexual abuse of children. Present figures indicate that young girls (below age 14) have a 7% greater chance of being molested by a residential stepfather than by their biofathers if they are living in a nuclear family (Russell, 1984). Researchers have advanced a number of hypotheses to explain these results, but as yet the theories have not been adequately tested (Finkelhor & Baron, 1986; Giles-Sims & Finkelhor, 1984; Parker & Parker, 1986). Suffice it to say that sexuality in stepfamily households can be an area of concern for stepfamilies and for the therapists who treat them.

Unfortunately, this present concern with child abuse is being used by warring ex-spouses and angry stepchildren to express their bitterness over their unwanted situation. One parent may accuse the other of child molestation in an attempt to sabotage the relationship of the child with his or her other parent, and stepchildren may accuse stepparents of abuse as a way to break up their parents' new marriage. In one family, the teenage daughter reported her stepfather's intimacies only later, a considerable time after they had ceased, when her mother and stepfather began, for the first time, to have a warm and loving relationship between them. For the girl, this signaled a loss of closeness with her mother and she used the most powerful weapon she could think of in her attempt to return the household to its former homeostasis.

When working with stepfamilies, therapists need to be aware that fear of loss, along with hurt and anger at rejection, can lead to reports of abuse when no such behavior has occurred. However, they must also recognize the increased potential for sexual abuse in stepfamilies. This is a specialized area of therapy in which there is an increasing body of literature. As Gardner (1979) states:

> Since stepparents and stepchildren do not have years of familiarization, the novelty of their relationships enhances sexual stimulation. Furthermore, the stepparent is likely to have a sexually charged "aura" to the child, since he or she has been brought in as the parent's "sexual object."

A. Attraction Between Stepparents and Stepchildren

In therapy, the area of sexuality often is not open to direct discussion. Even in educational groups for stepfamily adults, the topic of sexuality in stepfamilies sparks little discussion of intergenerational attraction. Even so, it is our impression that hearing group leaders give in a matter-of-fact way basic structural reasons for such attractions in this type of family relieves feelings of guilt that some stepparents may be experiencing.

By pointing out the difference between *feelings* and *behavior* and the need to control sexual *behavior*, leaders can also give stepparents a way to cope productively with such emotions. A more basic need is for help for the adults to form a strong and rewarding adult couple relationship. In addition, therapists can help stepparents give their stepchildren the nurturance and guidance that are appropriate for their ages.

Frequently, the observed hostility between stepparent and stepchildren may be covering conscious or unconscious sexual attractions. Fighting and anger become mechanisms by which they maintain distance and control over their sexual impulses.

> Christy and Paul had been married for a year when they sought therapeutic help. Paul's 19-year-old son, Robert, had moved in with the couple following the loss of his job as a clerk in a department store, and he was becoming increasingly verbally abusive to Christy when she was alone in the house with him. It seemed to the couple that Robert became particularly angry when Paul and Christy were going out for the evening. The precipitating event that led to the call for an appointment was Robert's scathing attack on Christy when she asked him to cook himself a hamburger when the couple was going out for the evening with

friends. At this point, Paul could no longer insist that Christy was exaggerating the content and negative emotion of Robert's interactions with her when his father was not there.

After talking once with the couple, the therapist met with Robert and his father and stepmother for a total of six times during a two-and-a-half month period. From the therapist's point of view, the dynamics that he saw emerging were not unusual for stepfamilies. Christy had not been previously married and was much younger than her husband. She was a warm and attractive woman and Robert felt drawn to her, particularly so because he was a very shy young man, was awkward in the presence of women, and had few friends and no girlfriend. In an effort to control his sexual attraction to his stepmother, Robert pushed her away by his angry and sarcastic remarks. He felt particularly lonely and upset when the couple went out together and he remained at home alone.

Sager et al. (1983) give several examples of situations in which they were able to deal directly with sexual acting out between adults and children in stepfamilies. When no overt sexual actions have occurred, we have found that dealing with these issues in a relevant but "nonsexual" context can often lead to satisfactory therapeutic movement. With Christy, Paul and Robert, the therapist dealt with the problem in the context of Robert's loneliness, pointing out Robert's unfamiliarity with the neighborhood in which Paul and Christy lived and his shyness in new situations (which Robert had previously acknowledged). They could all see that Robert's sense of personal inadequacy and emotions of loneliness and isolation would naturally be especially strong when Paul and Christy went out in the evening together.

Having recognized and acknowledged the dilemma, the three found little difficulty in deciding what they wished to do about it. They decided that Paul and Christy at times would invite Robert to go out with them (this worked satisfactorily for Robert since his father was present to act as an external control on Robert's attraction to Christy); that the couple would help Robert locate one or two groups of young people in their neighborhood with interests similar to his; and that Robert would search more diligently for another job.

These plans were implemented and Robert found a position in a grocery store. This gave him an important interest outside of the household, increased his social contacts, and significantly reduced his time alone in the household with Christy. At times, Robert reverted to his former sarcasm, but Christy could now handle the interchange in a nondefensive way and usually the tension would be quickly resolved.

B. Attraction Between Stepsiblings

We have encountered controversy as to whether or not sexual relations between steprelatives constitutes incest since there is no biological tie between them. We understand that Margaret Mead used the term "household incest" to describe the existence of sexual relations between household members living together as a family. From our perspective, this is a useful concept for stepfamily life since sexual relationships between stepfamily members, other than between the adult couple, can produce guilt, discomfort, and untenable family situations, even when involving two biologically unrelated young adults.

One young man recalls his reactions as a teenager when his father remarried:

> I was always thinking about girls and I was always thinking about sex in that house. One of my fantasy objects was my stepsister, but this was tough because I was both attracted to and afraid of women, and there she was in various states of undress (whether she actually was or not I don't remember). I was both attracted to her and curious about her as an individual and a female. As hard as I tried, I couldn't ignore her, nor place distance between us in that house. (Visher & Visher, 1979, p. 177)

We have been surprised at the number of adults who do not realize the need to alter previously casual "dress codes" that were comfortable in the single-parent household. Except for very young children, sudden confrontations between young people and children (or adults) of the opposite sex with whom they have not lived immediately brings sexual questions and interest into consciousness. For adolescents who are dealing with their emerging sexuality, these issues are particularly important.

Frequently, therapists need to help the adults realize that teenagers need external controls to help them deal with such feelings. The mother of a 15-year-old daughter was called upon to set household limits with her 17-year-old stepson soon after the stepfamily was formed. After several days of provocative behavior the 17-year-old came downstairs dressed only in a pair of revealing undershorts. His stepmother said sternly, "Go back and get dressed properly before you come downstairs where people are." The young man retreated with a few angry remarks, got dressed before reappearing, and never again was openly provocative. This stepmother was clear and unambivalent in setting helpful household limits.

However, we find that therapists are often put in the position of educating parents and stepparents to understand the children's need for external controls in sexual areas. In fact, adults often need to hear the message that affection between them is important for the children to see, but that passionate embraces are appropriate only in private. All too often the couple is unaware, or may wish to be unaware, of the sexual difficulties that can be exacerbated for children by their behavior.

Stepchildren have more extended family homes available to them than do children in nuclear families. Often, the availability of another place to live with adults who care about them is of benefit to stepchildren. Sexual attraction between stepsiblings is one situation that at times calls for more than a rearrangement of rooms or a discussion of the disadvantages of attachment and disillusionment with a person living in the same household. A move is indicated, and there often is another available household with the other parent.

In still other instances, young adults have been asked to move into some type of suitable living quarters. For example, in one stepfamily in which the husband's 21-year-old son and the wife's 18-year-old daughter became intimately involved, the young man was asked to move into an apartment of his own. The relationship between the two young people continued, but without the acute discomfort previously experienced by the others in the stepfamily household.

SUMMARY

Although clinical impressions and empirical data (Anderson & White, 1986) indicate that a *gradual* movement towards closeness speeds rather than delays integration, it is tempting for therapists to accept the unrealistic expectations of stepfamily adults to rush towards closeness between steprelatives. Such precipitousness, however, can lead to less, rather than greater, stepfamily integration because it does not allow for a gradual and solid building of familiarity and respect. The acute awareness of the presence of others brings with it a need to move slowly through the stages of discovery and familiarity. While the compression of this process can result in a wariness and springing apart following instant intimacy, the gradual building of trust between steprelatives can lead to sensitive and loving relationships that are marked by a conscious recognition of the specialness of their existence.

CHAPTER 13

Overview

We are surrounded by insurmountable opportunities.

—Pogo

It is our belief that when stepfamilies are able to integrate and experience the improved sense of self-esteem that comes from a solid identity as a family, they are families that bring great satisfaction for the adults and for the children. Losses have been replaced by gains, complexity has become richness and diversity, ambiguity has bred creativity and flexibility, and family caring and love have multiplied.

STEPFAMILY INTEGRATION

Ordinarily it is *not* a short journey from stepfamily ambiguity and fragility to solidity and integration. The process can take a minimum of one and a half to two years when the children are young to many more years when the children are older. As we illustrated at the beginning of the book, the relationships in stepfamilies need to shift and develop, going from loyalty patterns that are biologically based to encompassing new and enriching ties growing out of shared experiences and mutual respect.

Because of the structural characteristics common to American stepfamilies, each needs to accomplish a number of tasks to develop its family identity. Specific suggestions are outlined in Table 4. Even though these suggestions are basically self-explanatory, we find that stepfamilies often benefit from discussing them. With increasing frequency, therapists play a major role in helping these families with this understanding and with the delicate process of structuring new suprafamily systems.

TABLE 4*

STEPFAMILY TASKS
1. Dealing with losses and changes
2. Negotiating different developmental needs
3. Establishing new traditions
4. Developing a solid couple bond
5. Forming new relationships
6. Creating a "parenting coalition"
7. Accepting continual shifts in household composition
8. Risking involvement despite little societal support

1. **DEALING WITH LOSSES AND CHANGES**
   - Identify/recognize losses for all individuals
   - Support expressions of sadness
   - Help children talk and not act out feelings
   - Read stepfamily books
   - Make changes gradually
   - See that everyone gets a turn
   - Inform children of plans involving them
   - Accept the insecurity of change

2. **NEGOTIATING DIFFERENT DEVELOPMENTAL NEEDS**
   - Take a child development and/or parenting class
   - Accept validity of the different life cycle phases
   - Communicate individual needs clearly
   - Negotiate incompatible needs
   - Develop tolerance and flexibility

3. **ESTABLISHING NEW TRADITIONS**
   - Recognize ways are *different* not right or wrong
   - Concentrate on important situations only
   - Stepparents take on discipline enforcement slowly
   - Use "family meetings" for problem solving and giving appreciation
   - Shift "givens" slowly whenever possible
   - Retain/combine appropriate rituals
   - Enrich with new creative traditions

4. **DEVELOPING A SOLID COUPLE BOND**
   - Accept couple as primary long-term relationship
   - Nourish couple relationship
   - Plan for couple "alone time"
   - Decide general household rules as a couple
   - Support one another with the children
   - Expect and accept different parent-child stepparent-stepchild feelings
   - Work out money matters together

5. **FORMING NEW RELATIONSHIPS**
   - Fill in past histories
   - Make stepparent-stepchild 1:1 time
   - Make parent-child 1:1 time
   - Parent make space for stepparent-stepchild relationship
   - Do not expect "instant love" and adjustment
   - Be fair to stepchildren even when caring not developed
   - Follow children's lead in what to call stepparent
   - Do fun things together

6. **CREATING A "PARENTING COALITION"**
   - Deal directly with parenting adults in other household
   - Parents keep children out of the middle
   - Do not talk negatively about adults in other household
   - Control what you can and accept limitations
   - Avoid power struggles between households
   - Respect parenting skills of former spouse

(continued)

*From *Stepfamily Workshop Manual* (Visher & Visher, 1986) distributed by Stepfamily Association of America. Copyright 1986 by E.B. Visher and J.S. Visher.

TABLE 4 *(continued)*

• Contribute own "specialness" to children • Communicate between households in most effective manner	• Plan special times for various household constellations
7. ACCEPTING CONTINUAL SHIFTS IN HOUSEHOLD COMPOSITION • Allow children to enjoy their households • Give children time to adjust to household transitions • Avoid asking children to be "messengers" or "spies" • Consider teenager's serious desire to change residence • Respect privacy (boundaries) of all households • Set consequences that affect own household only • Provide personal place for non-resident children	8. RISKING INVOLVEMENT DESPITE LITTLE SOCIETAL SUPPORT • Include stepparents in school, religious, sports etc. activities • Give legal permission for stepparent to act when necessary • Continue stepparent-stepchild relationships after death or divorce of parent when caring has developed • Stepparent include self in stepchild's activities • Find groups supportive of stepfamilies • Remember that all relationships involve risk

THERAPEUTIC INTERVENTION

A. Initial Contact

During a recent conversation with a therapist, she commented that she often sees stepfamily adults for a first appointment, validates their feelings and situations, and finds that they do not return. They have been depressed and upset at the beginning of the session, but they leave smiling and saying how much better they feel. Knowing where you are going, having a road map and feeling confident that you are proceeding correctly can turn an intolerable trip into an adventurous journey. For a number of stepfamily individuals, validation and support from a person whom they feel is qualified to evaluate their progress are all they need to feel competent to continue to deal with the stepfamily situations they are encountering.

However, even though stepfamilies, on the average, appear to stay in therapy for a much shorter time than nuclear families, many will not disappear after an injection of validation. They will need a more extended treatment plan.

Since we wish to assess the strength of the couple relationship before including others in therapy, we initially see the adult who has made the contact or the couple if the person calling seems comfortable in asking the partner to come with him or her. (In some settings an adolescent may make the initial contact and be the first person seen.) Some therapists prefer to see the "family" for at least an evaluation appointment. If the presenting problem involves a child and the therapist's assessment on the telephone is that the household will come together with no major resistance, the family evaluation session can, of course, be productive. Our own approach is to start small and then enlarge the therapy group as seems advisable.

Initially we have several assessment questions:

1. When one maps the suprafamily system, where do key individuals tend to fit into the transitional process to stepfamily integration? (Following integration, most difficulties become similar to those in families in general.)
2. In which areas do the major difficulties appear to lie: Change and Loss, Unrealistic Beliefs, Insiders/Outsiders, Life Cycle Discrepancies, Loyalty Conflicts, Boundary Problems, Power Issues, Closeness and Distance?
3. Which members involved in the difficulties are potentially available for therapy, geographically and psychologically?
4. In what experiential stage of development does the family seem to be? The answer to this will be a crucial factor in determining whom it could be productive to see (see Chapter 4).

In evaluating the stepfamily, therapists have the task of stretching beyond nuclear family norms and thinking in terms of a suprafamily system that includes more than one household and more than two adults in the parenting coalition.

When the unique structure and characteristics of stepfamilies are kept in mind, productive shifts within the family can take place. We hear many stepfamilies talk about the help they have received from their therapeutic contacts. Maris, a stepmother, commented that in therapy she could be understood and say things to her husband, Cliff, that would upset their relationship if she said them to him at home. Her husband agreed and added:

It's really working out. Our therapist seems to understand us all. He's helping Maris realize that eight-year-old boys are messy and pretty noisy, and he's helping me set some limits for Teddy. And even Teddy likes him. He can really relate to kids.

In another family, the wife confided:

I've been married four years. I have a daughter who's in college and two teenage stepchildren. I am a professional person and have worked for many years. Then all of a sudden I couldn't cope. I absolutely fell apart and was in the hospital for several months. I think I was lucky it came to that, because then I saw a therapist. In the first couple of hours she validated me and what I was experiencing. All of a sudden I realized, "I'm not crazy after all." That made a lot of difference. It's still hard and we have a long way to go, but I'm really encouraged because we're all gradually beginning to have a good time together.

With the lack of stepfamily validation given in general by American society, validation is important throughout the therapeutic process, but initial validation by the therapist is particularly important in building therapeutic trust.

Educational materials and comments are intervention strategies that are especially valuable during the initial stage of therapy. It can also make a great deal of difference to give specific suggestions to families so they can feel less helpless and have a successful stepfamily experience. Learning about and building on success experiences can increase family self-esteem and provide a model for future positive action. In appropriate cases, homework tasks can give the message that there are things that members of the family can do *right now* to make the situation better. For example, the couple might agree to have some "alone time" during the next week, or parent and child might do something together such as reading a bedtime story, or the stepparent and stepchild might have fun doing something together. The two adults may be willing to write down (privately) their expectations of themselves and of their spouse, marking each expectation as to whether or not it is realistic or unrealistic, for discussion during the next therapy session. Or they may be willing to list five things they themselves are willing to change. These lists are shared and discussed in therapy. Initially, these tasks involving adults and children need to be suitable for individuals who do not know each other well and may have little trust of one another, even though they are living together under one roof.

B. Continuing Therapeutic Contact

As therapy continues, we consider that it is important initially to focus on the "transitional" rather than on the intrapsychic level. If personal intrapsychic reactions become the focus before some normalization and mastery of the interpersonal elements of stepfamily life, individuals can feel worse and cope less effectively because they feel increasingly guilty and are now convinced that there really is "something wrong with them." When there is the recognition that it is normal for the complexities of stepfamily life to produce stress for its individuals and that there are guidelines for coping with and reducing the stresses, then it may become productive to explore individual reactions to the situations occurring in the particular stepfamily. (In Chapter 3 we have discussed the therapeutic interventions we find to be the most helpful.) Many times, when the household chaos has subsided and anxiety and distress are less frequent, stepfamilies feel an emerging sense of organization and identity so that therapy no longer seems necessary to them. In these instances the deeper individual conflicts may not be addressed.

Common transitional tasks to be worked on in therapy include:

1. Dealing productively with losses and changes
2. Strengthening boundaries within the household and between households
3. Developing strong marital bonds
4. Building satisfying steprelationships since in stepfamilies these do not necessarily result from a good couple relationship
5. Creating a parenting coalition (see pp. 194 & 235-236)

Working out discipline issues differently than in nuclear families is helpful with some of these particular tasks. Stepparents who come in gradually and do not expect or are not expected to be a parent to stepchildren can make a positive contribution to the integration of the family. Frequently, however, the role expectations for stepparents are a major source of stress. Therapists can be extremely helpful by introducing the concept that stepparents and stepchildren cannot be expected to love one another when they first come together, and that strong caring may or may not develop depending on many factors such as age of the children, amount of contact, and more personal characteristics.

In many instances, therapists can also make a significant contribution by reframing for couples the limit-setting needs of the family, moving them away from a nuclear family model to one in which the parent plays an active role with his or her children, with the support of the stepparent. Helping parents remain or become active with their children and helping stepparents to step back until they have formed a friendly relationship with their stepchildren can be very important. Equally important is the concept that stepparents may not ever assume a parental role with their stepchildren (Mills, 1984).

The experience of therapists with whom we've talked mirrors our own, that stepfamilies often leave therapy without the planning and sense of closure that are more frequent with other families. If the therapeutic door is left open, they may return in the future at a time of stress. Working with stepfamilies can be exciting and rewarding because they tend to be highly motivated and aware of their emotions. However, their intensity and the complexity in terms of the numbers involved can become overwhelming to therapists and lead to therapist burnout. In this connection, therapist support groups are relieving and sustaining.

As individual and family self-esteem grows, and the many transitions of stepfamily life take on a normalcy, relationships become more positive, or at least neutralized. Stepfamilies then can begin to sense their solidity and their growth. Time itself can become a healer. The parent unit has shared memories and future plans, and a feeling of familiarity has replaced the barrage of the unfamiliar. The household unit finally has a foundation on which to absorb and deal with the daily fluctuations that occur. Significant family events involving the household or the larger suprasystem also can become growth experiences—bar mitzvahs, children leaving home, marriages, births, deaths. When this growth occurs, the stepfamily will have developed a satisfying identity that enriches the lives of its members and brings a satisfaction that is not taken for granted because there is a conscious awareness that it has been attained through much effort. It was not one of life's "givens."

STEPFAMILY RESOURCES

Educational, discussion, and therapy groups for stepfamily individuals are available. These are providing validation, support, and guidelines for adults and children. Group experience as an adjunct to therapy can be very effective and helpful. Program materials for such groups include the following:

Learning to Step Together: A Course for Stepfamily Adults, by Cecile Currier (1982). Stepfamily Association of America, 602 E. Joppa Rd., Baltimore, Maryland 21204.
Strengthening Stepfamilies, by Linda Albert & Elizabeth Einstein (1986). American Guidance Service, P.O. Box 99, Circle Pines, Minnesota 55014.
Banana Splits: A School-Based Program for the Survivors of the Divorce Wars, by Elizabeth M. McGonagle (1985). Ballston Spa Central Schools, Ballston Spa, New York 12020.

In addition, much help can be derived from books and other publications, such as:

Stepfamily Bulletin, quarterly publication of Stepfamily Association of America, 602 E. Joppa Road, Baltimore, Maryland 21204. This contains informative articles, personal experience stories, a column for therapists and counselors, a Kid's Corner, and other regular features.

Stepparent News, Listening Inc., 8717 Pine Ave., Gary, Indiana 46403. A newsletter with stepfamily information and personal experience stories, with an informal educational approach.

Educational Materials Program, Stepfamily Association of America, 602 E. Joppa Rd., Baltimore, Maryland 21204. A resource for ordering a wide variety of books for adults and children in stepfamilies which are frequently not available in bookstores.

(See the Appendix for a listing of books with relevance to both children and adults in stepfamilies.)

POSITIVE STEPFAMILY IDENTITY

After looking at the situations and dynamics that make the attainment of a satisfactory and rewarding identity difficult for many stepfamilies, it seems important that we return to the theme of the first chapter. "Opportunity," "challenge," "richness," "diversity," "love"—these are the words stepfamily members often use when they have successfully navigated the sometimes rocky shoals leading to family integration. Because there are many challenges, the rewards are all the more appreciated and valued. Even in stepfamilies who have had an easy time with their integration process, we have noticed that the individuals have an awareness of personal interactions and a sensitivity towards others that make for good human relationships. Because of society's stereotypes and the problems raised in therapy, it is easy for therapists to focus on stepfamily difficulties and overlook or discount the warm and moving observations that stepfamily children and adults share about their lives.

In Chinese, the word for *Crisis* combines the characters for both *Danger* and *Opportunity.* We have talked a great deal about the dangers. The opportunities are also there. A young child says:

Now there are a lot of new people in my life, and lots of grandparents. It can be really good, really fun.

And a teenager comments:

I hate to admit this, but since my stepfamily's new lifestyle is so different than what I was used to, I've learned that there is more than one way to live. There are parts of that lifestyle that I'm going to copy when I marry and have a family some day.

We think these and similar reflections are important because they come from young people who will be forming the families of the future. We are hopeful that their awareness will enable them to form good couple relationships in their first marriages and recognize the importance of nourishing those relationships so that they do not wither because they are neglected and taken for granted.

A woman asked about growing up in a stepfamily thoughtfully responded: "I was lucky, I had four adults to love me." Other adults, parents, and stepparents in stepfamilies say: "It's really comfortable now. When I get together with my stepchildren, the pressure's gone and we have fun." "I feel lucky to live with four really wonderful people." "I expected I'd be the boy's friend. I didn't think of myself as a parent, but I took a lot of responsibility. Now I have my own child and I realize my feelings for my own child and my stepchildren are the same. This really surprises me, and I like it."

With the likelihood that stepfamilies will be the predominant type of American family in less than 15 years (Glick, 1984), therapists are in an influential position because they can validate the value of remarriage. They can transmit to these families the emerging guidelines for productive roles and rules. And they can help stepfamilies build the personal satisfaction and pride that can evolve from coping successfully with the important challenges inherent in the maintaining of rewarding old loyalties and in the forging of meaningful new ties.

References

Adams, D. J. (1982). A comparison of confidence and degree of contentment in parental role of custodial and non-custodial stepmothers. Unpublished doctoral dissertation, Florida State University, Tallahassee, Florida.

Ahrons, C. R. (1981). The continuing co-parental relationship between divorced spouses. *American Journal of Orthopsychiatry, 51(3),* 415-428.

Ahrons, C. R. & Perlmutter, M. S. (1982). The relationship between former spouses: A fundamental subsystem in the remarriage family. In J. C. Hansen & L. Messinger (Eds.), *Therapy with Remarriage Families.* Rockville, Maryland: Aspen Publications.

Ahrons, C. R. & Wallisch, L. (1987). Parenting in the binuclear family: Relationships between biological and stepparents. In K. Pasley & M. Ihinger-Tallman (Eds.), *Remarriage and Stepparenting: Current Research and Theory.* New York: Guilford Press.

Anderson, J. Z. & White, G. D. (1986). An empirical investigation of interaction and relationship patterns in functional and dysfunctional nuclear families and stepfamilies. *Family Process, 25,* 407-422.

Aponte, H. J. (1976). Underorganization in the poor family. In P. J. Guerin (Ed.), *Family Therapy, Theory, and Practice.* New York: Gardner Press.

Aponte, H. J. & Van Deusen, J. M. (1981). Structural family therapy. In A. S. Gurman & D. P. Kniskern (Eds.), *Handbook of Family Therapy.* New York: Brunner/Mazel.

Becker, G. W., Landes, E. M., & Michael, R. T. (1977). An economic analysis of marital instability. *Journal of Political Economy, 85,* 1141-1187.

Bernard, J. (1956). *Remarriage: A Study of Marriage.* New York: Russell & Russell. (Second edition, 1971)

Bohannan, P. & Yahraes, H. (1979). Stepfathers as parents. In E. Corfman (Ed.), *Families Today: A Research Sampler on Families and Children.* Washington, D.C.: U.S. Government Printing Office.

Boss, P. & Greenberg, J. (1984). Family boundary ambiguity: A new variable in family stress theory. *Family Process, 23,* 535-546.

Boszormenyi-Nagy, I. & Spark, G. M. (1973). *Invisible Loyalties.* New York: Harper & Row. (Reprinted 1984, New York: Brunner/Mazel)

Bowman, M. E. & Ahrons, C. R. (1985). Impact of legal custody status on fathers' parenting post divorce. *Journal of Marriage and the Family, 47(2),* 481-485.

Bradt, J. O. & Bradt, C. M. (1986). Resources for remarried families. In M. S. Karpel (Ed.), *Family Resources.* New York: Guilford Press.

Brand, E. & Clingempeel, W. G. (1987). Interdependencies of marital and stepparent/ stepchild relationships and children's psychological adjustment: Research findings and clinical implications. *Family Relations, 36,* 140-146.

Brown, A. C. (1986). Factors associated with family functioning in non-counseling and counseling stepfamilies. Unpublished dissertation. California Graduate School of Marital and Family Therapy, San Rafael, Calif.

Bryan, L. R., Coleman, M., Ganong, L. H., & Bryan, S. H. (1986). Person perception: Family structure as a cue for stereotyping. *Journal of Marriage and the Family, 48,* 169-174.

Bryan, S. H., Ganong, L. H., Coleman, M., & Bryan, L. R. (1985). Counselors' perceptions of stepparents and stepchildren. *Journal of Counseling Psychology, 32,* 279-282.

Burchinal, L. G. (1964). Characteristics of adolescents from unbroken, broken, and reconstituted families. *Journal of Marriage and the Family, 26,* 44-51.

Chapman, M. (1977). Father absence, stepfathers, and the cognitive performance of college students. *Child Development, 48,* 1155-1158.

Cherlin, A. (1978). Remarriage as an incomplete institution. *American Journal of Sociology, 84(3),* 634-650.

Clingempeel, W. G., Brand, E., & Ievoli, R. (1984). Stepparent-stepchild relationships in stepmother and stepfather families: A multimethod study. *Family Relations, 33,* 465-473.

Clingempeel, W. G., Brand, E., & Segal, S. (1987). A multi-level, multi-variable developmental perspective for future research on stepfamilies. In K. Pasley & M. Ihinger-Tallman (Eds.), *Remarriage and Stepparenting: Current Research and Theory.* N.Y.: Guilford Press.

Clingempeel, W. G., Ievoli, R., & Brand, E. (1984). Structural complexity and the quality of stepfather-stepchild relationships. *Family Process, 23,* 547-560.

Clingempeel, G. & Segal, S. (1986), Stepparent and stepchild relationships and the psychological adjustment of children. *Child Development, 57,* 474-484.

Coleman, M. & Ganong, L. (1987). The cultural stereotyping of stepfamilies. In K. Pasley & M. Ihinger-Tallman (Eds.), *Remarriage and Stepparenting: Current Research and Theory.* New York: Guilford Press.

Coopersmith, S. (1967). *The Antecedents of Self-Esteem.* San Francisco: W. H. Freeman.

Crohn, H., Sager, C. J., Brown, H., Rodstein, E., & Walker, L. (1982). A basis for understanding and treating the remarried family. In J. C. Hansen & L. Messinger (Eds.), Therapy with Remarriage Families. Rockville, Maryland: Aspen Publications.

Crosbie-Burnett, M. (1984). The centrality of the steprelationship: A challenge to family theory and practice. *Family Relations, 33,* 459-463.

Crosbie-Burnett, M. (1985). Type of custody and involvement with children by father and stepfather. Unpublished paper presented at Annual Conference, National Council on Family Relations, November.

Crosbie-Burnett, M., Giles-Sims, J., & Plummer, C. (1986). Power in stepfamilies: A test of normative-resource theory. Unpublished paper presented at Annual Conference, National Council on Family Relations, November.

Currier, C. (1982). *Learning to Step Together: A Course for Stepfamily Adults.* Baltimore: Stepfamily Association of America.

Dahl, S. H. (1984). Marrying again. *Modern Bride,* October-November.

Derdeyn, A. P. & Scott, E. (1984). Joint custody: A critical analysis and appraisal. *American Journal of Orthopsychiatry, 54(2),* 199-209.

Dicks, H. V. (1967). *Marital Tensions: Clinical Studies Towards a Psychological Theory of Interaction.* London: Routledge and Kegan Paul.

Duberman, L. (1975). *The Reconstituted Family: A Study of Remarried Couples and Their Children.* Chicago: Nelson-Hall.

Fast, I. & Cain, A. C. (1966). The stepparent role: Potential for disturbances in family functioning. *American Journal of Orthopsychiatry, 36,* 485-491.

Ferri, E. (1984). *Stepchildren: A National Study.* Berkshire, England: Nfer-Nelson Publishing.

Fesler, B. (1985). Feeling like a stranger in a stepfamily. *Stepping Forward, 8(1),* p. 6. (Publication of Stepfamily Association, Calif. Division.)

Finkelhor, D. & Baron, L. (1986). Risk factors for child sexual abuse. *Journal of Interpersonal Violence, 1(1),* 43-71.

Framo, J. L. (1981). The integration of marital therapy with sessions with family of origin. In A. S. Gurman & D. P. Kniskern (Eds.), *Handbook of Family Therapy.* New York: Brunner/Mazel.

Furstenberg, F. F. (1981). Remarriage and intergenerational relations. In Fogel, R. W., Hatfield, E., Kiesler, S. B., & Shanas, E. (Eds.), *Aging: Stability and Change in the Family.* New York: Academic Press.

Furstenberg, F. F. (1987). The new extended family: The experience of parents and children after remarriage. In K. Pasley and M. Ihinger-Tallman (Eds.), *Remarriage and Stepparenting: Current Research and Theory.* New York: Guilford Press.

Furstenberg, F. F. & Nord, C. W. (1985). Parenting apart: Patterns of childrearing after marital disruption. *Journal of Marriage and the Family, 47(4),* 893-904.

Furstenberg, F. F., Nord, C. W., Peterson, J. L., & Zill, N. (1983). The life course of children of divorce: Marital disruption and parental contact. *American Sociological Review, 48,* 656-668.

Furstenberg, F. F. & Spanier, G. B. (1984). *Recycling the Family.* Beverly Hills, California: Sage Publications.

Ganong, L. H. & Coleman, M. (1983). Stepparent: A pejorative term? *Psychological Reports, 52,* 919-922.

Ganong, L. H. & Coleman, M. (1984). The effects of remarriage on children: A review of the empirical literature. *Family Relations, 33,* 389-408.

Ganong, L. H. & Coleman, M. (1986). A comparison of clinical and empirical literature on children in stepfamilies. *Journal of Marriage and the Family, 48,* 309-318.

Gardner, R. A. (1979). Intergenerational sexual tensions in second marriages. *Medical Aspects of Human Sexuality,* August 77-92.

Giles-Sims, J. (1984). The stepparent role: Expectations, behavior sanctions. *Journal of Family Issues, 5,* 116-130.

Giles-Sims, J. (1987). Social exchange in remarried families. In K. Pasley & M. Ihinger-Tallman (Eds.), *Remarriage and Stepparenting: Current Research and Theory.* New York: Guilford Press.

Giles-Sims, J. & Finkelhor, D. (1984). Child abuse in stepfamilies. *Family Relations, 33,* 407-413.

Glick, P. C. (1984). Marriage, divorce, and living arrangements: Prospective changes. *Journal of Family Issues, 5,* 7-26.

Glick, P. C. & Lin, Sung-Lin (1986). Recent changes in divorce and remarriage. *Journal of Marriage and the Family, 48,* 737-747.

Goldner, V. (1982). Remarriage family: Structure, system, future. In J. C. Hansen & L. Messinger (Eds.), *Therapy with Remarriage Families.* Rockville, Maryland: Aspen Publications.

Greif, J. B. (1979). Fathers, children, and joint custody. *American Journal of Orthopsychiatry, 49(2),* 311-328.

Greif, J. B. (1982). The father-child relationship subsequent to divorce. In J. C. Hansen & L. Messinger (Eds.), *Therapy with Remarriage Families.* Rockville, Maryland: Aspen Publications.

Hess, R. & Camara, K. (1979). Post-divorce family relationships as mediating factors in the consequences of divorce for children. *Journal of Social Issues, 35,* 79-96.

Hetherington, E. (1979). Divorce: A child's perspective. *American Psychologist, 34,* 851-858.

Hetherington, E. M. (1987). Family relations six years after divorce. In K. Pasley & M. Ihinger-Tallman (Eds.), *Remarriage and Stepparenting: Current Research and Theory.* New York: Guilford Press.

Hetherington, E. M., Cox, M., & Cox, R. (1976). Divorced fathers. *The Family Coordinator, 25(4),* 417-428.

Hetherington, E. M., Cox, M., & Cox, R. (1985). Long-term effects of divorce and remarriage on the adjustment of children. *Journal of the American Academy of Child Psychiatry, 24(5),* 518-530.

Huntington, D. S. (1986). Personal communication.

Ihinger-Tallman, M. (1985). Perspectives on change of custody among step-siblings. Presented at the Annual Conference of the National Council on Family Relations, Dallas.

Ihinger-Tallman, M. (1987). Sibling and stepsibling bonding in stepfamilies. In K. Pasley & M. Ihinger-Tallman (Eds.), *Remarriage and Stepparenting: Current Research and Theory.* New York: Guilford Press.

Isaacs, M. B. (1982). Facilitating family restructuring and linkage. In J. C. Hansen & L. Messinger (Eds.), *Therapy with Remarriage Families.* Rockville, Maryland: Aspen Publications.

Isaacs, M. B. (1986). Personal communication.

Jacobs, J. (1982). The effect of divorce on fathers: An overview of the literature. *American Journal of Psychiatry, 139,* 1235-1241.

Jacobson, D. S. (1987). Family type, visiting patterns, and children's behavior in the stepfamily: A linked family system. In K. Pasley & M. Ihinger-Tallman (Eds.), *Remarriage and Stepparenting: Current Research and Theory.* New York: Guilford Press.

Keshet, J. K. (1980). From separation to stepfamily. *Journal of Family Issues, 1,* 517-531.

Knaub, P. K., Hanna, S. L., & Stinnett, N. (1984). Strengths of remarried families. *Journal of Divorce, 7,* 41-55.

Landau, M. (1982). Therapy with families in cultural transition. In M. McGoldrick, J. K. Pearce, & J. Giordano (Eds.), *Ethnicity and Family Therapy.* New York: Guilford Press.

Landau-Stanton, J. (1985). Adolescents, families, and cultural transition: A treatment model. In M. P. Mirkin & S. Koman (Eds.), *Handbook of Adolescents and Family Therapy.* New York: Gardner Press.

Landau-Stanton, J., Griffiths, J., & Mason, J. (1982). The extended family in transition: Clinical implications. In Kaslow, F. (Ed.), *The International Book of Family Therapy.* New York: Brunner/Mazel.

Lewis, H. C. (1980). Clinical intervention with stepfamilies. Unpublished paper.

Lewis, H. C. (1981). What's in a word. *Stepfamily Bulletin, 3.* Baltimore, Maryland: Stepfamily Association of America.

Lewis, J. M., Beavers, W. R., Gossett, J. T., & Phillips, V. A. (1976). *No Single Thread: Psychological Health in Family Systems.* New York: Brunner/Mazel.

Luborsky, L., McLellan, A. T., Woody, G. E., O'Brien, C. P., & Auerbach, A. (1985). Therapist success and its determinants. *Archives of General Psychiatry, 42:*620-611.

Lutz, P. (1983). The stepfamily: An adolescent perspective. *Family Relations, 32,* 367-375.

McCarthy, J. (1978). A comparison of the probability of dissolution of first and second marriages. *Demography, 15,* 345-60.

McGoldrick, M. & Carter, E. A. (1980). Forming a remarried family. In E. A. Carter & M. McGoldrick (Eds.), *The Family Life Cycle: A Framework for Family Therapy.* New York: Gardner Press.

McGoldrick, M. & Gerson, R. (1985). *Genograms in Family Assessment.* New York: W. W. Norton & Co.

Mead, M. (1970). Aftermath. In P. Bohannon (Ed.), *Divorce and After.* Garden City, N.Y.: Doubleday.

Messinger, L. (1976). Remarriage between divorced people with children from previous marriages: A proposal for preparation for remarriage. *Journal of Marriage and Family Counseling, 2,* 193-200.

Messinger, L. & Walker, K. N. (1981). From marriage breakdown to remarriage: Parental tasks and therapeutic guidelines. *American Journal of Orthopsychiatry, 51(3),* 429-438.

Messinger, L., Walker, K. N., & Freeman, S. J. (1978). Preparation for remarriage following divorce. The use of group techniques. *American Journal of Orthopsychiatry, 78,* 263-272.

Mills, D. M. (1984). A model for stepfamily development. *Family Relations, 33,* 365-372.

Minuchin, S. (1984). *Family Kaleidoscope.* Cambridge, Mass.: Harvard University Press.

Minuchin, S., & Barcai, A. (1972). Therapeutically induced family crisis. In C. J. Sager & H. S. Kaplan (Eds.), *Progress in Group and Family Therapy.* New York: Brunner/Mazel.

Minuchin, S., Montalvo, B., Guerney, B., Rosman, B., & Schumer, F. (1967). *Families of the Slums.* New York: Basic Books.

Moos, R. F. (1978). Social-ecological perspectives on health. In C. Stone, F. Cohen, & N. E. Adler (Eds.), *Health Psychology.* San Francisco: Jossey Bass.

Morawetz, A. (1984). The single-parent family: An author's reflection. *Family Process, 23,* 571-576.

Mullen, B. (1987). Personal communication.

Muller-Paisner, V. (1983). Stepfamilies: A bid to come to terms. *Westchester Opinion, New York Times,* June 5.

Nadler, J. H. (1976). The psychological stress of the stepmother. Unpublished doctoral dissertation, California School of Professional Psychology, Los Angeles, California.

Papernow, P. (1980). A phenomenological study of the developmental stages of becoming a stepparent: A Gestalt and family systems approach. *Dissertation Abstracts International, 41,* 8B, 3192-3193.

Papernow, P. (1984). The stepfamily cycle: An experiential model of stepfamily development. *Family Relations, 33,* 355-363.

Papernow, P. (1986). The stepfamily cycle: The final steps to familydom. *Stepfamily Bulletin,* Winter issue. Baltimore, Maryland: Stepfamily Association of America.

Papernow, P. (1987). Stepping into parenting someone else's children. In J. Belovitch (Ed.), *Making Remarriage Work.* Lexington, Mass.: Lexington Press.

Parker, H. & Parker, S. (1986). Father-daughter sexual abuse. *American Journal of Orthopsychiatry, 56,* 531-549.

Pasley, K. (1987). Family boundary ambiguity: Perception of adult remarried family members. In K. Pasley & M. Ihinger-Tallman (Eds.), *Remarriage and Stepparenting: Current Research and Theory.* New York: Guilford Press.

Pasley, K. & Ihinger-Tallman, M. (1982). Stress in remarried families. *Family Perspective, 16(4),* 181-190.

Perkins, R. F. & Kahan, J. P. (1979). An empirical comparison of natural father and stepfather family systems. *Family Process, 18,* 175-183.

Peterson, J. L. & Zill, N. (1986). Marital disruption, parent-child relationships, and behavior problems in children. *Journal of Marriage and the Family, 48,* 245-307.

Ricci, I. (1980). *Mom's House, Dad's House: Making Shared Custody Work.* New York: Macmillan.

Rosen, R. (1979). Some crucial issues concerning children of divorce. *Journal of Divorce, 3,* 19-25.

Russell, D. E. H. (1984). *Sexual Exploitation: Rape, Child Sexual Abuse, and Sexual Harassment.* Beverly Hills, Calif.: Sage Publications.

Sager, C. J., Brown, H. S., Crohn, H., Engel, T., Rodstein, E., & Walker, L. (1983). *Treating the Remarried Family.* New York: Brunner/Mazel.

Sager, C. J., Walker, E., Brown, H. S., Crohn, H., & Rodstein, E. (1981). Improving functioning of the remarried family system. *Journal of Marital and Family Therapy, 7,* 3-13.

Santrock, J. W., Warshak, R. A., & Elliott, G. L. (1982). Social development and parent child interaction in father-custody and stepmother families. In M. E. Lamb (Ed.), *Nontraditional Families: Parenting and Child Development.* Hillsdale, N.J.: Lawrence Erlbaum.

Santrock, J. W. & Sitterle, K. A. (1987). Parent-child relationships in stepmother families. In K. Pasley & M. Ihinger-Tallman (Eds.), *Remarriage and Stepparenting: Current Research and Theory.* New York: Guilford Press.

Satir, V. (1972). *Peoplemaking.* Palo Alto, Calif.: Science and Behavior Books.

Schulman, G. L. (1972). Myths that intrude on the adaptation of the stepfamily. *Social Casework, 49,* 131-139.

Stanton, M. D. (1981). Strategic approaches to family therapy. In A. S. Gurman & D. P. Kniskern (Eds.), *Handbook of Family Therapy.* New York: Brunner/Mazel.

Steinman, S. (1981). The experience of children in a joint-custody arrangement: A report of a study. *American Journal of Orthopsychiatry, 51(3),* 403-414.

Steinman, S. B., Zemmelman, S. E., & Knoblauch, T. M. (1985). A study of parents who sought joint custody following divorce: Who reaches agreement and sustains joint custody and who returns to court. *Journal of the American Academy of Child Psychiatry, 24,* 554-562.

Stern, P. N. (1978). Stepfather families: Integration around child discipline. *Issues in Mental Health Nursing, 1(2),* 50-56.

Stern, P. N. (1982). Affiliating in stepfather families: Teachable strategies leading to stepfather-child friendship. *Western Journal of Nursing Research, 4,* 76-89.

Thies, J. M. (1977). Beyond divorce: The impact of remarriage on children. *Journal of Clinical Child Psychology.* Summer, *6,* 59-61.

Victor, R. (1986). Personal communication. Mr. Victor is Chair, Stepfamily Law Committee, Stepfamily Association of America.

Visher, J. S. (1984). Seven myths about stepfamilies. *Medical Aspects of Human Sexuality, 18(1).* (Jan.)

Visher, E. B. & Visher, J. S. (1978). Common problems of stepparents and their spouses. *American Journal of Orthopsychiatry, 48,* 252-262.

Visher, E. B. & Visher, J. S. (1979). *Stepfamilies: A Guide to Working with Stepparents and Stepchildren.* New York: Brunner/Mazel. (Also in paperback under the title: *Stepfamilies: Myths and Realities.* Secaucus, New Jersey: Citadel Press.)

Visher, E. & Visher, J. (1980). Once upon a time .... *Wellesley,* summer issue. Wellesley College, Wellesley, Mass.

Visher, E. B. & Visher, J. S. (1982). *How To Win as a Stepfamily.* New York: Dembner Books.

Visher, E. B. & Visher, J. S. (1985a). Stepfamilies are different. *Journal of Family Therapy, 7,* 9-18.

Visher, E. B. & Visher, J. S. (1985b). *Stepfamily Workshop Manual.* Baltimore, Maryland: Stepfamily Association of America.

Visher, E. B. & Visher, J. S. (1986). *Stepfamily Workshop Manual.* Baltimore, Maryland: Stepfamily Association of America.

Wald, E. (1981). *The Remarried Family: Challenge and Promise.* New York: Family Service Association of America.

Wallerstein, J. S. (1985). Children of divorce: Preliminary report of a ten-year follow-up of older children and adolescents. *Journal of the American Academy of Child Psychiatry, 24,* 545-553.

Wallerstein, J. S. & Kelly, J. B. (1980). *Surviving the Break Up: How Children and Parents Cope with Divorce.* New York: Basic Books.

Warren, L. W. & Tomlinson-Keasey, C. (1987). The context of suicide. *American Journal of Orthopsychiatry, 57(1),* 41-48.

White, L. K. & Booth, A. (1985). The quality and stability of remarriages: The role of stepchildren. *American Sociological Review, 50,* 689-698.

Wilson, K. L., Zurcher, L. A., McAdams, D. C., & Curtis, R. L. (1975). Stepfathers and stepchildren: An exploratory analysis from two national surveys. *Journal of Marriage and the Family, 37,* 526-536.

Appendix

READING LIST FOR ADULTS

Anderson, Joan Wester. *Teen is a Four Letter Word.* White Hall, Va.: Betterway Publications, Inc., 1983.
Provides thoughtful guidance on dealing with all the important stages of teen life. Especially helpful to "instant parents" of teens.

Bayard, Robert T. & Bayard, Jean. *How to Deal with Your Acting Up Teenager: Practical Self-Help for Desperate Parents.* San Jose, Cal.: The Accord Press, 1981.
The title accurately describes this excellent book.

Berman, Claire. *Making It as a Stepparent: New Roles/New Rules.* New York: Harper & Row, 1986.
Recommended as a "how-to" book, "this book is both sensitive and humorous. It looks at how to prevent or resolve the problems and takes an encouraging look at the potential rewards of stepfamily life."

Burns, Cherie. *Stepmotherhood: How to Survive Without Feeling Frustrated, Left-Out, or Wicked.* New York: Times Books, 1985.
"Based on research, consultation and inteviews with stepmothers, this book covers the entire range of experiences every stepmother faces: ex-wives, visitation schedules, discipline, guilt, and the happiness that can be found."

Einstein, Elizabeth. *Stepfamilies: Living, Loving and Learning.* New York: Macmillan, 1982. (Also in paperback.)
How to cope with both the larger issues and the day-to-day realities of stepfamily life. The author is both a stepchild and a stepmother.

Einstein, Elizabeth & Albert, Linda. Stepfamily Living Series. Ithaca, N.Y.: Einstein Enterprises, 1983.
Four booklets explore different aspects of stepfamily life.

Ephron, Delia. *Funny Sauce.* New York: Viking Press, 1986.
"If the book doesn't offer much in the way of solutions, it nevertheless remains a delightful romp. Additionally, it offers beleaguered stepparents recognition and support."

Gorman, Tony. *Stepfather.* Boulder, Colo.: Gentle Touch Press, 1983.
"The stories are told in everyday speech, and sociological facts are communicated through tone and accent. For those who look beyond the 'how-to' books on stepparenting, Gorman's account is valuable and interesting reading."

Juroe, David J. & Juroe, Bonnie B. *Successful Stepparenting.* Old Tappan, New Jersey: Fleming H. Revell, Co., 1983.
Two professional counselors offer a resourceful collection of guidelines based on their personal experiences and training as preparation for the responsibilities of successful stepparenting. Biblical emphasis.

Lansky, Vicki. *Practical Parenting Tips for the School-Age Years.* New York: Bantam Books, 1985.
"This book is directed to 'instant mothers' with no parenting experience. Offers more than 1000 'parent-tested' tips to guide you and your child or stepchild through the school age years."

Messinger, Lilian. *Remarriage: A Family Affair.* New York: Plenum Press, 1984. With a foreword by Mel Roman.
"A significant contribution to our appreciation of what some have called the new American extended family."

Newman, George. *101 Ways to be a Long Distance Superdad.* Mountain View, Cal.: Blossom Valley Press, 1981.
Aids mothers and fathers who are separated from their children. Offers ideas for "together type" activities.

Ricci, Isolina. *Mom's House, Dad's House: Making Shared Custody Work.* New York: Macmillan, 1980.
An excellent book illustrating how divorced parents can make two homes in the best interest of their children (and themselves).

Roosevelt, Ruth & Lofas, Jeanette. *Living in Step.* New York: Stein and Day, 1976. (Also in paperback.)
An easily read account of the experiences of the authors and a number of persons they interviewed about stepfamily problems. Particularly popular with stepparents.

Rosen, Mark Bruce. *Stepfathering: Stepfathers' Advice on Creating a New Stepfamily.* New York: Simon and Schuster, 1987.
Directed to the male adult in the stepfamily partnership, with practical suggestions and advice about many aspects of this experience.

Silver, Gerald & Silver, Myrna. *Second Loves: A Guide for Women Involved with Divorced Men.* New York: Praeger Pub., 1985.
"Written especially for those women who are second wives. Sound advice for coping with problems of stepchildren, in-laws, old friends, managing money and time. A wealth of information about life, love and happiness the second time around."

Stuart, Richard B. & Jacobson, Barbara. *Second Marriage: Make it Happy, Make it Last!* New York: W. W. Norton, 1985.
"What a help to have a book addressed to the millions of us who are forging couple relationships in the midst of remarriage complexity!" Filled with valuable suggestions for making the new couple relationship strong.

Visher, Emily B. & Visher, John S. *How to Win as a Stepfamily.* New York: Dembner Books, 1982.
"The book is filled with specific suggestions and guidelines on the various issues discussed. . . . The authors have succeeded in conveying that stepfamilies can indeed win."

Visher, Emily B. & Visher, John S. Stepfamilies: Myths and Realities. Secaucus, N.J.: Citadel Press, 1980.
This is a paperback edition of the Vishers' *Stepfamilies: A Guide To Working with Stepparents and Stepchildren* which is useful also to people in stepfamilies who want to better understand how their families work.

Wallerstein, Judith S. & Kelly, Joan B. *Surviving the Break Up.* New York: Basic Books, 1980.
A detailed and scientific report of a five-year study of the children of divorced families in Marin County, California.

Wooley, Persia. *The Custody Handbook.* New York: Simon and Shuster, 1980.
An excellent handbook on custody which presents a strong argument for coparenting, and deals with the legal issues in divorce.

READING LIST FOR CHILDREN

Berman, Claire. *What Am I Doing in a Stepfamily?* Secaucus, N.J.: Lyle Stuart, 1982.
A classic work, entertaining and informative.

Bradley, Buff. *Where Do I Belong? A Kids' Guide to Stepfamilies.* Reading, Mass.: Addison-Wesley, 1982.
An excellent book for children who are wondering about what is happening to them in their new stepfamily.

Craven, Linda. *Stepfamilies: New Patterns of Harmony.* New York: Julian Messner, 1982.
A helpful book for adolescents in stepfamilies.

Gardner, Richard A. *The Boys and Girls Book About Stepfamilies.* New York: Bantam Books, 1982.
A guide for children ages 9-12.

Getzoff, Ann & McClenahan, Carolyn. *Stepkids: A Survival Guide for Teenagers in Stepfamilies.* New York: Walker and Co., 1984.
A survival guide for teens and parents faced with a new family.

Green, Phyllis. *A New Mother for Martha.* New York: Human Sciences Press, 1978.
Deals sensitively with the feelings of a young girl whose mother has died, and whose father remarries.

LeShan, Eda. *What's Going to Happen to Me?* New York: Avon Books, 1976.
A book about the unspoken question which is in the minds of most children after a divorce and remarriage.

Lewis, Helen Coale. *All About Families — The Second Time Around.* Atlanta: Peach-
tree Publishers, 1980.
Explores children's feelings and opens adult-child discussion around important
and basic stepfamily issues.

Magid, Ken & Schreibman, Walt. *Divorce is . . . A Kid's Coloring Book.* Gretna, La.:
Pelican Publishers, 1980.
A coloring book for young children illustrated with scenes and captions regarding
the common dilemmas of children of divorce. Preface for parents.

Phillips, Carolyn E. *Our Family Got a Stepparent.* Ventura, Cal.: Regal Books, 1981.
"A book with a Christian emphasis for children who find themselves in families
where, through death or divorce, there is a stepparent in their lives. Discusses issues
chosen in an attempt to broaden understanding of children's common fears about
stepfamilies and stepparents."

Shyer, Marlene Fanta. *Stepdog.* New York: Charles Scribners Sons, 1983.
"A delightful story for children from the 'perspective' of the new family's dog,
who deals with becoming a 'stepdog.'"

Stenson, Janet Sinberg. *Now I Have a Stepparent and It's Kind of Confusing.* New
York: Avon Books, 1979.
To be read to younger children, with a preface for adults. Older children also
respond well to this book.

Vigna, Judith. *She's Not My Real Mother.* Chicago: Albert Whitman & Co., 1980.
A young boy must reevaluate his feelings toward his stepmother after she rescues him.

Vigna, Judith. *Daddy's New Baby.* Niles, Ill.: Albert Whitman & Co., 1982.
Tells how, through a near accident, a little girl changes her feelings towards her
father's new baby.

Vigna, Judith. *Grandma Without Me.* Niles, Ill.: Albert Whitman & Co., 1984.
A boy discovers a way to keep in touch with his grandmother after his parents'
divorce.

Many of these books can be ordered from Stepfamily Association of America, Inc.,
602 East Joppa Rd., Baltimore, Maryland 21204. Where descriptive material is
quoted, it is from the Educational Materials brochure of Stepfamily Association
of America.

Index